Arranging and Describing Archives and Manuscripts

by Fredric M. Miller

The Society of American Archivists
Chicago
1990

THE SOCIETY OF AMERICAN ARCHIVISTS
600 S. Federal, Suite 504, Chicago, IL 60605

© 1990 by the Society of American Archivists
All rights reserved. First edition 1990
Second printing 1997
Printed in the United States of America

ISBN 0-931828-75-9

Table of Contents

Preface

Like the Basic Manual Series that preceded it, and that for more than a dozen years excelled in articulating and advancing archival knowledge and skills, the seven new titles in SAA's Archival Fundamentals Series have been conceived and written to be a foundation for modern archival theory and practice. They too are intended for a *general* audience within the archival profession and should have widespread application within the profession. They will strengthen and augment the knowledge and skills of archivists, general practitioners and specialists alike, who are performing a wide range of archival duties in all types of archival and manuscript repositories.

From the beginning, these titles have been designed to encompass the basic archival functions enumerated by SAA's Guidelines for Graduate Archival Education. They discuss the theoretical principles that underlie archival practice, the functions and activities that are common within the archival profession, and the techniques that represent the best of current practice. They give practical advice for today's practitioners, enabling them to prepare for the challenges of rapid change within the archival profession.

Together with more specialized manuals also available from SAA, the Archival Fundamentals Series should form the core of any archivist's working library. The series has particular value for newcomers to the profession, including students, who wish to have a broad overview of archival work and an in-depth treatment of its major components. The volumes in the series will also serve as invaluable guides and reference works for more experienced archivists, especially in working with new staff members, volunteers, and others. It is our hope that the Archival Fundamentals Series will be a benchmark in the archival literature for many years to come.

Preparing these publications has been a collaborative effort. The authors have contributed the most, of course, but SAA readers, reviewers, staff members, and Editorial Board members have also assisted greatly. I would particularly like to thank Donn Neal, Executive Director, and Susan Grigg, Chair of the Editorial Board, whose good counsel and support never failed, Roger Fromm, Photographic Editor, and Teresa Brinati, Managing Editor, who brought the volumes from text to publication.

In addition, the Society expresses its deep appreciation to the National Historical Publications and Records Commission, which funded the preparation and initial printing of the series.

Mary Jo Pugh, Editor
Archival Fundamentals Series

Acknowledgments

I am indebted to several colleagues who either read and commented on various parts of this manual while it was in preparation or provided me with valuable unpublished materials. I would like to thank in particular Susan Davis, Kathleen Roe, Marion Matters, Lisa Weber, and especially the editor of the Archival Fundamentals Series, Mary Jo Pugh. I would also like to thank the managing editor of the series, Teresa Brinati, and the copy editor, Joyce Gianatasio. Contributions and suggestions from Greg Bradsher, David Bearman, Lydia Lucas, Katharine Morton, Michele Pacifico and Sharon Thibodeau were also of great assistance. Finally, I must thank my wife, Naomi, who read the successive drafts with the eye of an experienced librarian who had to be convinced that archival practices do indeed make sense.

Fredric M. Miller

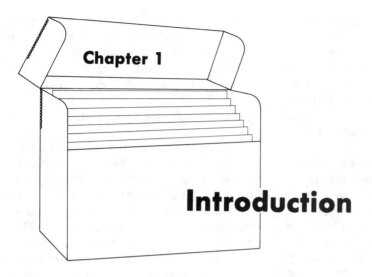

Chapter 1

Introduction

The Nature of Archives and Manuscripts

Archival and manuscript repositories exist to preserve historical records and make them available for use. The subject of this manual is the internal operations which link those two goals. These operations involve accessioning, arranging and describing various sets of records. Arranging and describing are commonly joined under the rubric of processing. By making possible the use of records, processing gives meaning to their acquisition and preservation. At the same time, processing is the key method by which archivists control and administer the records in their custody.

This manual covers generally accepted principles and techniques of archival accessioning and processing. After more than a century of development, these principles and techniques are now regarded as applicable to a wide variety of repositories, both public and private. They have been accepted because they are based firmly on the particular nature of archival materials and the logical progression of archival work.

In general terms, archives and historical manuscripts are the records, in any physical form, produced by organizations or individuals in the course of activity over time, and then saved permanently for some further use. The most important substantive characteristic of all archival and manuscript material is that it is the product of an activity, through which it was created or accumulated. Though normally thought of as "old files," archives are not in fact defined by any specific physical form. They can

be photographs, maps, or machine-readable files as well as traditional paper records. Equally important, archives and manuscripts are not simply all of the "old files" of an organization or individual. They are records saved because archivists have determined they have some probable future value. That process of evaluation is called appraisal. Records may have many different potential uses which justify their preservation after they are no longer needed in daily activity. They are most likely to be used for research by the general public and scholars, in administrative reference, during the establishment of legal rights and claims, and for fiscal accountability.

This manual deals with both archives and historical manuscripts. Following common usage, the term "archives" will generally include manuscript collections or repositories and "archivist" will include manuscript curators, unless stated otherwise. There are, however, important differences between archives and manuscripts. Strictly speaking, archives are the noncurrent but still useful records of an organization or institution *preserved by that organization or institution*. The term "archives" refers to the repository containing the records as well as to the records themselves. As organizational units, archives are part of the larger entity whose records they maintain, and their primary mission is to serve that institution. Thus the National Archives contains those records of the United States government deemed worthy of permanent preservation, while a small museum archives serves exactly the same function for the museum of which it is a part.

In contrast, manuscript collections are the records created or gathered by an organization or individual but transferred from the original custodian to a collecting repository, such as a local historical society or university library. Such repositories collect organizational records and personal papers from many different sources, primarily in order to serve researchers outside their own organization. A historical society retains its own records but will emphasize collecting the records of the key figures and institutions of its geographic area.

This difference between archives and manuscript repositories has significant implications for processing. Because the records in an archives come from only one source, they provide some measure of inherent unity and structure on which to base the work of arrangement and description. Because the records in a manuscript repository come from many sources, manuscripts curators must not only arrange and describe separate sets of records, but must also create a structure to relate the disparate records to each other in a repository-wide system.

While both archives and manuscript repositories contain records in a variety of formats, this manual will emphasize traditional textual records—the masses of paper files which still form the bulk of most holdings, even in contemporary "paperless offices." The principles of arranging and describing traditional non-textual media, such as maps and photographs, are usually consistent with those for textual records. However, their physical format, the type of information conveyed (visual or aural), their preservation requirements, and the ways in which they are used all dictate separate consideration. These matters are discussed in detail in publications available from the Society of American Archivists.[1]

New electronic or machine-readable records will not be discussed in this manual, primarily for two reasons. First, constant technical changes in software and hardware require major and continual modifications in acquisitions and preservation. Second, information in many computer systems is created and maintained in ways that are fundamentally different from the way information is fixed on a page of text, or even in a photograph or a map. Information in such complex machine-readable formats demands additional systems to arrange and describe it in ways compatible with traditional materials.[2]

Machine-readable records may someday render paper files obsolete. Nonetheless, records predating the 1980s, as well as much key contemporary documentation, will remain in traditional text whatever the eventual evolution of computer-based records.

Archives and Libraries

Archives and historical manuscripts form part of society's overall information resources, along with other resources such as books, journals, and automated data bases. Archivists share with librarians and other information professionals a commitment to organize their materials for use. This shared commitment should structure institutional processing programs, since most users desire information about a topic regardless of physical format. Nevertheless, the work described in this manual is dictated by the special character of archives, which may best be understood in contrast with universally familiar book-based library operations.

The physical difference between a shelf of newly acquired books and a stack of newly accessioned archival materials puts the operational differences into a practical context. The typical accession of archives or manuscripts arriving at a repository might take the form of twenty cartons of files, each containing an identifying label. The records will be primarily textual documents, but there might be other material such as photographs, rolled-up maps, floppy disks and artifacts. Unlike a book, a collection has no title page to identify author, title, and imprint, though the labels may indicate a source, such as a creator or donor. As a whole, the group of records is far larger than many runs of periodicals, let alone an individual book, and it is also heterogeneous in physical form. Unlike the individual books on a shelf, the boxes represent a set of related files and thus have an organic unity in which the whole is greater than the sum of its parts.

The archival collection derives not from a conscious act of intellectual creation, as a book or article does, but rather from a gradual accretion resulting from activity over time. The records are then saved not for a specific purpose determined by their creator, but for a range of hypothetical uses. Thus monthly statistical reports by a social worker to a welfare agency administrator serve immediate purposes for management, but historians in the future will use them for scholarly research projects wholly unrelated to their original function. Finally, though specific documents may not be unique copies, the collection as a whole will be unique, unlike books

---

[1] Mary Lynn Ritzenthaler, Gerald J. Munoff and Margery S. Long, *Archives and Manuscripts: Administration of Photographic Collections* (Chicago: Society of American Archivists, 1984) and Ralph E. Ehrenberg, *Archives and Manuscripts: Maps and Architectural Drawings* (Chicago: Society of American Archivists, 1982).

[2] Margaret L. Hedstrom, *Archives and Manuscripts: Machine-Readable Records* (Chicago: Society of American Archivists, 1984).

which are duplicated and collected in thousands of libraries.

Because archival records are the product of specific and unique activities, archival repositories do not share common holdings in the way libraries do. Without the impetus of common holdings, archives have no common classification system such as the Library of Congress or Dewey systems in libraries. Such systems organize the totality of a library's holdings and, in combination with other shorthand codes for author and edition, provide each book or journal with a symbol in the form of a call number that gives it a unique physical and intellectual location within a library. The book or journal will have the same relative place in every library that uses the same system.

Archives have no such methods for organizing their holdings or assigning predetermined places on the shelves. Despite important similarities in practices, responsibilities, and the nature of their materials, archives lack the large core of duplicated holdings and resultant shared cataloging and classification upon which modern library practice is based. In some ways, both the holdings and the internal catalogs of two state archives in adjacent states traditionally have had less in common than the smallest community library has with the Library of Congress.

The Nature of Archival Arrangement and Description

Processing is structured by the flow of archival work and the potential uses of the records as well as by the nature of archival and manuscript materials. Archival work in broad terms moves from acquisi-

tions and appraisal through processing and physical preservation to providing access and facilitating use. The nature and condition of newly received records are determined largely by institutional records management programs in the case of archives and by repository collecting policies in the case of manuscripts. (See Figure 1-1.)

In order to facilitate appropriate use, processing must be geared to the varied audiences for archival records. While books can generally be identified by type (popular, scholarly, or reference), as well as classified by subject, archival materials are not so easily categorized. A set of minutes may be useful for both internal planning and scholarly research; probate files might attract both attorneys and genealogists. Archival materials tend to attract fewer users than library materials, but they are often used more intensively, especially when the materials are being mined for scholarly research. At the same time, both archives and manuscript repositories acquire materials which may require restrictions on access to protect privacy and confidentiality.

Finally, while facilitating use, processing should also be designed to ensure the physical preservation of the records. Various types of preservation and conservation work occur simultaneously with processing. Each repository will develop an accessioning and processing program directed at its own holdings and its own users. However, such programs should be consistent with the common practices and standards developed or adopted by the archival profession.

The first step in examining those common accessioning and processing practices is to establish definitions. For accessioning, the following straightforward definition fits most cases: *Accessioning* is the process by which a repository takes physical custody and assumes legal and administrative control over a body of records.

The two components of processing—arrangement and description—are more difficult to define. At their most basic, they are simply the ordering and listing of records. They have also been described more theoretically as the archival equivalents of library classification and cataloging. The analogy has some validity, because the functions are similar. The underlying principles are very different, however, as are the results.

Archives and manuscript collections are arranged according to the principles of *provenance* and *original order*. The principle of provenance provides that records are maintained according to their creator or source rather than according to a subject or

Figure 1-1   Schematic of Archival Operations

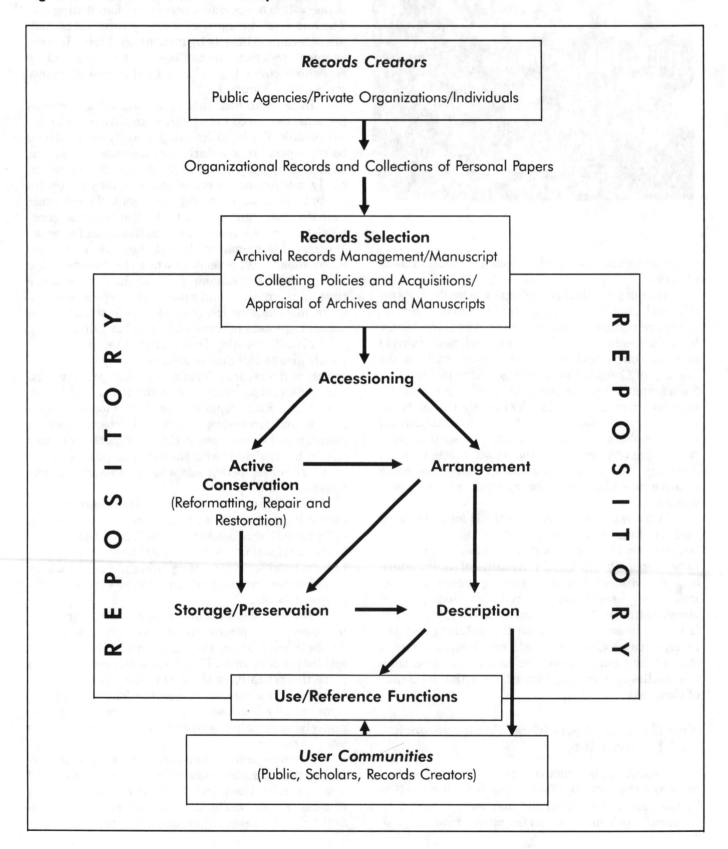

other form of classification system. Materials from different creators are not intermingled, even when they share a common subject. Provenance is the fundamental principle of archival organization. The principle of original order provides that the internal arrangement of files established by their creator be retained whenever feasible.

Groups of records are commonly described in multiple page inventories and other forms of narrative analysis as well as in card or computer catalogs similar to library systems. Inventories and narrative analyses are particularly suited to this *collective description* of all the records from a common source or within a common file order. Archivists emphasize collective description in contrast to individual description of items or documents.

In the context of these basic principles, the following operational definitions will be used in this manual, applying to both archives and historical manuscripts:[3]

Archival arrangement is the process of organizing and managing historical records by:

1) identifying or bringing together sets of records derived from a common source which have common characteristics and a common file structure, and
2) identifying relationships among such sets of records and between records and their creators.

Archival description is the process of capturing, collating, analyzing, controlling, exchanging, and providing access to information about

1) the origin, context, and provenance of different sets of records,
2) their filing structure,
3) their form and content,
4) their relationships with other records, and
5) the ways in which they can be found and used.

Both definitions refer to "sets" of records, primarily because other terms such as group and series have specific meanings to archivists. Here a set of records means two or more documents with some common characteristic. Sets of records range from all the holdings of a repository down to a single file folder and include all the possible subdivisions in between.

Following the principle of provenance, the major sets of records within public and institutional archives are the records of an agency or department, often called a "record group" in the United States. The records of agencies like the Federal Aviation Administration or the Freedman's Bureau are typical examples of record groups at the National Archives. In manuscript repositories, the records of a specific organization or the papers of an individual or family given to the repository and retained together on the basis of provenance are commonly termed a "collection." The records of the YMCA in a university library and the papers of William Penn in a historical society are examples of manuscript collections.

The series is another type of records set. It may be defined as follows:

> A *series* is a body of file units or documents arranged in accordance with a unified filing system or maintained as a unit by the organization or individual that created them because of some other relationship arising out of their creation, function, receipt, physical form, or use.[4]

Typical series include minutes, correspondence, case files, staff reports, ledgers, maps, and similar familiar record types. As this very partial list reveals, records are essentially organized, maintained, and used in the form of series. According to the principle of original order, such sets of records are kept together and in the order in which they were created. The series is generally accepted as the central unit for most aspects of processing work.

The definitions provided here stress that arrangement and description involve important intellectual activities, requiring analysis and decision making. Archivists and their staffs will continue to physically move boxes and folders and draw up lists, but that work should be understood in its larger context. In processing a typical body of records, an archivist will have to:

1) determine its origins and filing structure;
2) understand the activities it documents, how they were carried out, and how both changed over time;

---

[3] For standard definitions see Lewis and Lynn Bellardo, *The Glossary of Archivists, Manuscript Curators, and Records Managers* (Chicago: Society of American Archivists, forthcoming) and Frank B. Evans, Donald F. Harrison, Edwin A. Thompson and William L. Rofes, "A Basic Glossary for Archivists, Manuscript Curators and Records Managers," *American Archivist* 37 (July 1974): 415–433.

[4] This is a slightly modified version of the definition in Evans et al., "Basic Glossary," 430.

Work area in an archives/records center with supplies and manuals close at hand. *(Courtesy of Westchester County Archives, New York.)*

3) determine the informational content of the records and make some assumptions about the records' probable uses;

4) assess their physical characteristics and conditions; and

5) explain their relationship to other records.

Beyond such work on individual collections, some archivists emphasize as well the broad analytical value of the unique archival emphases on both the importance of record-creating activity and the different types of documentation which that activity produces. They see this perspective as a vital intellectual contribution to the whole world of information science.[5] It stresses the importance of process

---

[5] See David Bearman and Richard Lytle, "The Power of the Principle of Provenance," *Archivaria* 21 (Winter 1985/86): 14–27.

and form, an orientation crucial to the arrangement and description of archives.

Goals and Structure of the Manual

This manual will concentrate on such intellectual and decision-making activities and the principles and considerations that underlie them. It addresses as well the procedures and techniques that derive from these principles and decisions. The manual is designed to be especially helpful to the novice archivist coming to the profession either through educational programs or the assignment of new archival responsibilities.

This publication is not, however, designed to be used as an internal procedures manual. Such manuals, which every repository should have, provide de-

Figure 1-2   Schematic of Arrangement and Description

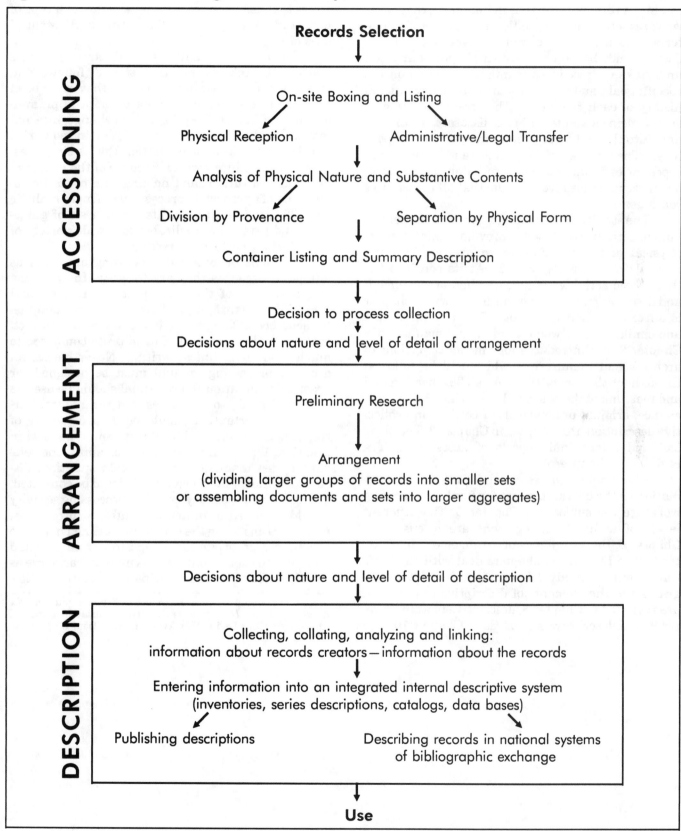

tailed instructions for all the steps involved in processing. As discussed further in Chapter 5, they cover work responsibilities, specific rules for handling materials, forms to be completed, standards to be obeyed, and the order in which all procedures are undertaken. Procedures manuals are based on the specific goals, audiences, resources, and institutional history of each repository. They translate the general principles and techniques discussed in this volume into the daily work requirements of the repository. The range of archives and manuscript repositories is far too broad to be encompassed in one internal procedures manual that all repositories could use.

The structure of the manual follows the continuum of activities designed to provide administrative, physical, and intellectual control over archives and manuscripts. (See Figure 1-2.) At its core are the three basic activities of accessioning, arrangement, and description. Following this introductory chapter is an examination in Chapter 2 of the differences and similarities between archives and manuscripts. Chapter 2 also introduces four model collections of archives and manuscripts which will be followed throughout the rest of the manual. The background and meaning of the basic archival principles of provenance, original order, levels of control and collective description are analyzed in Chapter 3. The physical and intellectual aspects of accessioning are reviewed in Chapter 4.

Planning, resources, administration, and automation as the overall context for further processing work are the subjects of Chapter 5. The different levels of archival arrangement are discussed in Chapter 6; the techniques of arrangement in Chapter 7. The final three chapters deal with the basic components of archival description. Descriptive programs and the elements of descriptive information are reviewed in Chapter 8, descriptive tools in Chapter 9, and descriptive standards in Chapter 10. The discussions of both arrangement and description stress the idea of options in the selection of a type of processing appropriate to the nature and potential uses of any given set of records.

Though this manual does discuss principles which all archival practice should follow, and strongly endorses standards where they have been created or accepted, it does not attempt to promulgate detailed rules. Despite gradual change, internal institutional archival procedures remain too varied to attempt the kind of regulation that is simply assumed in the library world. Because of the nature of archival institutions and holdings, an overall commonality of approach to processing is a more realistic goal. This manual represents a synthesis of guidelines and principles applicable to a wide variety of repositories and types of records.

Manuals on archival processing are often as difficult to read as they are to write. In 1898, the Dutch authors of the first great archival manual proclaimed forthrightly, "This is a tedious and meticulous book. The reader is forewarned."[6] In fact, that manual is a marvel of lucid prose compared to much modern technical writing. Nevertheless, an archival processing manual must be designed for practical adaptation. This manual should be used as a general guide to principles and techniques. Perhaps as important, it should be seen as a way of thinking about processing. But it cannot be used in isolation. Where national standards apply, the relevant guides, manuals and technical regulations discussed in the following chapters should be consulted. Within each repository, specific processing activity should be based on a detailed internal procedures manual, translating the principles outlined here into practices appropriate to the repository's mission and holdings. In such a context, this manual can serve as a bridge between broad principles and daily practice.

---

[6] Samuel Muller, J. A. Feith and R. Fruin, *Manual for the Arrangement and Description of Archives*. Translation of the 2nd edition by Arthur Levitt (New York: H. W. Wilson, 1968): 9.

Chapter 2

Archives and Manuscripts: Comparisons and Models

The institutions that preserve historical records in the United States fall broadly into the two categories of archives and manuscript repositories. The former includes both public archives at all government levels and private in-house institutional archives. The most common institutional repositories are university, corporate, religious, union, and museum archives. Manuscript repositories include historical societies, academic, public, and private libraries of all kinds and specialized research centers. In practice, arrangement and description are significantly different in the two types of repositories. The differences derive ultimately from differences in basic institutional goals and the types of records the institutions collect.

Institutional Missions and Holdings

Archives are first and foremost in-house operations. Their goal is to preserve records relevant to the ongoing functions of the organization of which they form a part, after those records are no longer needed for their original purpose. Though often used by scholars and the general public, the most important users of public and institutional archives are administrators and staff, even if they are not the most numerous constituency. Public archives also have important roles in protecting the rights of citizens by providing them with information about themselves and the policies that affect them. In contrast, the goal of most manuscript repositories is to serve researchers from outside the institution by collecting materials from a variety of external organizations and individuals. Rather than serving internal

administrative, fiscal or legal needs, they serve various cultural and research communities.

In pursuit of its institutional mission, an archives collects the records of its parent organization, whether a government, church, university, corporation or labor union. In pursuit of its mission, a manuscript repository usually acquires records and papers as a result of conscious solicitation according to an established collecting policy. Collections are gathered from many sources, but they share some common theme, whether a subject, a geographic area or the history of a group of people. The theme can be as broad as the history of an entire state or as narrow as the development of one religious denomination in a city.

A well-established archives receives its records through a records management program in which files having permanent value are selected and transferred internally in coherent and often ordered sets according to a regular schedule. In government and institutional archives, records appraised through such programs as having permanent value commonly form less than five percent of the total of inactive files. In manuscript repositories, collecting is rarely as regularized as in an efficient records management program. Manuscript curators instead have to identify appropriate materials and negotiate with organizations and individuals for their placement at the repository.

These differences dictate the nature of the holdings of archives and manuscript repositories. However complex the organization, an inherent unity binds the records of a public or institutional ar-

The stack area in an archives with scores of archival boxes. *(Courtesy of Brookings Institution Archives, Washington, D.C.)*

chives, since all the files derive from activities of that one organization. (See Figure 2-1.) No such inherent unity exists in manuscript repositories, which often contain materials from hundreds or even thousands of different sources. These can range from individual donations of valuable documents, letters or diaries to contributions of many cubic feet of records from organizations unwilling or unable to maintain them on their own. (See Figure 2-2.)

Yet while archives deal with only one donor, they commonly have to manage a larger bulk of records than most manuscript repositories. In public and corporate archives, records series comprising hundreds of cubic feet are not unusual. Entire manuscript collections only occasionally reach such proportions. Much more typical are the collections totalling a few boxes, or even only a few folders and bound volumes. Thus a typical historical society might have many more individual collections than the nearly five hundred Record Groups of the National Archives, but its average collection will be only a fraction of the size of such a Record Group. With few

exceptions such collections will also lack any natural "organic" relationship to the other collections in the historical society.

The nature and form of materials in the two types of repositories differ as well. In addition to organizational records and personal papers, manuscript repositories have two important types of collections unknown in archives. The first is the "artificial collection" of documents gathered by a collector, such as a group of letters signed by famous authors. The unity of such a collection derives from the collector and the subject, rather than from the way the documents were created. Such collections formed the core holdings of major repositories of the nineteenth and early twentieth centuries and they remain important today. Second, manuscript repositories commonly contain individual documents acquired by purchase, gift or bequest which have no natural relation to any other document. These are often assembled by the manuscript repository itself into a thematic collection with a title like "Civil War Documents," or "Early Deeds."

Figure 2-1   Record Groups at the Pennsylvania State Archives

Record Groups

NUMBER	TITLE	DATE SPAN FOR RECORDS
1	Department of Agriculture	1917–1969
2	Department of Auditor General	1802–1928
3	Civil Service Commission	1926–1970
4	Office of the Comptroller General	1720–1809
5	Constitutional Conventions and Council of Censors	1776–1968
6	Department of Forests and Waters	1897–1971
7	General Assembly	1776–1974
8	General Loan Office and State Treasurer	1773–1974
9	General State Authority	1935–1940
10	Office of the Governor	1917–1976
11	Department of Health	1904–1970
12	Department of Highways	1706–1967
13	Pennsylvania Historical and Museum Commission	1903–1977
14	Department of Internal Affairs	1859–1969
15	Department of Justice	1814–1970
16	Department of Labor and Industry	1914–1968
17	Bureau of Land Records	1675–1949
18	Loan and Transfer Agent	1817–1919
19	Department of Military Affairs	1793–1950
20	Department of General Services	1893–1967
21	Proprietary Government	1664–1776
22	Department of Education	1854–1969
23	Department of Public Welfare	1882–1967
24	Office of the Register General	1784–1809
25	Special Commissions	1858–1972
26	Department of State	1681–1978
27	Pennsylvania's Revolutionary Governments	1775–1790
28	Treasury Department	1763–1933
29	Pennsylvania Turnpike Commission	1875–1941
30	Pennsylvania State Police	1905–1964
31	Department of Commerce	1937–1977

Pennsylvania. Historical and Museum Commission. *Guide to the Record Groups in the Pennsylvania State Archives.* Frank M. Suran, compiler and editor. Harrisburg: Pennsylvania Historical and Museum Commission, 1980.

Figure 2-2   Manuscript Collections in the Swarthmore College Peace Collection

31 Dispatch News Service International. Records, 1968–1973.
5 meters (16½ feet)

Dispatch News Service International (DNSI) was formed in Saigon in 1968 by Michael Morrow and other freelance writers who hoped to give Westerners a deeper understanding of the people, problems, and cultures of Asia. An office of this non-profit news service was established in Washington in 1969 to aid in the distribution of investigative reports, in-depth features, human interest stories, and public interest articles submitted by writers who knew the languages, history, and culture of the areas from which they reported. Among the stories which Dispatch was first to circulate were articles on the Mylai massacre, the tiger cages at Con Son Island, and on CIA operations in Laos. Dispatch focused initially on news from Indochina but later distributed stories from all of Southeast and East Asia and from Latin America. Dispatch News Service International suspended its operations in March 1973 due to financial problems.

The records of DNSI in the Swarthmore College Peace Collection are primarily the records of the Washington office from 1970 to 1973. Under the direction of Richard A. Berliner and Joseph Gatins, a small staff edited and distributed articles and news releases, handled correspondence and financial matters, and tried to raise funds to support Dispatch. Included in the collection are unedited original manuscripts (many unpublished), articles and releases circulated by Dispatch, and clippings and photocopies of published articles (1968–1973). Correspondence (1970–1973). Correspondence (1970–1973), monthly memoranda sent to staff members and writers, newsletters, leaflets, financial records, fund-raising information, legal briefs, and photographs are also in the collection.

Correspondents include the following staff members and writers: Len Ackland, Edward Allan, Richard A. Berliner, Fred Branfman, Crystal Eastin, John Everingham, Thomas C. Fox, Joseph Gatins, Tim Hackler, Leon Howell, Don Luce, Emerson A. Manawis, Desmond McAllister, Michael Morrow, D. Gareth Porter, Donald E. Ronk, and Jonathan Unger.

FINDING AIDS: Preliminary checklist

RESTRICTIONS: None
DOCUMENT GROUP   108

32 Danilo Dolci. Papers, 1952–1978.
1.6 meters (5¼ feet)

Danilo Bruno Pietro Dolci (1924–   ), architect, social reformer, and writer originally from northern Italy, has worked to improve economic and social conditions in western Sicily since 1952. An advocate of nonviolent social change, Danilo Dolci has used such tactics as community education, demonstrations, and fasting and has developed the concept of the "strike in reverse" (in which unemployed persons voluntarily constructed a road in 1956 to demonstrate to the Italian government the great need for such a facility). He has confronted Mafia control as well as government and Church authority to bring about improving conditions in Sicily, notably by the construction of dams, agricultural training centers, and schools.

In his attempts to bring about a new social order in Sicily, Dolci, who has received international financial support and acclaim, has declared himself to be independent of political affiliations. Headquarters for Dolci's work is the Centro Studi E Iniziative Per La Pienze Occupazione in Partinico, Sicily. There are four other such pilot centers in other parts of western Sicily, each providing technical, educational, and cultural programs for residents of the region.

Danilo Dolci materials in the Peace Collection include correspondence (1959–1974), articles by and about Dolci, reports of the Centro Studi, international itineraries, pamphlets, leaflets, photographs, sound recordings, Dolci clippings from various sources, and Sicilian newspapers. Most of the Dolci materials are in Italian, with occasional English translations. The correspondence is mainly to and from Dolci's supporters in the United States and Great Britain; included are numerous Dolci letters to and from Jerre Mangione, author of *A Passion for Sicilians: The World Around Danilo Dolci* (1968). Mangione's notes for this book are also part of the Dolci collection.

Among the correspondents are Vero Ajello, Franco Alasia, Leslie A. Blanckensee, Patricia Coley, Robert Engler, Herbert J. Gans, Morris E. Garnsey, Frances Keene, Alfred McClung Lee, Lisa Aversa Richette, A. William Salomone, and Joan Simon.

FINDING AIDS: Checklist

RESTRICTIONS: None
DOCUMENT GROUP   105

33 Emergency Peace Campaign. Records, 1935–1938.
30 meters (99 feet)

The Emergency Peace Campaign (EPC) was a nation-wide campaign in 1936-1937 to keep the United States out of war and to promote world peace. The EPC was a member of the National Peace Conference and worked closely with the American Friends Service Committee and the National Council for Prevention of War.

The collection includes minutes; correspondence; administrative and departmental files; publications, releases, clippings; financial records, reports of field workers and peace caravans; material of local peace councils set up under EPC auspices; signed pledges of abstinence from war; and files of five of the twenty area offices of the EPC (Kansas City, New York, St. Louis, Chicago, Michigan).

Ray Newton served as Executive Director of EPC. Other staff members were Baruch Braunstein, Harold Chance, John Dillingham, Fred Atkins Moore, James P. Mullin, Kirby Page, and E. A. Schaal.

Important correspondents in the collection include: Devere Allen, Emily Greene Balch, Richard E. Byrd, Dorothy Detzer, Paul H. Douglas, Clark M. Eichelberger, Harold E. Fey, Harry Emerson Fosdick, Cordell Hull, Hannah Clothier Hull, Edwin C. Johnson, Abraham Kaufman, Frederick J. Libby, William O. Mendenhall, Mildred Scott Olmsted, Francis S. Onderdonk, Albert W. Palmer, Jeannette Rankin, A. Maude Royden, John Nevin Sayre, Guy W. Solt, Charles P. Taft, II, Jacob H. Taylor, Norman Thomas, and Norman J. Whitney.

FINDING AIDS: Checklist
MICROFILM: 190 reels

RESTRICTIONS: None
DOCUMENT GROUP   12

Swarthmore College. *Guide to the Swarthmore College Peace Collection.* 2nd edition. Swarthmore, Pennsylvania: 1981.

While lacking such collections, archives increasingly contain other types of records rare in manuscript repositories. Archives are affected by changes in record-keeping techniques and technologies far more quickly than manuscript repositories, because records management programs transfer to archives many records that are only seven to ten years old, and because archives exist in public and private environments where new systems are continually being implemented. Archives are confronted not only with the contemporary paper explosion, but also with an expansion of writing in a wide variety of electronic and micrographic formats. Although manuscript repositories hold many photographs, artifacts and other nontextual materials, the vast majority of their historic records are in the form of traditional paper files. These records generally come from individuals and small organizations. The time that passes between the creation of documents and their ultimate arrival at a manuscript repository is generally far greater than the time it takes for records to reach an archives. This is especially true in the case of personal papers. This preponderence of older material combined with the donors' lack of records management programs means that manuscript repositories contain a higher proportion of disordered and physically deteriorating materials than do archives.

Acquisitions and Processing

All of these variations naturally affect both the processing of individual sets of files and the way the repositories' holdings as a whole are described for users. For many decades, there were significant differences between the processing of archival records and historical manuscript collections in the United States. Only gradually did manuscript curators adopt basic archival processing principles and archivists begin to apply relevant manuscript and library-based descriptive practices.[1] The evolution of contemporary practice demonstrates that the best way to encourage the genuinely fundamental similarities in processing is to recognize and accommodate the appropriate differences.

These differences derive initially from the methods of acquisition. Established archives usually acquire subsets of the records of some organizational unit—such as the financial records of an office for the last ten years, or the files of a completed pro-

The preliminary examination of a new manuscript collection by an archivist. (Courtesy of The Balch Institute for Ethnic Studies, Philadelphia.)

gram. Manuscript repositories more commonly acquire a whole body of organizational records or personal papers, such as the records of a labor union local or the papers of a prominent politician. The two types of repositories thus often deal with very different types of groups of material. Further, in established archives with records management programs most records arrive as coherent series with an identifiable origin, or provenance, and an established file order. Manuscript repositories receive records in all conditions. The records of an organization making regular deposits in a manuscript repository may be in good file order. Other collections will exhibit a combination of one or more filing orders. Some manuscript collections are brought from attics and closets as piles of paper of unidentifiable provenance in no discernable order at all. These records often contain both unexplained gaps and unexpected riches. Manuscript staffs thus spend much more

---

[1] For a detailed interpretation of this process, see Richard C. Berner, *Archival Theory and Practice in the United States* (Seattle: University of Washington Press, 1983).

time than public or institutional archivists on the basic identification of provenance, filing order and subject matter.

Conversely, manuscript collections tend to be smaller and somewhat less complex than archival groups. Most manuscript collections—apart from the records of large modern organizations—are of a relatively manageable size, even if they are disordered. Archives, in contrast, are generated by mammoth, ever-changing bureaucracies with intricate reporting and organization charts. Archives need much more sophisticated methods of representing these changing relationships than manuscript repositories usually require to describe the internal characteristics of their individual collections. Writing from the point of view of a manuscript repository, Richard Berner stated that "every series has a parent."[2] In this perspective, most manuscript collections are typified by such straightforward series as the correspondence of Mr. Smith or the board minutes of the Chamber of Commerce. But in modern archives, a series may have multiple parents, twins, and an entire kinship network. Thus while physically arranging a manuscript collection may be more difficult than arranging an archival group of comparable size, once arranged it can be easier to describe as a unit.

Another set of problems arises when a repository tries to integrate all of its holdings in a repository-wide descriptive system. In theory, archives have a unity which flows from the organization of which they are a part. Know the structure and functions of the organization and you should know the arrangement and contents of its archives. Provenance and original order in this context should, in theory, produce an internal system that is to a large extent self-descriptive and self-indexing. That system is designed to be useful to internal personnel, with scholarly and public access a secondary consideration.

A manuscript repository can have no such self-indexing insitution-wide system. Although basic archival principles are employed in organizing each individual collection, some external structure has to be imposed to bring all the collections together. That structure has to serve all of the repository's constituencies, whether they be scholars, genealogists, land title searchers, local historians or any other group. Here methods drawn from librarianship to produce

appropriate indexes and catalogs have been and continue to be most relevant. Manuscript repositories, and archives to a lesser extent, also need to provide access through indexes to the kind of narrative information about records creators and records sets provided by traditional inventories. They need to employ a standardized terminology to translate and explain the meaning of series titles and file headings, some of which may be obsolete or obscure.

Archival principles like provenance and original order are of only limited help in providing access to the many small collections in manuscript repositories. For a collection of three diaries and fifty letters, the major challenge is not to arrange and describe the collection, but to inform users of its very existence in the repository and about its general content. Much more than archives, manuscript repositories will thus always rely on a common integrating index.

Commonalities

This stress on differences should not obscure the elements which archives and manuscripts have in common. A manuscript repository index or catalog locates and describes collections in that repository which are each arranged and described according to basic archival principles. Even personal papers of modern figures largely consist of bits of the archives of the activities and organizations in which the individual participated. Individuals active in six organizations will usually have some of the records of those six organizations as important components of their personal papers. Organizational records in manuscript repositories are, in Robert Brubaker's phrase, "fugitive archives,"[3] records which would be called archives if maintained by the institution which created them. Stripped of its pejorative connotations, this is a useful way of thinking about all modern manuscript collections. Lester Cappon used another image in an influential 1956 article. He explained that "the reputable curator of historical manuscripts must be an archivist at heart to do his job well; indeed he is a kind of multiple archivist."[4] The recognition of such similarities led to the application of common techniques to sets of records in all types of repositories.

Beyond the individual sets of records, similarities exist on the repository level as well. Even in

---

[2] Richard Berner and Uli Haller, "Principles of Archival Inventory Construction," *American Archivist* 47 (Spring 1984): 139.

[3] Robert L. Brubaker, "Archival Principles and the Curator of Manuscripts," *American Archivist* 29 (October 1966): 507.

[4] Lester Cappon, "Historical Manuscripts as Archives: Some Definitions and their Application," *American Archivist* 19 (April 1956): 110.

theory, archival record sets are only as self-descriptive and stable over time as the organizations they document. An ever-changing institution or government will produce confusing records; a complex organization will produce complex records. Given historical change and organizational complexity, it can in practice be as difficult to find the appropriate records documenting a subject even within a well-organized archives as it is in a manuscript repository with hundreds of different collections. Despite their inherent unity, archives, like manuscript repositories, need repository-wide integrated access systems. Archives and manuscript repositories also have more in common with regard to use than theory implies. It is a rare archives where administrators and other internal personnel outnumber researchers from the outside. Archives thus share with manuscript repositories a common responsibility to exchange information about their holdings in intra- and inter-institutional networks.

Models

The different types of repositories and holdings combine to produce endless possible variations. For the discussion of archival principles and practices in the rest of this manual, four idealized bodies of records representing the materials archivists are most likely to encounter will be used. Using idealized records both avoids focusing on a specific institution and illuminates common characteristics which are rarely combined neatly in real collections.

Our typical though fictional setting will be the State of Saratoga, appropriating one of the unused names suggested by Thomas Jefferson for the division of the Northwest Territory. In its state capital, Middletown, we find (1) the Historical Society of Saratoga (founded in 1857); (2) the Saratoga State University Graduate Research Library (built in 1966); (3) the Middletown Museum of Art (established 1889); and (4) the State Archives (established in 1915). Within these institutions we will concentrate on the following records, which typify their holdings. These descriptions will be further elaborated throughout the manual, but these brief summaries will convey a sense of typical situations.

1. Collection of Personal Papers. In accordance with its traditional concentration on prominent local individuals, the historical society acquires the papers of George Bailey (1911–1987), prominent local banker and civic leader, by a gift from his widow, Mary Hatch Bailey. The four filing cabinets of papers include records of Bailey's civic activities,

mainly with the Republican Party, the Chamber of Commerce, and the Southside Settlement/Community Center; his personal correspondence and other personal files approved for donation by the family; and some of his business records from his family-owned bank and the larger bank which absorbed it in 1970. The collection also includes some files relating to the civic and philanthropic activities of his wife, Mary Hatch Bailey, who was active in the Museum of Art, as well as several diaries of his father, Peter Bailey. Most of the files are arranged alphabetically or chronologically within topical or functional categories, such as "Settlement Board Minutes," or "Property Deeds." Mary Bailey also donated her husband's 150-item collection of handwritten letters of early Saratogans and presidential autographs, his plaques and awards, and his 500-volume library on Saratoga history and biography.

2. Organizational Manuscript Collection. The Graduate Research Library's Regional History Center acquires the records of Middletown's Southside Community Services, Inc., after years of negotiation. The records as boxed on-site by the library's staff consist of fifty cubic feet of textual files and ten cubic feet of photographs, pamphlets, maps, scrapbooks, and other printed material. About half the records are in file folders, but there are several different file systems. The rest of the records are loose papers or old bound volumes.

Southside Community Services was originally founded in 1878 as the Union Mission and was affiliated with the Episcopal Church until 1900. It then became the Southside Settlement, from 1900 to 1946. From 1946 to 1975 the agency was known as the Southside Community Center. The center absorbed two smaller settlement houses in 1948 and merged with the eighty year old Southside Day Nurseries in 1963. In 1975 it changed its name to Southside Community Services, to reflect the fact that from the late 1960s on it was responsible for administering a variety of urban renewal and community organization programs funded by government agencies.

3. Institutional Archives Record Group. As a result of a comprehensive records survey, the newly established Archives of the Museum of Art accessions forty-five cubic feet of records documenting the work of the Education Division from its creation in 1927 through 1982. The records include administrative and policy files for the division as a whole and files for each of its current departments (Public Education, Volunteers, International Programs, Children's Programs, Adult Programs). The Education Division's records also include the records of the Public Relations Department before it became a separate division in 1965. The records identified as having permanent value are boxed and transferred to the archives as they were maintained in office filing cabinets—by department, then by type of record (reports, memoranda, correspondence, brochures, announcements, proposals, etc.) and thereunder alphabetically or chronologically.

4. Series of Public Records. As part of the state's records management plan, the state archives receives a total of thirty cubic feet of Office of Park Planning files relating to state and county park planning for the years 1967 to 1980. The records arrive in two separate deliveries over the course of two months, one directly from the Office of Park Planning, the other from the State Records Center. In addition to about twenty-five cubic feet of paper files, the records include maps, audio tapes of public meetings, photographic prints and slides, and three computer tapes. The Office of Park Planning was established in 1958, although a park planner was on the staff of the old Department of Conservation beginning in 1935. The agency of which the office is now a part, the Department of Natural Resources (DNR), was created in 1972. The Office of Park Planning is a unit of the department's Bureau of Parks and Recreation. The textual files are in order alphabetically within four categories (Divisional Files, State Parks, County Parks, Maps). The archives already

has similar state and county park planning files for 1935 to 1971. Other records series produced by the Office of Park Planning such as administrative files and land acquisition files are also in the archives.

These four situations are not unusual or complex. Two of the sets of records represent the traditional collections of archives and manuscript libraries respectively—the files of a public agency (DNR) and the papers of a prominent individual (George Bailey). The other two collections are private organizational records. In the case of the Museum Education Division they are part of an in-house archives; in the case of Southside Community Services they have been transferred to a manuscript repository and form one of its collections. It is important to note that the only reason the first is called an archival group and the second a manuscript collection relates to their custody. Had the museum deposited its records at the historical society, they would have been called a manuscript collection like the Southside Community Services materials. In addition to these four ideal types, other types of collections, such as personal papers of public officials and artificial collections assembled by collectors, will be mentioned as appropriate. But the records outlined above illuminate most of the issues and challenges facing contemporary archivists. Following these records from accessioning through the completion of description will illustrate the interplay between archival principles and practices in four typical settings.

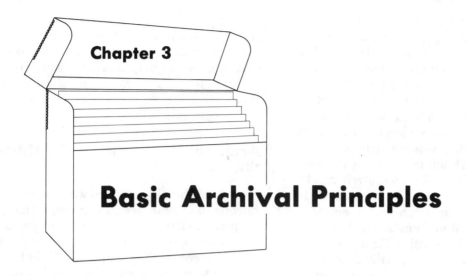

Chapter 3

Basic Archival Principles

Archival processing is based on the principles of provenance, original order and collective description developed in nineteenth-century Europe. In addition, American archivists have developed the concept of "levels of control" over records as a way of managing arrangement and description. Taken together, these four principles form a coherent system for organizing archives and manuscripts and making them available for use. Some have argued that archival principles are merely operational guidelines without substantive theoretical content. Concentrating on their practical applications within repositories can, however, mask the underlying conceptual framework. Embedded in the basic principles is an archival ideology or world-view with a significant historical pedigree.

Emergence of an Archival Ideology

From the time of the earliest civilizations of the Middle East, governments have commonly employed some system of preserving and organizing important records according to their official function and file arrangement. As modern state bureaucracies were created in Europe, government departments established registry systems and registry offices to control the growing mass of paper. Registry systems include lists and summaries of every document created or received by a department, together with classification schemes for grouping individual documents into physical files. Registry officials often maintained indexes to files and documents by name, place and subject.[1]

The first centralized national archives was created in France in 1794. Only then did records-keepers face the problems of organizing inactive files brought together from many departments. Between 1839 and 1841, following several decades of experimentation, French officials adopted the practice of *respect des fonds*; in essence, the principle of provenance. *Respect des fonds* provided that all the documents from one department—a *fonds*—would be kept together. But it did not address the order of the records within the *fonds*. In 1881, German archivists formalized archival arrangement at all levels by combining the principle of provenance with that of original order—the retention of the original file structure as established by the creating agency. In Germany, this system of maintaining records by office and established filing order relied on the existence of departmental registry control of files before they were transferred to the archives. Hence, original order is sometimes called the "registry principle."[2] The system as a whole is designed to express the indissoluble link between activity over time and the records produced by that activity.

---

[1] For registries see Theodore R. Schellenberg, *Modern Archives: Principles and Techniques* (Chicago: University of Chicago Press, 1956), 65–77.

[2] For nineteenth-century European archival history see Ernst Posner, "Max Lehmann and the Genesis of the Principle of Provenance," in *Archives and the Public Interest: Selected Essays by Ernst Posner*, edited by Ken Munden (Washington: Public Affairs Press, 1967), 36–44; and "Some Aspects of Archival Development since the French Revolution," *American Archivist* 3 (July 1940): 159–172.

The principles of archival arrangement were definitively codified by three Dutch archivists—Samuel Muller, J. A. Feith and R. Fruin— in their still useful 1898 *Manual for the Arrangement and Description of Archives*. In addition to discussing provenance and original order, they emphasized the collective description of records in page format inventories, as opposed to catalog card descriptions of individual items. Though it was not translated into English until 1940, the Dutch manual was the basis for Hilary Jenkinson's 1922 *Manual of Archival Administration*, and it had a profound impact on the founding generations of American archivists.

The 1898 Dutch manual summarized the new archival ideology in two key rules. Its authors proclaimed at the beginning that "an archival collection is an organic whole," derived from a common source or creating agency.[3] The repeated use of the term "organic" in archival literature emphasized that, in contrast to artificial groupings, the documents in archival collections relate to each other in ways that transcend the information in each document. The archival whole is greater than the sum of its parts; the relationships are as important as the particulars.

In a second rule, the Dutch archivists stated that the original filing order and overall structure of a collection "is not the result of chance, but the logical consequence of the organization of the administrative body of whose functions the archival collection is the product."[4] In this perspective, the Office of Park Planning files in one of our examples are created and organized in a way that can tell researchers something about the process of park planning in Saratoga, independent of the actual contents of those files. The separation of state and county park plans, for example, reveals an approach to planning based on political rather than topographic subdivisions. In this way, not only are records organic, but their organic development is represented in their filing structure.

Sir Hilary Jenkinson added a legal perspective by stressing the presumptive impartiality of records in their original state. For Jenkinson the preservation of the "sanctity of evidence" as represented by official records was the central archival responsibility. Records in their pure state, undisturbed by any rearrangement, conveyed the unvarnished truth about an activity or process.[5] The practice of archival arrangement flows logically from this belief that the uniquely impartial and organic characteristics of archives are reflected in their origin and filing structure. Provenance and original order provide information *about* a group of records which is not *in* those records, but which is essential to understanding them. Hence these two principles are central to archival operations.

Archival Principles in the United States

As archival principles were being developed in Europe in the nineteenth century, American archival practice hardly existed. Without a strong centralized government or departmental registry systems, federal records were maintained haphazardly. The first state archives was not founded until 1901. A rich variety of private historical societies did, however, develop in the United States. By the early twentieth century, major public and academic libraries were also collecting manuscripts from prominent families and individuals.[6]

In handling their collections, American libraries and historical societies drew upon the traditions of the great European rare book libraries and manuscript repositories, rather than drawing upon the new archival practices. They sorted their holdings into various classification schemes, developed detailed catalog cards for individual documents, and published document-level catalog lists. For especially important sets of documents, they prepared item summaries called calendars.[7] (See Figure 3-1.) This approach was supported by the rapid codification of library techniques in the last quarter of the nineteenth century, when such familiar tools as the Dewey and Library of Congress classification systems, the standard card catalog, and modern cataloging rules were developed. When the Library of Congress issued a manuscript cataloging manual in 1913, it concentrated on cataloging individual documents in a way consistent with newly developed standard catalogs for books. European archival principles seemed irrelevant. In fact, the emphasis of writers like Jenkinson and the Dutch archivists on service to administrators reinforced the view of many American manuscript librarians that archival principles were not oriented towards advancing research.

---

[3] Muller, Feith and Fruin, *Manual*, 19.

[4] Ibid., 57.

[5] Hilary Jenkinson, *A Manual of Archival Administration* (London: P. Land, Humphries, 1937), 20–21.

[6] See O. Lawrence Burnette, *Beneath the Footnote: A Guide to the Use and Preservation of Historical Sources* (Madison: State Historical Society of Wisconsin, 1969), 43–67 and 132–192.

[7] Theodore R. Schellenberg, *The Management of Archives* (New York: Columbia University Press, 1965), 33–52.

Figure 3-1   Calendar of Early New York Records

VOL. IV.]   **DUTCH MANUSCRIPTS.**   **75**

COUNCIL MINUTES.

1641.   PAGE.

April   18. Ordinance.   Regulating the currency of Wampum, and prohibiting the circulation of a foreign inferior description, which has driven "the splendid Manhattan wampum" out of sight, ... 90

May   2. Court proceedings.   Everardus Bogardus et al., guardians of the minor children of Cornelis van Vorst vs. Hendrick Jansen, tailor; to testify respecting an alleged indebtedness of Hendrick van Vorst to his deceased father's estate; defendant declares he knows nothing about it, ... 91

May   23. Court proceedings.   Jan Damen and David Provoost vs. Everardus Bogardus and Tymen Jansen, guardians of the estate of the late Hendrick van Vorst, on a claim as guardians of the Jan van Vorst, to one-half of the estate of said Hendrick, in his right, as full brother of deceased, and then to an equal share of the remainder with his half brother and sister; court awarded judgment for plaintiffs as claimed. Jacob Stoffelsen vs. Everardus Bogardus et al., guardians, &c., that defendant, before dividing Hendrick van Vorst's estate, pay what he owed his father; judgment for plaintiff. Hendrick Jansen, father and guardian of Elsie Hendrick, vs. the guardians of the late Hendrick van Vorst's heirs, for three cows which said Van Vorst verbally promised his daughter, in case he died on the passage to Fatherland; judgment for defendants, 91, 92

May   30. Court proceedings.   Frederick Jansen vs. Claes Sybrantsen Veringh, action of debt; judgment for plaintiff, .   93

June   6. Minute permitting a considerable number of Englishmen to settle with their clergyman, in New Netherland, on the following conditions: 1. They shall take the oath of allegiance; 2. They shall enjoy free exercise of their religion; 3. They shall nominate three persons, one of whom shall be appointed magistrate by the governor of New Netherland, with power to decide civil cases under 40 guilders ($16), without appeal, and criminal cases not deserving of capital punishment; 4. They shall not erect forts unless by permission; 5. Their lands shall be free of taxes for ten years, after which they shall pay the tenths; 6. They shall enjoy free trade, and free hunting and fishing; but, 7. Must use Dutch weights and measures, ... 93

June   6. Resolution.   Dr. Johannes La Montagne to go with a force of fifty men to Fort Hope, to curb the insolence of the English thereabout, who, not content with having usurped the lands which the Dutch bought and paid for, have committed various other outrages, ... 94

June   6. Court proceedings.   Fiscal vs. Ulrich Lupold for satisfaction to the company; defendant acknowledges his faults and requests to be again employed; judgment for plaintiff; meanwhile defendant to be allowed his rations until the arrival of the ships.   Fiscal vs. Maryn Adriaensen, slander; defendant begs pardon of the director, and is forgiven for the sake of wife and children, ... 94

June   13. Court proceedings.   The guardians of Cornelis van Vorst's children vs. Jacob Stoffelsen, husband of said Van Vorst's widow; plaintiffs claim the corn growing on said Van Vorst's bouwery; defendant ordered to prove that Hendrick van Vorst made the widow a present of his share, &c., and to pay 420 guilders, which he acknowledges to be indebted. Dirck Cornelissen vs. Jan Evertsen Bout; action of debt; judgment for plaintiff. Thomas Hall vs. . . . .

O'Callaghan, E.B., Editor. *Calendar of Historical Manuscripts in the Office of the Secretary of State, Albany N.Y.* Albany: Weed, Parsons and Co, 1865.

The American situation changed dramatically in 1934 with the establishment of the National Archives. Because it was founded well into the twentieth century, it was dominated from its inception by the huge masses of files created by modern bureaucracies. The United States government generated about one hundred thousand cubic feet of records between the Revolution and the Civil War; it produced 3.5 million cubic feet between 1917 and 1930 alone.[8] The manuscript library approach of arrangement by various topical and chronological classes and item cataloging, which had been influential in many of the early state archives, was clearly inappropriate in this context. From the first, the National Archives accepted provenance and original order as its organizing principles.

Adapting these principles to American conditions, including the lack of registries, proved challenging. Workable solutions were finally adopted in 1940–41. Government records were to be organized according to "Record Groups." These were generally the records of commonly identifiable agencies, bureaus, and commissions, like the Interstate Commerce Commission. No overall topical classification

[8] Ibid., 129.

scheme was to be imposed upon the several hundred Record Groups which were soon identified; there would be no attempt to group, for example, agencies related to aspects of social services under one large classification.[9]

For description, the basic National Archives "finding aid" was not a card catalog, but a pamphlet-like descriptive inventory of each Record Group, containing introductory information about the records as a whole and a list of all the constituent series. Within each series, the principle of orginal order would be maintained for the files themselves.[10] An indexed, published guide provided an integrated overview of all the Record Groups. (See Figure 3-2.)

The techniques developed by the National Archives were widely adopted by state, local and institutional archives. In 1950 a new Library of Congress manuscript cataloging manual endorsed the collection, not the document, as the proper unit for cataloging. The library soon afterwards adopted a variation of the archival inventory, called the "register," for describing manuscript collections. From the 1950s on, many other manuscript repositories recognized that archival principles could be applied to their collections as well. The organizational records and even the personal papers acquired by libraries and historical societies to document the twentieth century were more similar in size and complexity to government records than they were to eighteenth- and early nineteenth-century manuscript collections.

The application of archival principles to modern manuscripts was a dominant theme of the next two decades, with Theodore Schellenberg its most influential advocate. The culmination of this trend came in 1977 when the Society of American Archivists published a manual on arrangement and description by David B. Gracy II. The SAA also published a separate volume of sample inventories and registers.[11] Both were addressed simultaneously to

archives and manuscript collections. In contrast to the standardization of the library world, archivists and manuscripts curators accepted the individuality of each repository's application of the basic archival principles. Provenance did not produce identical results in all government archives; inventories did not have the same format and terminology in all historical societies. This diversity was regarded as an inevitable consequence of the uniqueness of each repository's holdings.

However, important elements of manuscript library practice remained useful for all types of repositories. Archival principles minimized the practical need for an integrative catalog or index describing all of an institution's holdings. By relying on provenance and file structure to organize their materials, archivists underemphasized as well the subject access so important to many researchers. Archival principles also provided little guidance to the repository which wanted to describe its manuscipts and its library holdings in the same catalog.

To meet these needs, manuscript practice continued to use methods of detailed descriptive cataloging and subject indexing drawn from librarianship, while respecting provenance, original order and collective description. This combination of techniques was exemplified by the thousands of forms which repositories prepared to describe their collections in the Library of Congress' *National Union Catalog of Manuscript Collections* (*NUCMC*), beginning in 1959. The forms were used by *NUCMC* staff to generate catalog cards with name and subject headings consistent with library standards.[12] Public and institutional archives, in contrast, maintained through the 1960s and 1970s their independence from library practice. This separation was explained on the basis of the uniqueness of each records creator and records set in contrast to the duplication of library materials.

Rapidly developing national automated library systems and the advantages to users of including archives and manuscripts in such systems finally led to a fruitful convergence of the archival and library traditions in the early 1980s. The National Information Systems Task Force (NISTF) of the Society of American Archivists identified the common pieces of information, such as creator, title, dates, and size, which all repositories gathered about their holdings, whatever the nature of the internal forms they used

[9] For these developments, see Philip M. Hamer, "Finding Mediums in the National Archives: An Appraisal of Six Years Experience," *American Archivist* 5 (April 1942): 82–92; Donald McCoy, *The National Archives: America's Ministry of Documents* (Chapel Hill: University of North Carolina Press, 1978): 79–81, 106; Frank B. Evans, "Modern Methods of Arrangement of Archives in the United States," *American Archivist* 29 (April 1966): 241–263; and United States National Archives, *Control of Records at the Record Group Level* (Washington: GPO, 1950) and *Principles of Arrangement* (Washington: GPO, 1951).

[10] Edward Hill, *Preparation of Preliminary Inventories* National Archives Staff Information Paper no. 14 (Washington: GPO, 1950). Reprinted by the National Archives and Records Service in 1982.

[11] David B. Gracy II, *Archives and Manuscripts: Arrangement and Description* (Chicago: Society of American Archivists, 1977) and *Inventories and Registers: A Handbook of Techniques and Examples* (Chicago: Society of American Archivists, 1976).

[12] Gracy, *Arrangement and Description*, 34; and Terry Abraham, "NUCMC and the Local Repository," *American Archivist* 40 (January 1977): 31–42.

Figure 3-2   National Archives and Records Service Inventory Page

6   RECORDS OF THE CIVILIAN CONSERVATION CORPS

Secretary of the Interior designated a rock outcrop at the north end of Big Meadows in the Shenandoah National Park as the "Robert Fechner Rock." Executive Order 8673 established the Massanutten Unit of the George Washington National Forest as the "Robert Fechner Memorial Forest." Included are a large-scale map of the George Washington National Forest and photographs of Camp Roosevelt, the first CCC camp.

23.   BLUEPRINTS. 1935–40. 2 in.
Arranged by type of building.
Plans for typical buildings and interior furnishings in CCC camps. Some plans for portable buildings are included.

24.   REPORT INSTRUCTIONS AND FORMS. 1941. 2 in.
Arranged by subject.
Instructions and forms used in reporting both at the level of the Office of the Director and at the individual camps.

25.   REPORTS OF SALVAGE AND RECLAMATION ACTIVITIES. 1934–39. 2 vols. 3 in.
Arranged by supply depot.
Reports sent to Director Fechner about CCC repair activities operated by the Quartermaster Corps at the supply depots at New Cumberland, Pa., for the III Army Corps area and at Columbus, Ohio, for the V Army Corps area. The narrative and photographic reports show the repair of CCC clothing, equipment, and supplies for future use by the CCC.

Records of Divisions

DIVISION OF SELECTION

The Department of Labor supervised the selection of junior enrollees from April 1933 to May 1939. The President directed the transfer of this function to the Director of the CCC by Executive Order 8133, May 15, 1939. There were no fundamental changes in selection policy, procedure, or personnel incident to the transfer. On May 25, 1939, the Secretary of Labor authorized the transfer to the Director's office of all records pertaining to the selection of junior enrollees. These records were combined with those subsequently created by the Division of Selection of the CCC.

The Division was responsible for preparing standards of eligibility and procedures for the selection of junior enrollees. Initially there were strict requirements that enrollees be primarily from families on relief. The CCC act of June 28, 1937 (50 Stat. 319), altered the requirements to permit the enrollment of those unemployed or in need of employment. State and local public welfare agencies selected the enrollees, but the Division of Selection had wide latitude in designating the State selecting agency and in reviewing State plans of operation to ensure conformity with established standards. The Division required extensive reporting by State agencies on the number and characteristics of the selectees. It advised the Director on matters of policy regarding the selection and welfare of enrollees and

cooperated with the War Department in determining State quotas for enrollees.

26.   GENERAL CORRESPONDENCE. 1933–42. 10 ft.
Arranged alphabetically by subject.
Relates to all CCC selection activities and accomplishments.

27.   RECORDS RELATING TO THE ORGANIZATION AND OPERATIONS OF THE SELECTION WORK. 1933–42. 10 ft.
Arranged alphabetically by subject.
Correspondence with the Director's staff and with the Secretary of Labor; correspondence about the appointment of State directors of selection; and records relating to budget and financial matters, personnel, the development and revision of CCC and State forms used in the selection work, and the organization of selection work.

28.   POLICY FILE. 1933–42. 8 ft.
Arranged alphabetically by subject.
Primarily correspondence with State selecting agencies regarding policy decisions on the selection of enrollees and other matters for which the Division of Selection had responsibility, such as allotment payments. The records also include information on discharges and other actions in which the Division had an interest but not responsibility.

United States. National Archives and Records Service. *Preliminary Inventory of the Records of the Civilian Conservation Corps. Record Group 35.* Compiled by Douglas Helms. Washington: National Archives, 1980.

Figure 3-3 Chronological Outline

Separate Traditions

	ARCHIVES	*MANUSCRIPTS (& LIBRARIES)*
1791		Massachusetts Historical Society—First Historical Society in the United States
1794	French National Archives created	
1839/41	Development of principle of *respect des fonds*	
(1876)		(American Library Association founded; Dewey Classification published)
1881	Principles of provenance and original order codified in Germany	
1895		Historical Manuscripts Commission created by American Historical Association
1897		Library of Congress Manuscript Division founded
1898	Dutch archives manual published	(Library of Congress classification system emerging)
1899	Public Archives Commission created by American Historical Association	
1901	First American state archives created in Alabama	
1907		(ALA cataloging rules developed)
1912	First American publication discussing European archival principles (W.G. Leland)	
1913		Library of Congress issues *Manuscript Cataloging Manual*
1934	U.S. National Archives created	
1936	Society of American Archivists founded	
1940/41	National Archives adopts record groups/inventories as basis for processing	

Merging Traditions

	ARCHIVES	*MANUSCRIPTS (& LIBRARIES)*
1950		New Library of Congress manuscripts cataloging manual adopts archival principles
1952–54		Development of rules for National Union Catalog of Manuscript Collections (NUCMC)
1956	Cappon article on "Historical Manuscripts as Archives" published	
1962		First volumes of NUCMC issued
1964	Holmes article on levels of archival arrangement published	
1965	Schellenberg, *Management of Archives* published	
1967		(Anglo-American Cataloging Rules developed)
1968		(Machine Readable Cataloging—MARC—begins at Library of Congress for books)
1976/77	SAA *Basic Manual Series for Archives and Manuscripts* published	
1980–82	SAA National Information Systems Task Force formed	
1983	MARC format and cataloging rules for archives and manuscripts developed	

to describe that information.[13] NISTF emphasized how such archival "data elements" could be described and information about them exchanged within existing library-based bibliographic networks, without violating the fundamental archival principles.

Based upon this work, archivists and librarians developed by 1983 a mutually acceptable machine-readable cataloging (MARC) format for archives and manuscript collections compatible with national library standards. At the same time, Steven Hensen prepared rules for describing holdings in his cataloging manual, *Archives, Personal Papers and Manuscripts*.[14] Archivists were now able to describe their holdings in bibliographic data bases like the Research Libraries Information Network (RLIN) and the On-line Computer Library Center (OCLC).

These achievements were all founded upon the retention of arrangement by provenance and original order, and collective description through inventories and other finding aids. Thus a cycle had been completed. In the 1950s, archival principles were successfully applied to processing modern manuscripts. Three decades later, in the world of automated information exchange, those principles were reconciled with modern bibliographic techniques. A system of archival arrangement and description had been created which allowed archives and manuscripts to be accessible along with other information resources, while respecting the basic archival principles. These remain the foundation of archival processing, and deserve further explication.

Provenance

Provenance is the fundamental principle of modern archival practice. In essence, it simply means that "archives of a given records creator must not be intermingled with those of other records cre-

ators."[15] Records about parks from the Saratoga Department of Natural Resources must not be filed with records about parks from the state's Department of Transportation. The records creator is the organization or individual which generated or accumulated the materials. Under the latter provision, letters received by Bailey from Smith in Bailey's papers are part of the Bailey collection. Letters sent belong to the recipient (Bailey) and do not get moved into a Smith collection. The files of most organizations and individuals usually include records created, records received and records accumulated in the course of daily activity.

Provenance is identified primarily with the creator rather than the donor if the two are different. Even if the donor of the Bailey papers had been an unrelated heir with a different last name, they would still be the Bailey papers, because Bailey is the creator. It is essential to understand that provenance emphasizes record creators rather than record keepers, and the relationships between records and their creators. As Richard Szary has written, provenance is "a concept that seeks to integrate information about historical materials with information about the context in which they were created."[16] Thus for each set of records archivists need to understand fully two inter-related elements—the materials themselves and the context in which they were created.

Archivists have proposed a number of practical and theoretical justifications for provenance. A key practical argument is that a set of records must be put in one place physically and/or administratively, and that the selection of a location strongly influences intellectual arrangement and description. Provenance permits archivists to avoid the librarian's need to select only one predefined subject for purposes of classification, by accepting the creator or source as the substitute for some devised system of classification. As Michel Duchein wrote, without provenance "all archival work must be arbitrary, inexact and subjective, simply because all the documents could be classified by subject in two or three ways."[17] In addition, provenance allows for an uncomplicated archival organization and a simple description of repository holdings. Collections and se-

---

[13] Richard Lytle, "An Analysis of the Work of the National Information Systems Task Force," *American Archivist* 47 (Fall 1984): 357–365; and David Bearman, *Towards National Information Systems for Archives and Manuscript Repositories: The National Information Systems Task Force (NISTF) Papers, 1981–1984* (Chicago: Society of American Archivists, 1987).

[14] Nancy Sahli, *MARC for Archives and Manuscripts: The AMC Format* (Chicago: Society of American Archivists, 1985, with 1987 update by Lisa Weber); Max Evans and Lisa Weber, *MARC for Archives and Manuscripts: A Compendium of Practice* (Chicago: Society of American Archivists, 1985); and Steven Hensen, *Archives, Personal Papers and Manuscripts: A Cataloging Manual for Archival Repositories, Historical Societies and Manuscript Libraries* (Washington: Library of Congress, 1983). A second edition of *APPM* was published by the Society of American Archivists in 1989.

[15] Evans et al., "Basic Glossary," 427–428.

[16] Richard Szary, review of *Towards Descriptive Standards: Report and Recommendations of the Canadian Working Group on Archival Descriptive Standards*, by the Bureau of Canadian Archivists, *American Archivist* 50 (Spring 1987): 270.

[17] Michel Duchein, "Theoretical Principles and Practical Problems of *Respect des Fonds* in Archival Science," *Archivaria* 16 (Summer 1983): 68.

ries are generally maintained as they were received. The holdings of archives and manuscripts repositories are described and organized on the general level according to inherited administrative structures or the names of individuals and families.

This simplicity does have a price. Organization according to provenance precludes the uniformity of arrangement provided by library classification systems. There are naturally similarities among the holdings of archives. For example, every state produces records about parks. However, no two states will have identical administrative structures relating to parks; hence the archival arrangements for park records cannot be identical.

With automation making it possible to arrange any set of records on paper several different ways without any concern for physical location, the justification for provenance should be and is more than mere convenience. The fundamental point is that provenance remains conceptually the most appropriate way to maintain archives and modern manuscripts. It is the way to preserve the key information inherent in any group of records as a whole—the organizational context and course of activity which led to their creation. As Schellenberg wrote, "There is no information which is more revealing of the content and significance of records than information relating to their functional origins."[18] This is the essential justification for the application of provenance as an organizing principle from the broadest level of government down to the different activities involved in administering a program. Information relating to provenance is at least as important in relation to records as information about an author is to a book.

Actual practice and further refinement bring inevitable complications. In theory, provenance means that the records of two government departments should be maintained separately, even if within those departments there are specific sets of records relating to the same subject or the same program. The Saratoga Department of Natural Resources (DNR) and Department of Transportation may both be involved in highway landscaping, but the records of that activity generated by the two departments will be maintained separately. This is the most basic type of application of provenance. But archivists have had difficulty identifying precisely the organizational or functional levels at which provenance should apply, especially in large and complex organizations. A state bureaucracy like the DNR will include a great many layers of divisions, offices, bureaus and programs. What is the smallest "office" that can be called an "office of origin" for record-creating purposes?

Definitions have varied by country as well as over time and must be adaptable. But there is a general agreement that in the administrative sense the concept of provenance should apply throughout an organization down to the smallest identifiable and relatively stable organizational unit with some defined and coherent function for which it has substantive responsibility. Thus, within the DNR the Office of Park Planning meets those criteria as the record-creating entity for the planning files. One-person units or very transitory programs within that office would generally not meet the criteria.

It is also important to understand, however, that provenance should apply to activity and function as well as organizational structure. Though provenance is often thought of only in terms of the latter, its application to the former is also vitally important. This is the sense in which provenance is applicable to the basic unit of records administration— the series. Series of files derived from particular functions within an office should not be intermingled with files documenting other functions. The person who constitutes the staff of the Public Education Department of the Museum Education Division may conduct programs for both elementary school students and the elderly. If filed separately, the records of the two programs should be maintained separately, even though there is no organizational structure involved. Similarly, series documenting different activities relating to a common function— such as planning proposals for a county park versus planning meetings about that park—will usually be separate. While the most important aspect of provenance and its historical origin relates to the integrity of records *creators*, for practical purposes it extends in modern records to keeping distinct the activity of record *creation* as well. Through this simultaneous documention of organization, function and activity, provenance documents change over time.

Original Order

The principle of original order as formulated in Germany provided that records "are to be maintained in the order and with the designations which they received in the course of the official activity of the agency concerned."[19] Original order is meant to

---

[18] Schellenberg, *Management of Archives*, 81.

[19] Posner, "Archival Development since the French Revolution," 168.

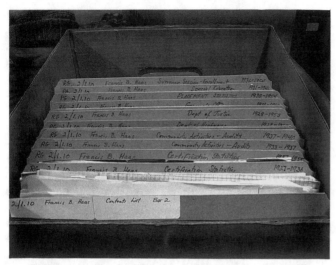

Record storage box with files in order. *(Courtesy of David Scott Husky Photos, Pennsylvania.)*

function within a system organized generally according to provenance. Though developed before the full advent of modern office systems, original order proved to be well adapted to a practice such as the maintenance of loose documents in file folders within boxes and cabinets. Original order preserves the physical arrangement of individual documents within file units such as folders, of those units within filing systems, and of groups of files in relation to each other. Whether the principle can be adapted to automated systems is very much an open question.

Original order was designed to preserve a governmental unit's entire filing structure, including the specific series of records and their inter-relationships. The Dutch system was "based on the original organization of the archival collection, which in the main corresponds to the organization of the administrative body that produced it."[20] In Germany and elsewhere in Europe, all such arrangement was governed by the agency registry officials. In contrast to the emphasis on records creators and functional activity in provenance, original order thus relates mainly to records-keeping and filing systems. Archivists tend to retain almost all coherent filing systems, even if a better one is obvious. Largely because rearrangement is so time consuming and often subjective, original order is generally retained unless it is positively detrimental to the uses for which the records are being preserved. Original order is innocent until proven guilty.

In both theory and practice, however, repositories have been perfectly able to respect provenance

and ignore original order. Unlike the former, the latter principle always contained some flexibility. Archivists recognized that some filing systems they received were capricious or no longer comprehensible. In other cases records were received in disorder and archivists had to devise their own system. The 1898 Dutch manual suggested that faced with recreating an original order, an archivist should "judge whether and to what extent it is desirable to deviate from that order."[21] In theory, original order should be retained when it satisfies certain conditions. That order should:

- preserve some inherent documentary relationships;
- provide information about the creation and use of or activity documented in the records; or
- add to the value of the archives as unbiased evidence of that activity.

The basic justification for original order was, in Jenkinson's words, "the exposition of the Administrative objects which the Archive originally served."[22] Schellenberg maintained that where the original order did not reflect "organic activity" it could be replaced by one that did.[23] Though these principles remain valid for textual records, they are certainly less applicable to complex automated data bases in which information is stored randomly and can form part of several files at once.

The issue of automated records is a reminder that original order is based on the assumption that the overall structure of an agency's records can and should mirror its organizational structure. This is far from being an absolute truth. The more controlled an organization's internal structure and record system, the more valid this assumption tends to become. In American national and local governments, such controlled environments historically have been rare. The series themselves were generally not in a fixed and controlled system. Original order therefore applied mainly to filing order within series. American archivists usually had to devise their own systems for arranging the series in relation to each other.

Levels of Control

"Levels of control" is not a theoretical principle but rather a way of implementing provenance and

[20] Muller, Feith and Fruin, *Manual*, 52.

[21] Ibid., 17.
[22] Jenkinson, *Archival Administration*, 97.
[23] Schellenberg, *Management of Archives*, 100.

original order in the management and processing of records. Both of those principles have traditionally mandated the description or preservation of hierarchical structures. Arrangement by provenance attempts to replicate bureaucratic organization by grouping sets of records produced by subordinate offices under the rubric of a larger agency. The records of the Museum of Art's Adult Programs Department are thus a subordinate part of the larger record group of the Education Division. In original order, documents are parts of file units which are parts of series which in turn may be part of a larger filing system. A letter from Smith to Bailey in 1941 is in a folder marked "Smith, 1940–44," which in turn is in the "Incoming Correspondence" series of Bailey's "Personal Files." As American archivists confronted the mass of modern documentation without benefit of controlled record systems, they turned to these hierarchies as a way to manage their vast holdings.

The result was the development of the concept of levels of control, best described in 1964 in an article by Oliver Wendell Holmes.[24] The essential point is that most modern archival work involves progressively grouping and describing sets of records along a continuum from the largest and most general to the smallest and most specific. Thus the records of an agency can be successively both physically subdivided and intellectually described in terms of its constituent offices, activities, or functions; the file series documenting each office, activity, or function; the files within each series; and the documents within each file. Each of these refinements is regarded as a different level of control.

Each level of control has its own implications for administration, processing needs, and access. Depending on resources and priorities, records can be processed at any level without necessarily proceeding to more detailed work. Thus the park planning series could be listed to what is called the subseries level by noting that a certain range of boxes contained county park files, without necessarily proceeding to the level of listing the file folder headings in those boxes. But even in the most complete processing, different levels of organization provide different kinds of information. At the broadest level of an agency's records or an individual's papers, archivists can gather information about overall history or biography and the general coverage of the records. Series reveal infomation about specific record-creat-

ing activities and file structures, while individual file units and documents convey detailed content information and provide names for indexing. The archival emphasis on the interdependence of records means that all levels of control are related, and thus individual file units cannot be fully understood without an understanding of the larger aggregates.

Like provenance and original order, the concept of levels of control is a necessary oversimplification. The type of straightforward organizational and filing hierarchies it assumes apply mainly to records predating the mid-twentieth century. It becomes less useful as networks of relationships replace hierarchies in both organizations and filing systems. An office may "report" to more than one superior, or be part of changing groups of task-oriented structures. A file may be simultaneously in several offices, through either mechanical reproduction or an automated system, and it may serve a different function in each office. Such changes mean that archival thinking about levels of control should be modified, but not replaced. However complex the structure or network, most organizational units are parts of larger units, and most paper files are still maintained within filing systems. Given the continued applicability of provenance and original order, there remain good reasons for conceptualizing arrangement and description in terms of levels of control.

Collective Description

The principle of describing sets of records collectively rather than as discrete items also derives from the preservation of provenance and original order. The description of an archival collection is to a considerable degree the description of its arrangement; a sequential discussion of its different components. The essentials have changed little since the Dutch manual mandated that "[s]eries must not be described document by document. . . . In the description of an archival collection the important point is that the inventory should serve merely as a guide; it therefore should give an outline of the contents of the collection and not of the contents of the documents."[25] The goal of collective description is to provide a unified overview of the archival or manuscript collection. To borrow a metaphor used by Schellenberg, it deliberately aims to show the forest rather than the trees.[26]

Like provenance and original order, collective description can be understood in terms of the differ-

[24] Oliver W. Holmes, "Archival Arrangement—Five Different Operations at Five Different Levels," *American Archivist* 27 (January 1964): 21–41.

[25] Muller, Feith and Fruin, *Manual*, 108.
[26] Schellenberg, *Management of Archives*, 281.

ences between library and archival practices. In library cataloging, the typical book is described individually according to author, title, publisher and the date and place of publication. The process is essentially a transcription of information from a title page according to standardized rules. Such descriptive cataloging emphasizes the individuality of the book as a separate unit. There is no need to have an overview of other books in the same subject class to find one item.

Archival description, in the absence of title pages, does not and cannot rely on the transcription of information from a prescribed location. Instead, archivists must formulate descriptive information through an examination of the whole corpus of the records themselves and a study of the context in which they were created. In effect, archivists and not the creators have to establish who the "author" is, and what the "title" of the records should be. Further, archivists use collective finding aids to provide meaningful pathways guiding users to specific records. Researchers have to understand the entire record set and its context before being able to retrieve a particular file or group of files. In contrast to this common world-view of archivists, there is very little that is collective or organic about the library system.

In addition to justifications based on the essential nature of archival materials, collective description is also an eminently practical way of dealing with voluminous modern records. Schellenberg wrote that the "technique of collective description provides a short cut to attaining control over the holdings of a repository."[27] The hypothetical thirty cubic foot park planning series, for example, might include more than one hundred thousand individual documents in a thousand file folders, clearly precluding any item-level approach.

Along with others, Schellenberg linked collective description explicitly to levels of control. Description begins with the largest aggregates of records and proceeds to successively finer subdivisions. Archivists can and should describe collectively every logical grouping of records larger than a single item, and every logical grouping will have its own common characteristics. By describing such characteristics for aggregates starting with the broadest level, collective description eliminates the redundancy of describing them for each separate set of records. There is no need to describe the history of the Southside Settlement for every one of the several dozen series generated by the settlement, since all the series de-

---

[27] Ibid., 113.

Figure 3-4 Collective Description of Series

Container Numbers	Series
A. Board of Directors File	
1-14	Minutes, 1909-59. 14 containers. Typed copies of the minutes of the meetings of the board, kept by the secretary, chronologically arranged to the month. Containers 8–14 consist of photocopies of the same material.
15-18	Reports, 1919-39. 4 containers. Copies of reports issued by committees and officers of the Association, including the secretary, treasurer, field secretary, and director of publicity, chronologically arranged to the month.
19-22	Correspondence, 1919-39. 4 containers. Letters, memoranda, and telegrams between board members and officers of the Association, chronologically arranged to the day.
23-24	Annual Meetings, 1915-34. 2 containers. Correspondence, reports, telegrams, and a few speeches, chronologically arranged to the day.
25	Annual Reports, 1919-39. 1 container. Correspondence, memoranda, and some annotated articles prepared for the yearly reports, chronologically arranged to the day.
26-29	Committee Correspondence and Reports, 1920-39. 4 containers. Correspondence, memoranda, statements, and reports, alphabetically arranged by committee and chronologically arranged to the day.
B. Annual Conference File	
1-17	Annual Conferences, 1913-39. 17 containers. Correspondence, telegrams, clippings, resolutions, speeches, reports, and printed matter, chronologically arranged to the day, with speeches, reports, and resolutions filed at the end of each conference.

United States. Library of Congress. Manuscript Division. *National Association for the Advancement of Colored People; A Register of its Records in the Library of Congress, vol. 1.* Washington: Library of Congress, 1972.

scriptions can be subsumed under or related to a single history description. Collective description is thus an efficient as well as an appropriate method of intellectual control.

Provenance, original order, levels of control, and collective description form a coherent system of organization for archives. In our public archives example, the system would work conceptually (though not necessarily physically) as follows:

- Department of Natural Resources records (maintained together administratively on the basis of provenance, including common origin and manageable size) include records of the
- Bureau of Parks and Recreation (also maintained together adminstratively on the basis of provenance) which include records of the
- Office of Park Planning (maintained together both because of provenance and on the basis of original order because the records form a unified filing system).

The Office of Park Planning has a group of records which it maintains together and calls "Planning Files" (retained as a series on the basis of provenance, in the sense of the documentation of a function, and original order), which include

- County park plans arranged alphabetically by county, within county alphabetically by township and within township by date (maintained in original order, despite not being an ideal filing system).

Archivists would maintain this structure and describe the different collective characteristics of the records and record creators at each of these levels. They would also bring together intellectually sets of records regardless of their physical location. The implementation and consequences of this system need to be explored and understood in some detail by all archivists.

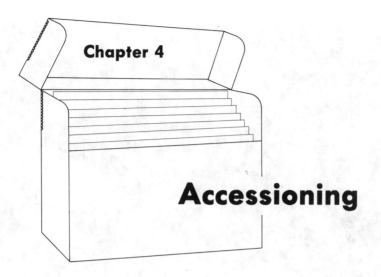

Chapter 4

Accessioning

Accessioning comprises all the steps that repositories take to gain initial physical, administrative, legal, and intellectual control over newly acquired material. The most basic and necessary operation is the transfer of custody from an organization or individual to the archives. But accessioning also involves such crucial activities as the identification of the nature and provenance of records and the summary analysis of their physical condition and intellectual content.

Taken together, these activities make accessioning a rudimentary or preliminary form of complete arrangement and description. Records are grouped roughly by origin and by physical form and condition. They are described according to the key elements of creator, official title or record type, volume, dates, and source. As a result, during accessioning repositories generate a variety of control forms providing both legal and jurisdictional custody and initial physical and intellectual access. Further work of arrangement and description will build upon the information gathered during accessioning. It is important therefore that accessioning should be seen as the first stage of a coordinated repository processing program, and that the information collected at this stage be in a format and terminology usable in later stages of processing.

However, accessioning is not the same as processing. Accessioning involves a cursory examination of *all* records as they enter the repository. Processing, as we shall see, is applied to records *selected* according to institutional priorities rather than merely according to the order in which they are received. In accessioning, the secure transfer of records remains the first requirement, with additional information about the records a secondary concern. Further, the unit of work in accessioning is not necessarily a logical grouping of files, but whatever materials arrive at one time from the same source. A single accession may later be processed as several different groups or collections, as will be the case with the Southside Community Services accession. Conversely, several accessions may eventually be processed together, such as our Office of Park Planning series which came to the state archives at two different times. Accessioning is not the time to process, but it is the time to identify appropriate sets of records for processing in the future.

Despite important differences between archives and manuscript repositories, accessioning at all repositories commonly involves five related activities:

1) preparatory on-site work;
2) physical, legal, and administrative transfer;
3) physical records analysis;
4) content analysis; and
5) preliminary listing.

Each of these activities provides information which is recorded on one or more internal control documents. These forms and the accessioning procedures should be standardized and described in the repository's internal procedures manual.

Preparatory On-site Work

Accessioning should begin as soon as the acquisition and appraisal procedures are completed; as

"Rough" accessioning of Pennsylvania Railroad Company records. *(Courtesy of Pennsylvania Historical and Museum Commission.)*

soon as the repository knows it will receive a certain body of records. In a public or institutional archives with a records management program, records are maintained in order while in active use, and those destined for the archives are identified on disposition schedules. Much archival accessioning is in effect the implementation of the records disposition plan through cooperation between the archives and agency officials responsible for records. Records from series to be preserved at the archives should be scheduled for transfer every few years. In newly established archives, the archivists undertake an initial institutional survey to identify all such series. Though the situation is rarely ideal, most archives do receive regular accretions of scheduled departmental records. (See Figure 4-1).

Records ready to be transfered to the archives should be reviewed by an archivist before being boxed. They should be placed in acid-free archival boxes, maintaining their internal file order, and the boxes labelled on site. Archivists may prepare instructions for boxing and labeling by agency staff. Labels should identify the office of origin, the type of records and the beginning and end of the file groups in the boxes. The label should also indicate the total number of boxes transfered as well as the individual number of each box (e. g., "Box 4 of 17"). A listing of all the label information from each box provides a commonly used initial control document. Archives should also have a general transfer form summarizing the records and the authorizations for their transfer. This form should indicate as well any restrictions on the use of the material and any legal considerations of which users should be aware. (See Figure 4-2.)

Manuscript collections rarely arrive so neatly. The repository can begin accessioning only after the identification of organizations and individuals according to the repository's collecting policy and the successful conclusion of negotiations. Normally, no

Figure 4-1 State of Saratoga, State Archives

RECORDS DISPOSITION SCHEDULE # 12-345 (revised 9/88)

DEPARTMENT Natural Resources
Division Outdoor Recreation
Bureau Parks and Recreation
Office Park Planning

FILE SERIES	MINIMUM RETENTION BY AGENCY (In office or State Records Center)	DISPOSITION
Annual Reports	10 years	Archives
Applications—Jobs	3 years	Destroy
Audits	7 years	Destroy
Budget Submissions	7 years	Destroy
:		
:		
Land Acquisition—parcel files	20 years	Destroy
Ledgers	7 years	Destroy
Legislative Liaison reports	4 years	Archives
:		
:		
Planning files	7 years	Archives
Purchase Orders	2 years	Destroy
Research materials	2 years	Destroy
:		
:		

transfer should take place until after an agreement has been reached between the repository and the donor or depositor which authorizes the transfer of the records and their processing by the repository. Most important, the agreement must stipulate the conditions according to which the records will be opened and used. The most common transfer documents in the case of gifts—usually personal papers—are letters, wills, or formal deeds. Deposit agreements between the repository and the organization are generally used in the case of organizational records. These transfer documents should ensure that the repository has some level of physical and legal control over both the records and, in terms of copyright, over their intellectual contents as well. All restrictions, such as the closing of records for a term of years or limitations on publication, should be clearly established.[1] (See Figure 4-3.)

Because negotiations over acquisitions and agreements dominate manuscript collecting, collections are frequently acquired without having been appraised in detail to determine which specific files are of permanent value. A repository must often either conduct the appraisal process and the on-site boxing simultaneously or receive a substantial body of unappraised material which must then be reviewed. During the boxing of records, manuscript curators try to identify and maintain the order of the files—in fact there are often several different file orders. However, as with institutional records, the file order of manuscript collections should be evaluated during boxing and boxes should be labeled in order to generate initial lists. On-site work is especially crucial for manuscripts since, in the absence of a formal records management program for small organizations and individuals, the people on site are a prime source of information about the records.

Two of our model collections illustrate the contrasts between archives and manuscripts. Records relating to planning generated by the Office of Park Planning of the Department of Natural Resources are to be transferred to the state archives at a time chosen by the DNR once the records are at least seven years old. After a regular agency review by the archives staff, the agency agrees that it can transfer

---

[1] For information on gifts and deposits, see Gary M. Peterson and Trudy Huskamp Peterson, *Archives and Manuscripts: Law* (Chicago: Society of American Archivists, 1985), 24–38.

both 1972–80 planning files still in the office and 1967–78 files stored in the state records center. The files at the records center are already in acid-free archival boxes and have been listed; the records at the office are boxed and listed by the staff using a manual provided by the archives. Except for some photographs and audio tapes, all the records are delivered to the archives in a good file order. However, since they arrive at two separate times from two sources, they are treated as two separate accessions.

A different course of events unfolds once the deposit of the Southside Community Services records at the university library is approved. The archivists find their way to the old community center housing the agency. Told by the staff to take "whatever old stuff you find," they spend the next four days searching through every nook and cranny. One storeroom has five filing cabinets of records from the 1920s to 1960s in good order. In the main administrative office, post-1975 records are also well maintained. But files and papers from other periods and predecessor agencies are scattered all over the building. Lacking an overview of the records, the archivists box everything except duplicates and housekeeping records such as recent staff time sheets. They preserve existing filing orders and note the building location from which each box came, as well as the contents of each box. On the last day of the transfer an agency staffer asks if old books count as archives, and the minutes dating back to 1878 are thus uncovered, next to a box of lantern slides from the 1910s. In the end, fifty boxes of files arrive at the university with no overall structure.

An archivist peruses the manuscript material in a new collection from the Jewish Publication Society of Philadelphia. *(Courtesy of The Balch Institute for Ethnic Studies.)*

Physical and Administrative Transfer

The physical transfer of records can be the responsibility of either the donor or the repository. It is the archivists' responsibility, however, to guarantee the physical integrity of the materials. Records such as glass plate photographs, phonograph records, and computer tapes require special handling and should be boxed and transferred under archival supervision. The physical transfer of all records should be accompanied by a standard form which authorizes transfer of authority and relates specifically to the physical movement of the records. The safest procedure is for the repository to check the total volume of records received and the box labels against lists prepared at the source of the records. The archives should ensure that it is receiving the materials it is agreeing to preserve. A quick review of overall physical condition is also appropriate at the time of receipt to guard against any damage that occurred during transfer.

The first internal procedure after the arrival of records is to enter information about them into the repository's listing of accessions. Every repository should have some minimal information about everything that it contains. If the records lack a formal title, one should be created. The common convention is to call organizational files "records" and personal files "papers." The entirety of the records of an office or the papers of an individual are designated according to their provenance—e.g., George Bailey Papers, Southside Community Services Records. Series titles combine function and record type—e.g., Executive Committee minutes. The accession should also now receive an accession number, used to control it until further processing. The simplest numbering system is usually the best. A combination of a year and an accession sequence is often used, as in 90-01, 90-02,

Figure 4-2

SARATOGA STATE ARCHIVES RECORD TRANSMITTAL FORM	D81789	89-767
	Leave blank – Archives use only	

AGENCY REQUESTING TRANSFER:

Agency   Department of Natural Resources

Major
Subdivision   Bureau of Parks and Recreation

Minor
Subdivision

Office/Unit   Office of Park Planning

Person with whom to confer about contents, location, and shipping of records:
Name   F. Olmstead

2. RECORDS DISPOSITION SCHEDULE
NUMBER: 12-345

3. CURRENT LOCATION OF RECORDS:
[ ] State Records Center
[X] Agency Space (specify):
Room 27 of DNR Building

Phone number   706-1234

4. DESCRIPTION OF RECORDS: (Give overall title of records, contents of individual containers and volumes, dates, or attach Office of General Services Records Center Transfer List if the records are now in the State Records Center.)

[ ] OGS Records Center Transfer List attached   [X] Additional sheet(s) attached

General Title–Planning Files

Box #	Records	Dates
1	Departmental/Divisional Files, A-F	1976-1980
2	Departmental/Divisional Files, G-L	1976-1980
3	Departmental/Divisional Files, M-P	1976-1980
4	Departmental/Divisional Files, P-Z	1976-1980
5	State Park Plans, A-C	1972-1978
6	State Park Plans, D-G	1972-1980

5. ESTIMATED VOLUME: 15   cubic feet _____ items (specify) _____

6. STATEMENT OF AGENCY REPRESENTATIVE: The records described above and on the attached pages are hereby transferred to the Saratoga State Archives in accordance with Section 142 of the State Records Law. It is agreed that these records will be administered in accordance with the provisions of this law and the rules and regulations of the Commissioner of Records and the State Archives. The State Archives may dispose of any containers, unused forms, blank stationary, duplicate records, or other nonrecord material in any manner authorized by law or regulation without further consent of this agency. I certify that I am authorized to act for this agency on matters pertaining to the disposition of agency records.

SIGNATURE _____ TITLE   Administrator   DATE   8/15/89

7. REMARKS CONCERNING SHIPPING/DISPOSITION: Note pickup of Planning Files at State Records Center (Acc89-768) and coordinate storage

8. RESTRICTIONS: Unrestricted

9. RECORDS RECEIVED AT STATE ARCHIVES:

SIGNATURE _____ TITLE   Archivist I   DATE   8/15/89

SR 1-80-3

Figure 4-3

SARATOGA HISTORICAL SOCIETY

DEED OF GIFT

I, Mary Bailey, hereby donate the books, papers, and other historical materials described in Attachment A to the Saratoga Historical Society. I am the owner of these materials and now give and assign to the Historical Society legal title, property rights, and all rights of copyright which I have in them, including the rights to reproduce, publish and display the materials.

The materials shall be maintained, organized and made available for research under the usual procedures of the Historical Society. I understand that any time after delivery of the materials I shall be able to examine them during the regular working hours of the Historical Society. The papers will not be made available to researchers until a standard inventory of their contents has been prepared and a copy received by me.

The Historical Society may dispose of any materials which its representatives determine to have no historical value or permanent interest, providing that prior to any disposal and during my lifetime I shall be notified of such determination, and that at my request the materials proposed for disposal shall be returned to me.

Signed: *Mary Bailey*

Date:

This gift of books, papers and other historical materials is accepted on behalf of the Saratoga Historical Society, subject to the terms and conditions above.

Signed: Curator of Manuscripts

Date:

Attachment A

The following materials were donated by Mary Bailey to the Saratoga Historical Society on (date). The list of materials accepted forms part of the instrument of gift.

4 4-drawer filing cabinets of personal papers generated or assembled and owned by George Bailey and Mary Bailey,

153 autographed historical letters purchased by George Bailey,

509 volumes on American and Saratogan history and biography purchased by George Bailey, and

3 boxes of plaques, diplomas and awards given to George Bailey and Mary Bailey.

for the first two accessions of 1990. Where there are major internal repository divisions the system may be more elaborate, as in A90-01 for internal archives and M90-01 for acquired manuscript collections in an institution preserving both. Other information on the accession form usually includes date received, immediate source, volume, dates of the records, a brief note about their contents and arrangement, and location of the records once shelved. The form can also include references to the authority under which the records were acquired and to related records in the repository. (See Figure 4-4.)

The accession form has traditionally been a page or a card filled out for each accession. Increasingly, repositories use an automated format. Whether duplicated by photocopying or through the computer, the information from accession forms can be used to control records in many different ways. Such information can subsequently be arranged to provide a list of accessions by date acquired and alphabetical listings by donor or originating agency. Files for each donor or agency are especially important for ensuring administrative control and suggesting future acquisitions in both archives and manuscript repositories. Donor/originating agency files generally contain all of the correspondence and related documents concerning a given donor, including the data about each separate accession from that donor. During processing, donor files provide vital information about the context and provenance of every set of records. Accession information can also be used for physical control of records through the generation of a shelf list of records by location. Other types of lists of newly accessioned records—by title, type, and period—can assist intellectual access.

The information recorded on accession forms can be used as the initial stage of a permanent record that is continually refined as processing proceeds. This approach allows information about acquisitions to be immediately represented in a repository-wide descriptive system, and also provides a measure of administrative control over new accessions. The ability to continually refine information about materials as archival processing proceeds was built into the MARC format for the description of archives when it was created in the 1980s. Even the most basic and preliminary data collected at the time of accessioning can be organized in a structure compatible with that format. This basic data can be recorded without any need to fill out all of the information that will be eventually collected or to employ all the elements of standardization to be discussed in Chapter 10.

In the best circumstances, all the work involving accessioning is done while the records are in a special receiving area. Barring complications, they are then moved to one or more stack areas. The final step in initial accessioning is to select and record the location of the materials, which must be updated at every change. Every records container should at the minimum carry the accession number and a unique container number. If possible, all boxes from an accession should be shelved together, except for the separation by physical form discussed below. Most repositories control their records physically in terms of straightforward indicators of room, bay, row, stack, and shelf numbers. The location information should indicate the specific range of rows, stacks, and/or shelves for every set of records described.

In contrast to library systems, there is no intellectual significance attached to the location of archival records in relation to each other. This is primarily because there is no governing classification scheme in archives, but also because archives do not have open stacks in which users can browse. The park planning series for 1967–80 will not necessarily be near other records from the Office of Park Planning, nor will they be in a general area reserved for DNR records. Archives stress instead the most efficient use of space in which the purpose of notation systems is primarily physical access to records by the staff, not by researchers.

Physical Analysis of the Records

Soon after the listing of an accession, an archivist should examine its physical condition and intellectual contents. The physical analysis should concentrate on the records containers, the condition of the enclosed files and papers, and the disposition of nontextual and nonarchival materials. This is especially important in manuscript repositories, where collections commonly arrive in everything from cardboard transfiles to the proverbial shoebox. Such poor storage conditions also mean serious problems of paper deterioration. Textual files should be transferred to acid-free archival storage containers of one cubic foot or less, with oversized material and bound volumes stored in flat boxes. Such archival-quality containers are available from a variety of library and archives supply and equipment companies.

The physical state of records is best assessed by a trained conservator, especially if the records are clearly fragile, valuable or damaged. But all profes-

Figure 4-4 Saratoga Historical Society, Department of Manuscripts

---

ACCESSION FORM

Accession Number 89062   **Collection Number** To be assigned

Creator: Bailey, George Rogers (1911-1987) **Title (Type of Materials):** Family Papers

Inclusive dates: 1802-1986   **Bulk Dates:** 1879-1982

Volume: cu. ft. _____ **items** 150 **other** 4 4-drawer filing cabinets

Donor/Depositor: Mrs. Mary Bailey

123 Elm Street, Bedford Falls, SA

 (address/phone):   (322) BU8-3002

Rights transferred: All

Restrictions: Papers closed until final inventory produced

Accompanying finding aids: Bailey's list of 150 autograph letters

Physical condition: Generally good, with some fragile scrapbooks and letter copies

Place transferred from: 123 Elm Street, Bedford Falls, SA

Individual approving transfer: Mary Bailey   **Transfer Date:** 3/22/89

Description of collection: Personal papers of prominent banker and civic leader, documenting business career and involvement with many civic, political and social service organizations, especially Chamber of Commerce, Republican Party and Southside Community Center. Also includes diaries of father (Peter) and some papers of wife, Mary, documenting work with Middletown Museum of Art, and 150 item autograph collection of US Presidents and early Saratogans.

Related collections: Middletown Chamber of Commerce

Key personal names: Bailey, Mary; Bailey, Peter; Chambers, Henry; . . . .

Key Corporate names: First National Bank of Middletown; Bedford Falls Savings and Loan; Middletown Chamber of Commerce; Middletown Museum of Art; Republican Party; . . .

Key places described: Bedford Falls, Middletown, Saratoga

Major subjects: Banking; Politics; Social Services

Location of materials in repository: File Cabinets in Accessioning Area;
                            Autographs in Vault, Stack 8, Shelf 5

Initial accession date: Nov. 15, 1989   **Date of last update:** 11/18/89

  Compiler: D. Reed   **Compiler:** D. Reed

---

sional archivists should be able to determine if the papers or their folders suffer from mold damage, moisture, insect infiltration, or excessive brittleness. The work during accessioning will be a general review rather than the file-by-file examination that can be done later during processing. Damaged records may need to be repaired or copied. Archivists should also consider which records must be fumigated, cleaned or unfolded. The condition of records as received should be noted on accession forms. Further work such as deacidification will be determined by the policies, procedures and facilities that every repository should have for conservation and preservation. For guidance, archivists should consult the Society of American Archivists' manual entitled *Pre-*

serving Archives and Manuscripts and where necessary obtain the advice of trained conservators and preservation experts.[2]

An equally important aspect of physical analysis deals with nontextual records. Photographs of all kinds, motion picture films, blueprints, maps, audio recordings, magnetic tapes and discs and other types of historical documentation require different systems for storage and handling. In addition, the nature of their use and the information they contain

[2] See Mary Lynn Ritzenthaler, *Preserving Archives and Manuscripts* (Chicago: Society of American Archivists, forthcoming). For a review of the technical aspects of conservation see National Research Council, *Preservation of Historical Records* (Washington: National Academy Press, 1986), which is available from the Society of American Archivists.

often dictate retrieval systems geared to individual items rather than the collective description appropriate for textual records.

Specific procedures for dealing with the many kinds of nontextual records vary enormously among repositories. Some repositories have separately staffed units for the major types of nontextual records—such as a Photographic Archives Section—while others rely on separate stacks or shelving. In some cases, nontextual materials are simply maintained as separate series within a collection, without any other physical separation. During accessioning, archivists should identify coherent sets of material which might deserve separate physical and/or intellectual treatment, such as boxes of photographs or sets of maps. Again, this is not the time for consideration of individual items or files. Thus within the park planning series a coherent body of maps maintained exclusively as such can be treated separately, but not so a single file of maps within a box of paper records about a given park. The contents of an individual folder should ordinarily not be divided, unless there are compelling reasons relating to physical deterioration or storage problems. In most cases, every effort should also be made to keep together a clearly unified set of folders, even if some folders are nontextual records and others are not. (The handling of the major different types of nontextual records is discussed in the separate Society of American Archivists manuals as noted in Chapter 1.)

When nontextual records are to be removed from the accessioned group for special storage or handling, archivists list them on separation forms. A form is used for each different set of material, noting its contents, volume and dates, the original location of the material within the accession, and its new location. All of the forms providing information about the accession remain together throughout processing, so that staff and users can always identify the entirety of an accession, regardless of format. Whatever the physical location, the materials will thus remain intellectually and administratively part of the original accession and will be processed together with the rest of the materials. This is especially crucial in cases where a series remains intellectually the same while its physical form changes. For example, the public meetings of the Office of Park Planning may have been documented through typed transcripts up to 1972, then on reel-to-reel audio tape until 1978 and thereafter on videotape. In such cases, repositories should always be able to intellectually reconstitute accessions and series regardless of divisions by format. Intellectual unity is

more important than physical divisions. (See Figure 4-5.)

Newly accessioned records are also often found to contain publications. Publications can be considered archival if created or received in the course of business, or if they form an integral part of a file documenting some activity. A series relating to child labor in the Southside Settlement records may contain a variety of published reports filed with original correspondence as well as typed reports. Publications which have been annotated in some way that relates to the activity documented in the records should also be retained with the regular records. Often organizational records or personal papers are accompanied by a related yet separately maintained library or research collection. Manuscript repositories are usually part of institutions containing their own libraries, to which the publications can be offered. The manuscripts department would retain only a list of the transferred material. Thus Bailey's five hundred history books would be sent from the historical society's manuscript department to its library for possible addition to its holdings, after a separation form has been prepared.

Content Analysis

The physical and intellectual analyses of a new accession should proceed simultaneously. This is obviously convenient and efficient, since in practice the records need only be spread out once for examination. But the analyses are also interrelated conceptually. The Southside Community Services collection contains a large number of photographs which should be physically separated from the other records for purposes of storage and perhaps for item-level description. But if those photographs came from different predecessor agencies, intellectual as well as physical distinctions will be necessary. Some of the lantern slides, for example, might be identified as having come from the Tenth Street Settlement rather than the Southside Settlement. In this case it is not enough simply to identify a collection as "Lantern Slides;" it must also be distinguished by provenance.

The most important intellectual activity performed during accessioning is this identification of the accession by provenance and/or type of record series. The identity—or identities—provided here will structure all future processing. In most public or institutional archives, the provenance is the creating office, or the most recent creating office if there have been organizational changes. Accessions are often

Figure 4-5   Saratoga State University, University Libraries—Department of Special Collections

---

REGIONAL HISTORY CENTER

MANUSCRIPT COLLECTION SEPARATION SHEET

Collection Name: Southside Community Services   **Acc. No.** 89−305 **Coll. No.** M725
Type of Material: Photographs   **Physical Format:** Lantern Slides   **Size:** 3″ × 4″
Number of Items: 150   **Total volume:** 1 linear foot (2 Archives boxes)
Dates of Material: c.1905−1920
Description (list each container and folder where necessary):
  Box 1−"Neighborhood Views" # 1−40
        "Settlement House Staff and Activities" # 41−72
  Box 2 "Settlement House Staff and Activities" # 73−105
        "Social and Housing Problems" # 106−150
Originally filed in Container: Box 57
    as part of (filing system): "Photographs"
Now located in: Photographic Archives Section
    specific location: Range R5/ Stack 3/ Shelf 9
Separation date: Oct 13, 1989   **Separated by:** D. Toner
Remarks: Images to be copied to produce one master negative for preservation, one negative for reproduction and one set of prints for users
NOTE— File 1 copy in original location, 1 copy with materials in new location, 1 copy in collection file and 1 copy with finding aid.

---

one or more series rather than the records of a whole office or agency. The series should be already identified through the records management program. Occasionally the archivist will have to determine how many separate series exist in a given accession, through an analysis of the records' forms and filing structures and the functions or activities they document.

Manuscript collections more commonly than archives raise questions at the basic level of provenance. Records from an organization can include the records of predecessor agencies, merged agencies or even tangentially related organizations. Whatever divisions are eventually made, it should always be possible to reconstitute any original accession. Where a related group of accessioned files independently documents the history of an organization, those records can be treated as a separate collection for processing and use. Generally records of direct predecessors or merged organizations are maintained as subdivisions of the collection of the current organization. This is often justifiable on the grounds of both historical context and merged filing systems. Where such continuity is lacking, it is more appropriate to establish a separate collection. An older

organization's records may simply have been stored with a newer one, and then transferred with the latter to the archives.

Personal papers present similar challenges. They may be the papers of more than one person, with collections including ancestors' papers as well as those of contemporary family members. The determination of whether separate collections should be established will again depend on the individuals and the integrity of the filing structure. Personal papers may also include whole sets of business or organizational records, though these are rarely complete or independent enough to warrant consideration as separate collections. In reviewing such subsets of organizational records and determining their proper provenance, archivists should be aware of the concept of *replevin*, according to which many types of public records found in private custody are theoretically recoverable by public authorities.[3] The determination of provenance and the division of accessions into separate series should in general be marked by caution. It is very difficult to accurately reconstitute the structure of divided accessions.

---

[3] Peterson and Peterson, *Law,* 90–93.

Our sample collections illustrate the key issues. Though created under two different departments (Conservation and Natural Resources), the park planning records constitute one series having a common filing structure and content. For administrative purposes within the state archives, the series is identified with the DNR because that is the organization which has existed since 1972. The museum's Education Division files are also kept together, despite the presence of early files from the Public Relations Department which later became an independent division. Embedded within the division's file system and part of its history, those public relations records remain where they are.

In contrast, the Southside Community Services collection contains the records of several organizations which had separate histories before being absorbed into the present agency. Those which formed direct constituent parts of the current agency, such as the original Union Mission, should not be treated as separate collections. But one organization—the Whomsoever Mission—simply left its records to the Southside Community Center when it dissolved in 1957 without any formal merger. Those records should form a separate collection, since they have no integral link to the other records. The connection that did exist will be reflected in the accession form's information that the records arrived together. Similarly, if Mary Bailey's relatively few files are interfiled with those of her husband, they will remain in the George Bailey collection, though eventually they will be described under her name. But the three diaries of Bailey's father, dating from 1901 to 1919, were not part of any filing system and relate in no way to the son's papers. They should constitute a separate collection. Repositories should have specific policies for dealing with issues such as these. It might be simpler to entitle the entirety of the accession as the "Bailey Family Papers," rather than try to divide it according to family members.

Archivists should take the time to verify and refine basic information about the title, volume, time span, contents, and arrangement of the records listed on the initial accession form. Since final processing may be months or years away, a summary description of the contents may be prepared, indicating significant names, dates, topics, and types of records. This can provide a basic level of intellectual access, while also serving as the foundation for future descriptive work. As in the case of the initial form, the summary description should be organized in terms of the different elements of information that will be refined or retained throughout process-

ing. This organization will also facilitate the standardization and exchange of information about the records at a later date. (See Figure 4-6.)

Repositories, especially manuscript repositories, may also find it necessary to do some unfinished work of appraisal and weeding during accessioning. Weeding will usually involve the automatic disposal of duplicates and blank forms. Appraisal will commonly mean the identification of large groups of detailed housekeeping and financial records, as well as other records which an experienced archivist might reasonably suspect as having no permanent value. None of these records should be disposed of without the approval of archivists responsible for appraisal.

Restricted records should also be separately identified during accessioning. These may include:

a) security classified records such as those at the National Archives or Presidential Libraries, or in the manuscript collections of government officials;

b) personnel records, case files and contracts in public and institutional collections; and

c) materials restricted for a term of years under gift or deposit agreements in manuscript repositories.

Such restrictions should be noted and the records labeled accordingly so that they are not handled by unauthorized staff or made available for use before full processing. A more subjective area requiring judgment by the archivist concerns possible breaches of privacy or confidentiality, or potential cases of libel in records lacking any imposed restrictions. Since it is usually impossible to read every document in a collection, sets of records posing potential difficulties—such as purely personal correspondence and diaries of fairly recent date—should be noted during accessioning. They can be reviewed later by an archivist qualified to make the relevant legal assessments.

Preliminary Listing

Archival records should come from offices or records centers with a summary list already prepared. If records arrive without any indication of the contents of the individual boxes, such a description should be prepared. This can be merely a list of box numbers with the briefest indication of contents, such as "Box 8: Correspondence, 1976–78, E–H" Even for large bodies of records, the list can usually be prepared by clerical staff. Attached to the other accession information, the box list is a vital tool for

Figure 4-6   Saratoga State University, University Libraries—Department of Special Collections

REGIONAL HISTORY CENTER
COLLECTION SUMMARY DESCRIPTION

Collection Name: Southside   **Accession No.:** 89-305   **Collection No.:** M725
Community Services, Inc.

Dates: Inclusive 1874-1983   **Bulk** 1878-1980

Volume: 61 cu. ft. (rec. ctr. cartons) **Location of Records:** A3-5-7 through
A4-2-3

History/Biography: Founded in 1878 as Episcopal Church-affiliated Union Mission. Became Southside Settlement House in 1900, ending church affiliation. Absorbed Tenth Street House (est. 1903) and St. John's House (est. 1915) in 1948, both becoming branches. In 1963 merged with Southside Day Nursery and Children's Center (est. 1886) to form Southside Community Center. Reflecting new urban renewal and community organization responsibilities, became Southside Community Services in 1975. Since 1922 has maintained various camp facilities on Lake Superior.

Scope and Contents of Records: Early records include bound volumes (minutes, correspondance, etc.) and Matron's reports for Union Mission (1878-1900, 3.5 cu. ft.); reports, minutes and other records of Tenth Street House (1904-48, 3 cu. ft) and St. John's House (1915-48, 2.5 cu. ft.). Administration, programs and services of Southside Settlement (1900-63), Community Center (1963-75) and Community Services (1975-) documented fairly comprehensively in 41 cu. ft. of textual records. Day Nursery (1886-1963) and associated Children's Center (est. 1916) documented in 2 cu. ft. of minutes, reports and correspondance. Collection also includes photographs, scrapbooks, clippings, and pamphlets

Arrangement of Records:
Records of Union Mission, Tenth Street House and St. John's House, and Day Nursery are separate from main body of material. Southside Settlement/Community Center files 1900-1968 are in varying file groups with folder titles. Records for 1968-74 are disordered. Post-1974 records are organized by Division and program, then alphabetically or chronologically.

Finding Aids: Box summary list prepared   **Published References:** Bronstein, L., The
during accessioning   History of Midwestern Social
Services (Middletown, 1981)

Restrictions/Conditions of Use:
Post-1920 case files open only with agency permission; no citation of
names of employees or clients

Key terms

Personal: Addams, Jane; Bailey, George; Bowman, Henry; . . .
Corporate: Middletown Day Nursery; South Middletown Children's
Center; . . . .
Geographical: Middletown; South Middletown
Subject: African Americans; Children, Immigrants; Housing; Settlement
Houses; Social Conditions; Social Services
Form of materials: Photographic prints; photographic negatives; lantern
slides; scrapbooks; clippings

Prepared by: R. Woods   **Date:** Sept. 7, 1989

Figure 4-7 Middletown Museum of Art, Museum Archives

Initial Container List

Record Creator (administrative unit or individual/title): Education Division

Record Group No.: 06   **Acc. No.:** A89077

List prepared by: N. Intern   **Date:** 3/17/89

Box #	Records title (creator/type)	Dates	Location*
1	Division Director/Administrative Files	1927-75	15/3/1
2	Division Director/Program Files A-P	1930-82	15/3/1
3	Division Director/Program Files R-Z	1937-82	15/3/2
	Division Director/Staff Reports	1972-79	15/3/2
	Division Director/Correspondence A-F	1941-82	15/3/2
4	Division Director/Correspondence G-Z	1941-82	15/3/2
5	Children's Department/School District	1935-66	15/3/3
6	Children's Department/School District	1967-82	15/3/3
	Children's Department/Community Programs	1940-82	15/3/3
7	Adult Programs/Project Files	1955-82	15/3/4
8	Adult Programs/Administrative Files	1952-82	15/3/4
.			
.			
.			
42	Admin. Secretary/Personnel Records	1973-79	18/3/1
	Admin. Secretary/Financial Records	1967-79	18/3/1
43	Public Relations/General Files	1948-65	18/3/1
	Public Relations/Publicity Listings	1948-65	18/3/1
44	Education Division/Minutes	1927-77	18/3/2
	Education Division/Annual Reports	1928-88	18/3/2
45	Education Division/Publications	1927-82	18/3/2

*Location symbol— Range/Stack/Shelf

physical, administrative and intellectual control and access. (See Figure 4-7.)

Lists prepared for manuscript collections are often more detailed than lists for archival groups or series. Because such collections are usually smaller, more heterogeneous, and less organized, listing on the folder level is usually advisable. The final box/folder listing should also include nontextual materials. If resources permit and the collection is disorganized, staff should check supplied folder titles against contents.

The preparation of box and folder lists will be especially important if the repository allows access to collections after accessioning but before full arrangement and description is completed. This is an important policy decision which every repository must make based on the nature of its holdings, the needs of its users, and its institutional resources. The decision need not be uniform for all records in a repository. Collections which have little recent personal information, contain few valuable documents, are of interest primarily to scholars and may not be fully processed for years can often be opened for research once a basic list is completed. Collections which are more sensitive or will be processed sooner because of their small size or important contents will usually be closed to external use until processing is completed. However, even such collections should be listed at least at the box level during accessioning for effective physical and administrative control.

For modern records, control during accessioning rarely goes below the folder level. However, valuable documents like those in Bailey's autograph collection should be promptly listed for purposes of insurance and security as well as future access. Such individually valuable items should also be marked in a nondamaging manner with a unique identifying symbol. The simplest procedure is to mark the document on its reverse side in pencil with the accession number, container number, and a sequential document number.

At the end of accessioning an archivist should have gained legal and physical control over a newly received body of records and laid the foundation for future processing. The records should be boxed, listed, and shelved. They should be separated where appropriate by physical form, and by provenance or file series. Unwanted materials should have been disposed of and fragile, restricted, or valuable records identified. The repository should have basic data about the records' physical and intellectual attributes, gathered in such standardized control documents as accession forms, separation lists, and box and folder lists.

In this way accessioning is a summary of processing as a whole. For many uncomplicated archival collections in good order much of the work of processing is indeed completed during accessioning. Even in such cases, however, information about the records still has to be integrated into a repository-wide descriptive system and the records' context and contents more fully analyzed before they can be used effectively. For most manuscript collections, accessioning provides only the basis for the larger work of arrangement and description. Further processing will be determined by institutional policies and priorities, as well as by the information about the records collected during accessioning.

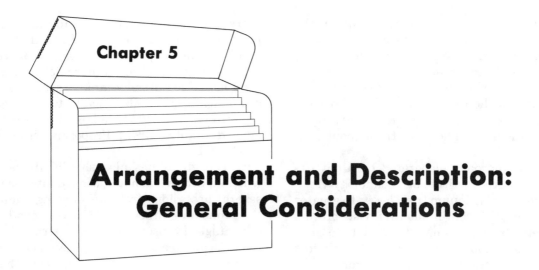

Chapter 5

Arrangement and Description: General Considerations

Establishing Priorities

All repositories have a backlog of accessioned records awaiting full arrangement and description. This is mainly the result of the bulk and complexity of modern records combined with limited insititutional resources. The larger the backlog, the more complete should be the information gathered during accessioning, for it will long serve as the basic physical, administrative, and intellectual control over the records. Archivists must select which of their backlogged records should be arranged and described, and decide how much detail in processing is appropriate for these records. Levels of control and progressively refined arrangement and description provide a useful framework for such decisions. But decisions about the processing of individual sets of records can be effectively formulated only in the context of a repository-wide processing program based on institutional goals and priorities. That program together with the nature of the records themselves will determine the best way to process a body of material.

The overall processing program should be based on the mission, resources, and clientele of the repository. Each repository should develop general guidelines for both the selection of records to be processed and the way they should be processed. Clearly the more salient a collection to the central institutional mission, the sooner it should be processed. The Southside Settlement records are of more importance to a university library documenting local social history than the Bailey papers would be, while the latter are more important to a historical society

preserving the legacy of the area's leading citizens. The selection of records to process will also employ criteria similar to those used in archival appraisal to weigh the comparative administrative utility and research value of various unprocessed records.[1]

The museum archivist may thus decide that the Education Division records—which are in relatively good order—can and should be processed quickly because they will interest a variety of internal and external users and provide a broader picture of the museum's activities than the disordered records of more mundane internal departments. Conversely, the historical society's manuscript curator may determine that the Bailey papers are less important than the papers of a more prominent local figure, and are too disordered to process without considerable effort. They will then await processing while being controlled and accessed through the existing accession forms and container list.

The repository processing program should extend beyond the selection of records and ensure that processing is a balanced and coordinated activity. Activities should be carried out in a logical order. Records should not be arranged but then left undescribed. Neither should arrangement and description be conducted in isolation from the work of preservation and conservation. Reference staff should be informed about new accessions and consulted about processing priorities, since they will be most familiar with user interests and needs. In the later stages

---

[1] See F. Gerald Ham, *Selecting and Appraising Archives and Manuscripts.* (Chicago: Society of American Archivists, forthcoming).

of processing, they should review the drafts of the inventories, guides, and catalog entries used to describe records. The processing program should generate summary data to provide both administrators and staff with a general overview of the state of work on all materials in the repository. No set of records should be seen in isolation, for the decision to process one set of records has implications throughout a repository.

A popular approach elaborated by archivists at the Massachusetts Institute of Technology views processing along a continuum from lesser to greater specificity.[2] Along this continuum archivists process each set of records in a manner appropriate to their particular nature and probable use. The choices range from simply retaining the order, summary description, and box list prepared during accessioning to item-level description and indexing. In the past, an emphasis on uniformly detailed processing to the item level resulted in repositories having immense backlogs of undescribed, inaccessible records and a small number of perfectly processed collections. The key goal of a processing program should be instead to maximize the proportion of a repository's holdings available for effective use. It is better to have a high proportion of records with general series-level descriptions than a small proportion with comprehensive item- or folder-level indexes.

General processing guidelines should indicate the level of detail considered appropriate for the arrangement and description of most of the repository's holdings. Essentially, this will be the level which facilitates most of the probable use of the materials without an excessive investment of repository resources. In most manuscript repositories, the standard of description is now the folder level. Records are arranged in folder order and, as part of the inventory, a folder title listing is provided. In most archives, records management should ensure that recent records are in a logical folder order, though the volume of such records commonly precludes individual folder-level listings. Archival processing is therefore generally at the level of the series and their major subdivisions.

Processing guidelines may also indicate what kinds of records most of the repository's clientele use, so that such records within a collection may receive more careful processing than other parts of the collection. It is important to understand that

there is no requirement that all sets of records be processed to the same level of detail. The museum archivist, for example, may want to provide within the Education Division a more detailed description for a box of lectures by famous speakers than for a box of grant proposals. Each lecture might be listed separately, while a whole box of proposals could be labeled simply "Grant Proposals—School District, 1968–1971."

The guidelines also should discuss how and when an archivist should consolidate for processing several accessions from an ongoing agency. While the immediate processing of accessions has obvious advantages for users and administrators, it can also result in an excessive fragmentation of a repository's holdings. A more controversial issue that may be broached is the selection of important records that may have been processed incorrectly or inappropriately in the past and need either refinement or reprocessing. As noted earlier, the guidelines should discuss as well the conditions under which unprocessed materials are made available for research.

It may be easier to decide *to* process a body of records than to decide *how* to process them—what kind of information to provide, how much detail to supply, and what formats to use. These decisions depend on available resources, possible uses of the material, and the nature of the records themselves. These factors will be assessed utilizing the information gathered during accessioning. The effort required to implement a usable arrangement varies in difficulty according to:

    a) the size of the collection,
    b) its current arrangement,
    c) changes over time in organizational structure,
    d) changes in filing structure, and
    e) the variety of physical formats present.

Similarly, the complexity of descriptive work will be largely determined by the time span, contents, and record type of the files. Thus a series of program files may include file names that may by their nature be self-descriptive (i.e., Job Corps, Staff Selection), but general minutes and correspondence files often need further elaboration. Similarly a subject may be identical with the name of a series or file, as in the plans for a specific park. However, there will also be cases in which the file titles give little indication of the subject of the records (e.g., the Southside Settlement servicing an Italian neighborhood without any file titles containing the word "Italian").

---

[2] Karen T. Lynch and Helen W. Slotkin, *Processing Manual for the Institute Archives and Special Collections* (Cambridge: MIT Libraries, 1981).

The estimation of possible uses of records is for the most part subjective. While public and institutional archives are commonly patronized by scholars, genealogists and the general public, theoretically they must process materials with a view first to potential internal uses by executives, legal and financial officials, and other staff. This requirement is to some extent mandated and predictable. But in practice, archives, like manuscript repositories, serve mainly outside users. Manuscript repositories have no official clientele comparable to that of archives.

The staff of all repositories should have a good idea what their users will want and how they can go about finding it. The university librarians may assume that the Southside records will be of interest mainly to scholars, and that they will be able to understand a file title like "House Reports, 1914–1917." The state archivists may suspect that public officials would come to the park planning files for specific information on a park, and would not find useful a listing of "Park Reports, 1970, A–F." The archivists may decide therefore that a list of the specific parks is required for effective description. In the planning of processing, understandings of current use should be combined with reasonable projections about patterns of future use. Such projections in the archival world are not based on scientific models. Archivists base their estimates instead on a combination of available quantitative data about research use, a knowledge of the reasons why given records were created, and an understanding of the evolving interests of various user communities.[3]

Resources and Facilities

Assessing available institutional resources is vitally important in planning processing. With limited resources, repositories should generally process collections only to the level of detail that makes the collection usable by most researchers. Within that constraint, archivists should try to weigh the relative costs of processing different groups of records. They should be able to calculate for their own institution the direct costs of labor, supplies, and equipment for work on each collection as a whole, and also on a per unit (per box) basis. The major direct

benefits of processing tend to be intangible, or difficult to quantify, such as an increase in "significant" research. Direct cost-benefit comparisons are thus questionable, though processing usually reduces the bulk of the records. The key issue remains comparative costs of processing one body of records as opposed to another.

Each repository must do its own calculation of processing costs because of the variables involved.[4] An archives' main expense is for labor. The use of student or volunteer labor can make hourly costs at academic repositories and historical societies much lower than those at public or institutional archives. On the other hand such archives may employ a higher proportion of clerical versus professional staff. If manuscript work means describing records to the folder level or refoldering records, it will involve far more time than archival work. The extent and nature of automation will also have a significant effect on processing costs. Automation entails significant start-up costs. Beyond that, it often does not result in long-term savings as much as in the ability to accomplish more processing for an equal or only marginally larger outlay of funds. Decisions relating to automation, personnel, and even the type of preservation storage supplies to be used are policy decisions that the repository has to make.

The cost of processing any given collection is thus a product of institutional policies and the nature of the records. Because they arrived in better order and better physical condition, the park planning and museum records should be easier to process than the Southside Community Services collection. However, they may not be less expensive to process, depending on the level of detail desired by users and the impact of institutional personnel policies.

A repository must commit resources to processing beyond staff costs and supplies. Processing requires space—a special area where records being processed can be stored and spread out for simultaneous work by several people. There should be separate tables or workbenches and sorting shelves for each collection being processed. The processing area as a whole should have its own supply storage cabinets, desks, and equipment such as a computer, a photocopier, and a microform reader. Other specialized equipment will be required for dealing with non-

---

[3] Model comprehensive approaches are discussed in Larry Hackman and Joan Warnow-Blewett, "The Documentation Strategy Process: A Model and a Case Study," *American Archivist* 50 (Winter 1987): 12–47; and Joan K. Haas, Helen W. Samuels and Barbara T. Simmons, *Appraising the Records of Modern Science and Technology: A Guide* (1985), available from the Society of American Archivists.

[4] See Terry Abraham, Stephen Balzarini and Anne Frantilla, "What is Backlog is Prologue: A Measurement of Archival Processing," *American Archivist* 48 (Winter 1985): 31–44; and Uli Haller, "Variations in the Processing Rates on the Magnuson and Jackson Senatorial Papers," *American Archivist* 50 (Winter 1987): 100–109.

An archivist works in the processing area with a manuscript collection. *(Courtesy of the Balch Institute for Ethnic Studies, Philadelphia.)*

textual records such as photographs, films, video tapes, and audio tapes. The processing area should be distinct from the general stacks, public use areas, and the separate area devoted to conservation work. (See Figure 5-1.)

The Administration of Processing

The allocation of resources to processing is one aspect of the overall administration of arrangement and description. By its nature, processing is the essence of orderliness. It places a premium on detail and precision, and therefore demands careful, logical and well-coordinated administration. The key aspects of that administration are: established procedures, explicit planning and decision making, and a sensible division of labor. The daily institutional processing environment will be a product of such policies and procedures combined with available institutional resources.

Established internal procedures should be codified in a procedures manual. Every repository should have its own manual, which should be regularly up-

dated. The manual will encompass all aspects of processing from accessioning to the final entry of information into the repository-wide descriptive system and, where appropriate, a national data base. The manual should cover matters ranging from routine tasks such as refoldering, removing metal fasteners, disposing of duplicates, and sorting items within folders to more challenging issues such as treating nontextual records, identifying series and subseries, and selecting indexing terms. Procedures for the physical treatment and storage of records should represent an adaptation of standard conservation and preservation techniques to the circumstances and resources of the repository. The same principle of adaptation will apply to repository procedures for accessioning, arrangement and description. The manual should proceed methodically through all the possible steps of processing. It should also indicate what options are available in the different stages of processing, who should decide which options to choose, and who should carry out the different tasks. (See Figure 5-2.)

Figure 5-1   Processing Facilities

General Environment of processing area should be:
- Large enough for storage and staff activities, often about 20% of the total repository area
- Near loading/delivery area
- Air-conditioned, dry and cool with monitored temperature and humidity
- Secure, with controlled entry and exit, locks and alarms, and smoke detection and fire suppression devices
- Exposed to little or no direct sunlight

Furnishings—Large tables (3' x 6') and/or workbenches
- Office desks and chairs
- Supply cabinets
- Filing cabinets

Equipment— Computer (microcomputer) or computer terminal with printer and computer workstation furniture
- Typewriter
- Ladder, kickstools, handtrucks and booktrucks
- Photocopier
- Microfilm reader
- Card catalog
- Cleaning equipment, including vacuum cleaner

Shelving/Storage—Adjustable metal shelving in various sizes and depths, placed around periphery of processing area
- Oversize flat cases (map cases) for maps, blueprints, posters, etc.
- Sorting shelves (file/literature organizers)

Supplies— Acid-free boxes, document cases, and containers for all sizes and types of records, textual and nontextual
- Acid-free folders, envelopes, and sleeves for textual and photographic records
- Archival-quality fasteners
- Archival-quality copying paper
- Labels
- Cleaning supplies
- General office supplies

Reference collection—
- Materials on archival processing and preservation
- Materials on history of institutions/themes/areas which collections document

Media-specific equipment as needed—
- Reel-to-reel and cassette audio tape player
- Motion picture viewer
- Videotape player
- Light table and related photographic equipment

NOTE: This does not include most conservation equipment and supplies, which should be in separate conservation area.

The procedures manual will in this way be supportive of the ongoing planning and decision making crucial to effective processing. Every major activity should include some time for reflection and group decisions. The MIT system suggests that the archivist responsible for a collection prepare a processing proposal for discussion with colleagues. Though not always necessary, that level of formality ensures an explicit review and documentation of processing. Efficient processing requires the creation of a work plan for each group of records to be processed. A well conceived plan will permit several staff members to be working on different parts of the collection at the same time. However, all processing plans will have to take into account general institutional personnel policies, which may restrict their flexibility. The preparation of an overall processing plan will force the archivist to consider repository-wide policies and priorities, and decide among alternatives.

The plan for each set of records need not be long or detailed, but it should prompt the staff to:

1) outline the current state of the records;
2) indicate the preferred state of arrangement, stressing the nature and proposed arrangement of the different components;

Figure 5-2   Outline of a Model Procedures Manual

Overview of processing:
    Principles of arrangement and description
    Administration and staff responsibilities
    Physical facilities and rules for handling records
Accessioning:
    Boxing and listing on site
    Physical transfer procedures and forms
    Accessioning forms
    Acknowledgement procedures
    Separation of nontextual records
        photographs
        films
        sound recordings
        videotapes
        computer tapes and disks
        maps and architectural materials
        posters and broadsides
        publications
    Identifying separate collections within an accession
    Reboxing and labeling
    Recording basic information and checking for related collections
    Preparing container lists
Arrangement:
    Reviewing collection file and surveying collection
    Preparation and approval of work plan
    Basic research on records and creators
    Intellectual organization by creators and file sets
    Physical organization by file sets and boxes
    Deciding when to retain/discard original order
    Imposing an arrangement—choosing a system
    Folder-level organization and folder labeling
    Item-level organization
    Weeding duplicates and identifying routine records for appraisal
    Identifying restricted records
    Identifying records with potential confidentiality problems
    Labeling boxes and folders
Preservation during processing:
    Boxing records
    Refoldering
    Photocopying
    Flattening
    Removing fasteners
    Cleaning
    Identifying problems for Conservation Department
Description:
    Internal finding aids—nature and structure
    Deciding on level of detail and type of finding aids
    Staff responsibilities
    Describing records creators

Figure 5-2   Outline of a Model Procedures Manual—Continued

Description (continued):
    Describing records
    Describing archival activities
    Final container listings
    Entering information into repository catalogs and indexes
    Preparing the descriptive information—
        finding standard forms of names and places
        finding standard subject index terms
        applying standard forms and terms
    Style
        punctuation
        spelling
        spacing
        abbreviations
    Filing rules
    Editing descriptions
    Preparing summary descriptions for:
        institutional publications (narrative descriptions)
        bibliographic utility (MARC entry or entries)
Administrative requirements:
    Reporting procedures
    Keeping track of supplies, time, and facilities used
    Updating information as processing proceeds
Appendices:
    Forms—blank and samples
    Processing checklist
    Sources of information for terms
    Technical cataloging manuals
    Structure of USMARC format and applicable AACR2 rules

3) explain how the proposed arrangement relates to the desired level of description and the probable uses of the records;
4) indicate which staff members will perform which tasks;
5) discuss special problems such as conservation needs, care of nontextual records and collection restrictions;
6) estimate the time and resources required for both arrangement and description; and
7) outline a general work flow, work schedule and division of labor among the staff.

A processing plan such as this will be especially valuable for collections such as the Southside Community Services records, which are both disordered and complex. Without some overall restraints and decisions about priorities, the processing of such a collection to an arbitrary level of common detail can strain institutional resources. At the same time, the collection is ideal for coordinated parallel processing, since some staff members can be working on the turn-of-the-century bound volumes from predecessor agencies, while others concentrate on the comparatively well ordered files of the 1930s through the 1950s, and a third group processes the scattered documents of 1968–1974. All the groups can benefit from a sense of the overall structure of the collection, and from guidelines relating to the treatment of deteriorating paper and the variety of nontextual records found in the collection. (See Figure 5-3.)

The division of tasks between professional and nonprofessional staff in such processing projects is especially important, even in small institutions where there are only one or two professional archivists. A strict delineation of professional tasks is impossible. In general, professional archivists should be responsible for:

Figure 5-3 Saratoga State University, University Libraries—Department of Special Collections

REGIONAL HISTORY CENTER

Archival Work Plan

Collection: Southside Community Services   **Acc. No.:** 89-305   **Coll. No.:** M725
Archivist: R. Woods   **Date:** 1/7/90

Current Condition of Records

Arrangement: Records of Union Mission, Tenth Street House, St. John's House and Day Nursery/Children's Center are in separate groups. Southside Settlement/Community Center files 1900–1968 are in various file groups, potentially series and subseries. Records for Community Center, 1968–74 are in considerable disorder, with many scattered documents. Post–1974 records are organized by division and program, and thereunder alphabetically and chronologically

Description: Summary box list prepared during accessioning includes most major sets of folders with dates.

Physical Condition: Bound volumes intact but with some mold damage and leather binding deterioration. Folders and copied letters, clippings and scrapbooks, 1910–50 seriously brittle.

Proposed level of arrangement:
1) All records organized at series, subseries, and folder/volume levels
2) No item–level rearrangement within folders
3) Mission, Houses, and Nursery kept as separate record subgroups

Proposed level of description:
1) Collection–level summary, organization histories, series descriptions, relational and index terms on in–house data base management system
2) MARC AMC records for collection and each corporate body and record subgroup

Special considerations:
1) Main series for 1900–80 will overlap organizational changes
2) Disordered 1968–74 files should be formed into series compatible with immediately preceding or succeeding series organization

Staff assigned: R. Woods, Archivist (.25 FT); F. Turner, grad. assistant; 2 student assistants (1 FTE); M. Cutter, manuscript cataloger (.1 FT)

Estimated time for arrangement: 2 months   **description:** 2 months

Work schedule and assigned staff:
    Month 1—Woods surveys collection and prepares overall arrangement system
           Turner and students organize series and rebox records, supervised by Woods
    Month 2—Turner and students arrange folders/volumes and refolder
           Woods prepares summary histories and series descriptions
    Month 3—Students prepare container list
           Woods and Turner prepare final inventory
    Month 4—Final inventory completed
           Woods and Cutter prepare MARC AMC records and index entries
           Information entered into national and in–house data bases

Approved: **Date:**_____

1) decisions affecting overall arrangement, description, preservation, and records disposition;

2) monitoring and supervising physical rearrangement and listing; and

3) preparing descriptions of the origin, scope, contents and components of the records.

Clerical staff, students and volunteers should be responsible for:

1) routine refiling of individual items, refoldering, boxing, and listing;

2) basic conservation measures such as photocopying and the removal of fasteners; and

3) the preparation of box and folder listings.

Such clerical operations should usually be rotated fairly regularly among the staff, since most people find them less than stimulating over long periods of time.

There is naturally a grey area between professional and nonprofessional tasks, especially the tasks assigned to paraprofessionals who usually have college degrees. Paraprofessionals will often implement the organization of a collection like the Southside Community Services records into series after the archivist outlines the series to be formed. Similarly, a paraprofessional can be directly responsible for the division of a group of records such as those from the Museum Education Division into series under the supervision of a professional archivist. Paraprofessionals and clerical staff can review the contents of folders to identify key names and subjects within an indexing strategy determined by the archivist. All of these divisions of labor are guided by outside forces such as staff interests and abilities and union and personnel rules. Above all, processing has been revolutionized by the use of automation both for clerical tasks like sorting and listing and for professional tasks like information retrieval and the supervision of the flow of work.

Automation

For textual records, automation has transformed processing work without transforming processing principles. This has occurred because the type of information gathered during processing proved so amenable to computerized operations. Computers are particularly efficient at storing, sorting, rearranging, merging, finding, and printing or

Computer used in processing of photograph archives. *(Courtesy of the Metropolitan Transit Authority, New York.)*

displaying the phrases and numerical data found in descriptions of archival materials. Descriptions amenable to automation include accession forms, location registers and lists (e.g., archival inventories and box/folder lists), catalog entries, administrative data and narratives describing sets of records.

Automation is an extremely complex topic, and archivists should familiarize themselves with the ever-changing world of computer equipment, systems and programs in adapting automation to their own processing operations. They should make a special effort to keep abreast of the literature in archival, library and information science journals.[5] Regardless of changes in technology, however, automation of the control of textual records should be understood as a tool for the implementation of archival principles, not as a principle in itself. Such archival automation has traditionally taken two forms: enhancement of physical and administrative control, and improved description and retrieval. Increasingly sophisticated integrated systems are able to carry out both kinds of operations simultaneously, greatly reducing duplication of effort.

The application of automation to the physical control of archives resembles its application in any warehousing situation. It allows the repository to know the contents and location of every box of records, to group and review holdings without physi-

---

[5] Among the best journals to consult regularly are *Journal of Library Automation, Information Technology and Libraries* (published by the ALA Library and Information Technology Association), *Library Hi Tech, Journal of the American Society for Information Science (ASIS)* and *Archives and Museum Informatics.*

cally moving them, and to make rapid modifications as additions to collections or series arrive. The park planning records from 1967 to 1980 are an addition to a records series which extends back to 1935. The computer facilitates the updating of the overall series record and can provide a complete overview of the location of all the components of the series.

Beyond simple physical control, computers can provide administrative control by allowing archivists a comprehensive review of the course of work and the allocation of staff time to every group of records. By including information about archival operations in the computerized data form for each set of records, an archivist can determine, for example, which accessioned records have been awaiting processing for more than a year, or which records have been reviewed by the conservation specialist. During processing of disordered collections, archivists can experiment with alternative arrangements by manipulating listings without physically moving any records. Automation also permits the identification of multiple creators of a body of records where appropriate. None of these operations is impossible without computer programs, but all have been made considerably easier and more efficient.

The uses of automation for description and retrieval have brought similar improvements. The ease with which listings can be modified and updated is one obvious advantage. More significant is the computer's assistance in the perennial archival problem of having to file a document physically in one place according to archival principles while making it accessible from a variety of perspectives. By applying automation to different descriptive tools, archivists can assign one or more subject, name or place index terms to the entirety of a set of records, or to any subset of those records from series down to item. A 1919 report on child health in the Southside Community Services records has to be placed in one folder within a sequence of folders, and its title would appear in only one place in the folder listing in the collection inventory. Using a computer with the proper programs, the report could still be filed in the place determined by provenance and original order, while being indexed under terms such as "children" and "health." Here again, automation can facilitate and provide significant enhancements to what was a laborious and often neglected manual operation.

A more innovative use of archival automation is the production of different types of file listings through rearrangement of an original list. (See Fig-

ure 5-4.) Common and relatively inexpensive data base programs allow repositories to produce file lists which can be sorted and printed according to creator, time span, title, and any other variables properly designated. Such programs can also permit listing files and series according to key words appearing in the file lists, narratives, and other descriptive summaries. Repository-wide systems and programs can combine indexes and summary information from a variety of collections into repository-wide descriptive tools. In the historical society, they could produce a listing of all entries of George Bailey appearing in any inventory, not just in the Bailey collection.

On a more advanced level, archivists use sophisticated data base programs to supplement collection-based printed descriptions such as inventories with interactive retrieval directly from a repository-wide data base. If the repository has exercised consistency and standardization in assigning index terms to descriptive tools, users of these programs can sit at a terminal and look for any mention of records, from individual documents to entire collections, that fit some combination of terms. These terms can describe subjects, names and places as well as record attributes such as provenance, file type and time span.

Researchers at the university library could thus request social service case files dealing with both children and South Middletown in the 1920s—combining subject, record type, geographic terms and chronological terms—and be rewarded promptly with the name of the Southside Community Services collection. Researchers could request personal papers about the Republican Party in the historical society and find Bailey's papers, among others. It is important to note that in both cases the automated system should not send the users directly to the specific records, but to the inventories that describe the records. It is even more important to remember that the quality of the result of such searches depends on the quality of the basic archival processing of the collections themselves.

Beyond the walls of individual repositories, archivists use computer systems to exchange automated descriptive information according to national standards for format and vocabulary. Such rules, which are the subject of Chapter 10, must be followed in order for others to both find and understand the descriptions of the holdings of individual repositories in national systems. In turn, observing these standards will structure some of the internal work of processing, especially description and indexing. Standards, like basic archival principles, institu-

Figure 5-4

MUSEUM RECORDS LISTED IN CHAPTER 4 "INITIAL CONTAINER LIST" COMPUTER SORTINGS

I. Sorted alphabetically by records title:

Title	Box #	Dates	Location
Admin. Secretary/Financial Records	42	1973–79	18/3/1
Admin. Secretary/Personnel Records	42	1967–79	18/3/1
Adult Programs/Administrative Files	8	1952–82	15/3/4
Adult Programs/Project Files	7	1955–82	15/3/4
Children's Department/Community Programs	6	1940–82	15/3/3
Children's Department/School District	5	1935–66	15/3/3
Children's Department/School District	6	1967–82	15/3/3
Division Director/Administrative Files	1	1927–75	15/3/1
Division Director/Correspondence A–F	3	1941–82	15/3/2
Division Director/Correspondence G–Z	4	1941–82	15/3/2
Division Director/Programs Files A–P	2	1930–82	15/3/1
Division Director/Program Files R–Z	3	1937–82	15/3/2
Division Director/Staff Reports	3	1972–79	15/3/2
Education Division/Annual Reports	44	1928–88	18/3/2
Education Division/Minutes	44	1927–77	18/3/2
Education Division/Publications	45	1927–82	18/3/2
Public Relations/General Files	43	1948–65	18/3/1
Public Relations/Publicity Listings	43	1948–65	18/3/1

II. Sorted chronologically by starting date:

Dates	Title	Box #	Location
1927–75	Division Director/Administrative Files	1	15/3/1
1927–77	Education Division/Minutes	44	18/3/2
1927–82	Education Division/Publications	45	18/3/2
1928–88	Education Division/Annual Reports	44	18/3/2
1930–82	Division Director/Program Files A–P	2	15/3/1
1935–66	Children's Department/School District	5	15/3/3
1937–82	Division Director/Program Files R–Z	3	15/3/2
1940–82	Children's Department/Community Programs	6	15/3/3
1941–82	Division Director/Correspondence A–F	3	15/3/2
1941–82	Division Director/Correspondence G–Z	4	15/3/2
1948–65	Public Relations/General Files	43	18/3/1
1948–65	Public Relations/Publicity Listings	43	18/3/1
1952–82	Adult Programs/Administrative Files	8	15/3/4
1955–82	Adult Programs/Project Files	7	15/3/4
1967–79	Admin. Secretary/Financial Records	42	18/3/1
1967–82	Children's Department/School District	5	15/3/3
1972–79	Division Director/Staff Reports	3	15/3/2
1973–79	Admin. Secretary/Personnel Files	42	18/3/1

tional missions and resources, and changing automation technology, form the larger environment in which arrangement and description should be considered.

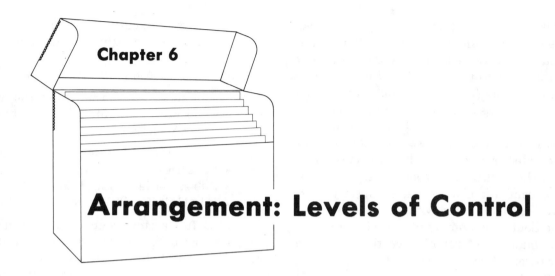

Chapter 6

Arrangement: Levels of Control

Archival arrangement involves both ensuring that a body of records is in a meaningful internal order and placing the records within the overall system according to which the repository's holdings are organized. The distinction between these two related operations is important. Equally important is the difference between physical and intellectual arrangement—between arranging actual boxes and manipulating information about records. With these distinctions in mind we can apply our definition of arrangement as the process of organizing and managing historical records by:

1) identifying or bringing together sets of records derived from a common source which have common characteristics and a common file structure, and

2) identifying relationships among sets of records and between records and their creators.

This definition can be applied to any set of records that is to be arranged, from the records of an entire organization to a few boxes from a small program within an agency.

General Approach to Arrangement

The operational approach which has dominated arrangement in the United States is straightforward and practical. It emanates mainly from the experience of the National Archives in controlling masses of modern records. Its core is the concept of a five-level hierarchy of arrangement moving from the larger scale to the smaller—repository, record group/manuscript collection, series, file unit, and document. The classic exposition of this approach came in a 1964 *American Archivist* article by Oliver W. Holmes.[1] This way of proceeding was driven by the perceived requirement on the part of archivists to assign every document to one file unit (such as a folder), every file unit to one series and every series to one office of origin. This system for physical control and arrangement proved easy to apply. Using it for documents in two of our sample record sets would produce the following:

(Repository)	*State Archives*	*University Library*
1) Repository Division	Public Records	Regional History Center
2) Rec. Grp./ Coll.	Dept. of Nat. Res.	Southside Comm. Serv.
3) Series	Park Planning Files	House Matron's Monthly Reports
4) File Unit (folder title)	Capital County Park Plans, 1976–78	Reports, 1910–15
5) Document	1977 Middletown Municipal Park Plan	January 1911 Report

The difference between archives and manuscripts in cases like these derives from the way records are acquired. The actual work of physical arrangement in archives usually begins at the series level, because that is the set of records most com-

---

[1] Holmes, "Archival Arrangement," 21–41.

monly acquired. Rather than receiving all the records of the DNR or even of the Office of Park Planning, the state archives is far more likely on a daily basis to receive part of some series of files such as the planning records. The record group, such as the DNR, which serves as a general administrative construct, has already been established, though of course new record groups are established when records are received from agencies not previously represented in the archives. In contrast to the usual archival concentration on series, manuscripts arrangement deals more often with entire collections, such as the Southside Community Services records, because in manuscript repositories these are the more typical sets of records acquired.

The five-part model was soon modified to fit actual practice by the addition of two other "levels"—*subgroups* within record groups/collections and *subseries* within series. They may be defined as follows:

- Subgroups are bodies of records maintained or created by a subordinate administrative body, or groups of series related by a common activity or use.
- Subseries are records filed together in subsystems within larger file structures.

The number of stages of subgroups and subseries can in theory be extended endlessly. There can be subgroups of subgroups in complex organizations, and subseries of subseries in complex filing structures. However, archivists should try to minimize the complexity of arrangement, so that both levels should be limited if possible to a few stages. But the usefulness of the additional levels is apparent if we return to our model collections. The DNR records would be much more understandable if the whole agency structure could be displayed:

- Record Group: Department of Natural Resources
- Subgroup: Bureau of Parks and Recreation
- Sub-subgroup: Office of Park Planning

The example of the Southside Community Services records is perhaps more important. At the time the Monthly House Matron's reports were created there was no Southside Community Services, but instead the Southside Settlement. The organizational origin of the reports is best represented by the following:

- Collection: Southside Community Services
- Subgroup: Southside Settlement House (1900–1946)
- Series: House Matron's Monthly Reports

In terms of subseries, the full file structure within the Office of Park Planning leading to the 1976–78 Capital County plans is:

- Series: Park Planning Files
- Subseries: County Parks
- Sub-subseries: Capital County Plans
- File Unit: Capital County, 1976–1978

This full system emphasizes organization in terms of the provenance and original order of the records. It also helps illustrate what archivists call the "evidential value" of records. Evidential value refers to the way the creation and file structure of records reveals information about the functions and activities of an organization. However, this way of organizing records works best with records arriving intact from extinct organizations which had a relatively stable existence and a simple structure.

Such situations are fairly common in both archives and manuscript repositories. Organizational records might consist of a few well-defined series of files—such as annual reports, minutes, executive director's correspondence, financial records and alphabetically arranged program files—covering a few decades. The repository can physically organize the series on the shelves in an order moving from the general to the specific, such as from annual reports to program files. The conventions archivists use to order series are discussed in more detail in the next chapter. The lists of the files will reflect their physical order on the shelves. This very basic, but not uncommon, type of arrangement preserves both the provenance of the files as a whole and the integrity of the filing structure through the series. (See Figure 6-1.)

The major difficulties with the system derive from its overemphasis on physical grouping and fixed hierarchical structures. Maintenance of physical unity and original order is appropriate for the actual files in a filing system. It is not necessary in relating sets of records sharing a common provenance. Arrangement by provenance is independent of the physical proximity of records. As the Dutch knew in 1898, "by description of an archival collection in a single inventory, that collection from a scientific point of view becomes whole again. From that point of view, it matters little where the archival

Figure 6-1 Records Structure Reflected in Physical File Organization, Museum Education Division

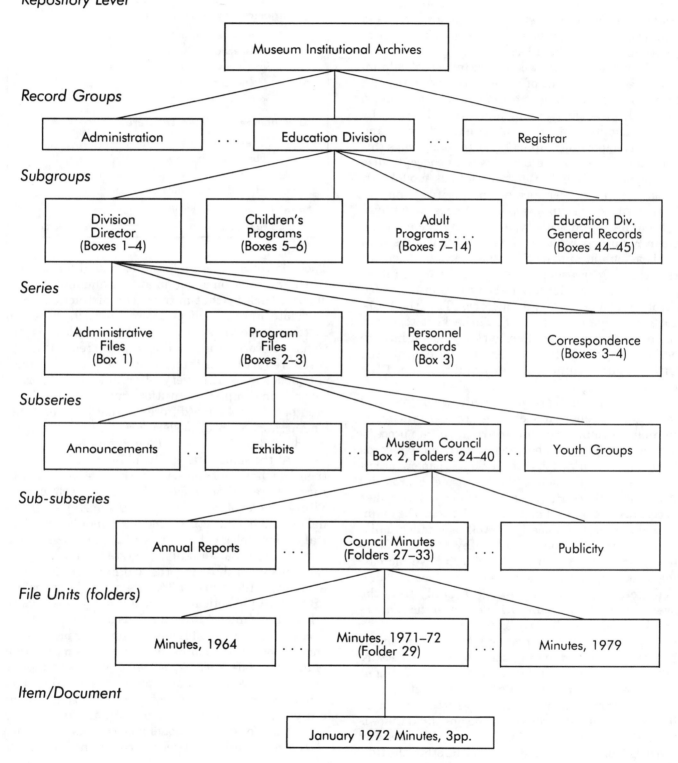

documents are kept."[2] The major practical reason for keeping records with a common provenance together would be for user convenience in browsing and retrieval, as in library stacks. Since archives and manuscript repositories have closed stacks, physical location becomes much less crucial.

The difference between the intellectual/administrative arrangement of records by provenance (in terms of record groups, collections and subgroups) and their physical grouping and internal sorting by filing structure (in terms of series, subseries and files) has important implications. In many ways this basic duality is a more useful way to conceptualize arrangement than the classic Holmes model. Arrangement by provenance on the record group/collection and subgroup levels has no necessary physical manifestation. This type of arrangement can be entirely on paper. Given the complexity and size of modern public and institutional records, such arrangement increasingly *is* only on paper, as an organizing structure for a large body of records shelved throughout a repository's stack area. Thus the 1967–1980 park planning files should be kept together, since they arrived together, but they do not have to be kept anywhere near other files series from the Office of Park Planning, let alone all the other DNR records.

As the planning files illustrate, where physical integrity of a coherent body of records exists at accessioning, it should be maintained to facilitate processing and use. That will be possible with many records from old organizations or personal papers accessioned as a group, such as the Southside records and the Bailey papers. Having arrived as complete bodies of records, the textual materials at least can be maintained together physically as well as intellectually. However, this is a convenient but by no means absolutely necessary situation. Archivists have increasingly recognized that their traditional idea of a unified hierarchy of levels flowing naturally from the overall repository organization down to the individual documents was overly simplistic.

Archivists now understand that arrangement by provenance and arrangement by filing structure are two different but related systems. Arrangement by provenance provides information about records creators; arrangement by filing structure provides information about records. On the one hand there is the history of the Southside Comunity Services and the biography of George Bailey; on the other the type of records which that history and that life generated.

---
[2] Muller, Feith and Fruin, *Manual*, 42.

Figure 6-2   The Two Types of Arrangement

Arrangement by provenance

> Archival record groups and manuscript collections
> Subgroups (archives and manuscripts), sub-subgroups . . .
> Series documenting activity/function

Arrangement by filing structure

> Series of records filed together
> Subseries, sub-subseries . . .
> File units
> Individual documents and items

Note: *The same series will often represent arrangement by both provenance and filing structure*

The difference is as profound as the difference between information about an author and information about a book by that author. The distinction helps elucidate other complications within each of the two systems. Archivists are aware that complex institutional networks and relationships increasingly represent reality better than the simple monohierarchical model in which every office has one superior. Records in complex institutions may have no single creator or may have different creators over time. The arrangement of modern archival records must be adapted to this reality. (See Figure 6-2.)

At the same time, as David Bearman and other theorists have noted, sets of records as such are rarely in a hierarchical relation to each other.[3] While a group of records will have some type of internal organizing structure—most commonly alphabetical or chronological—there will usually be no comparable external organizing system dictating the relationship of those records to other records. While a program file marked "A" clearly belongs before "B" in an alphabetical system, it is not so clear where all the files under "Programs" as a whole belong in relation to "Financial Reports," for example. Unless there is some built-in derivation or summarization of information—such as a series of indexes to a series of cases—records are not superior or subordinate to other records; program files are not at some inherently "lower" structural level than minutes.

The hierarchical model has even less relevance to the relationship between records and the offices

---
[3] For an outstanding discussion of the confusion over hierarchy in archival writing, see Bearman and Lytle, "The Power of the Principle of Provenance," 16–21.

that generated them. Minutes and other records do not "report" to their creating body in the way that body reports to its superior unit. The latter relationship can be illustrated on an organization chart, but not the former. Records have relationships to their creating body and organizational environment, as well as to other records, but these relationships are not hierarchical.

Archival arrangement should thus not be thought of as one unified system in which physical files and file series are at some lower level than record groups, collections, and subgroups. These are instead two different kinds of arrangement—arrangement by provenance/records creator and arrangement by filing structure. Each works best when separated from the other. There is no need for a fixed physical reproduction on the shelves of a hierarchy extending all the way through an entire organizational structure and then file structure. With both types of arrangement regarded as more flexible, information about records and information about records creators can be represented separately and then related through links that illuminate the full range of their historical development. The complex history of the DNR and the responsibility for park planning in Saratoga constitutes one kind of information; the descriptions of the various records generated by planning activities are another type of information. The relationships among these different pieces of information constitute the framework for arranging and describing records. In an imperfect but useful analogy to libraries, we can note that bibliographic information about a book brings together information about both the author, who may have written several books, and information about that specific book in order to make a complete description.

In practice this perspective may have little impact on the arrangement of many traditional records and papers. For personal papers and many small organizational collections, especially collections no longer growing, the simplicity of structure often allows a simultaneous physical and intellectual arrangement. The arrangement of the Bailey papers would not necessarily require a sophisticated analysis of relationships between files and creators, nor would the few minutes and reports from the old St. Joseph's Settlement taken over by the Southside Settlement. But even in these cases it is useful to conceptualize physical and intellectual arrangement separately. For more modern organizational records, it is certainly more appropriate than the original system on which it is based.

Levels of Control

In this more complex environment, the series remains the most useful unit of analysis. As noted in Chapter 1, a *series* is:

> a body of file units or documents arranged in accordance with a unified filing system or maintained as a unit by the organization or individual that created them because of some other relationship arising out of their creation, function, receipt, physical form, or use.

Arrangement is based on working with coherent sets of records and relating those records to their origins and organizational context. Series form the link between arrangement by provenance and arrangement by filing structure because they commonly combine physical integrity with the documentation of an ongoing function or activity. Thus in the records of the Museum's Education Division, monthly reports of the various department heads not only constitute a coherent set of records, but also manifest a specific responsibility and activity. Series are thus at the center of the contemporary organization and management of records by (1) repository-level arrangement, (2) provenance, (3) filing structure, and (4) physical file units and documents.

1. Repository-Level Arrangement. Many repositories have physically and administratively separate divisions to which different types of record groups or collections are assigned. Such arrangement at the repository level is concerned primarily with facilitating the logical and efficient administration of the institution. The most common division is the division between manuscripts and archives in institutions which collect both. The University Library may include the University Archives as well as the Regional History Center, so that the first act of arrangement is to assign the Southside records to the Regional History Center. A similar division is the one often made within institutional archives between organizational records and the personal papers of prominent officials or participants when those individuals donate their records to the archives.

Other divisions vary according to the nature of the repository, its holdings, and its clientele. Divisions on the basis of physical form (such as maps, films and photographs) are common. In these cases, the repository must keep careful separation records so that the intellectual unity of collections is maintained. Some repositories have separate sections of record groups or collections devoted to time periods (pre- versus post-1800) or even topics, such as military history. All such divisions should retain the integrity of record groups, rather than divide them among different parts of the archives. In manuscript repositories, valuable individual documents may go to a separate secure area. In general, the number of separate physical divisions within a repository should be minimized, to avoid wasting space.

2. Arrangement by Provenance. Though repository-level arrangement is convenient for administrative and physical purposes, the most important organization of repository holdings is in accordance with the principle of provenance. Repositories organize their holdings according to origin and all records are linked to at least one creator. Where records arrive from that creator over time, arrangement by provenance is largely an intellectual and administrative activity. However, archives and manuscript repositories apply provenance in different ways according to the respective concepts of record group and manuscript collection.

As developed by the National Archives, a *record group* is "a body of organizationally related records established on the basis of provenance with particular regard for the complexity and volume of the records and the administrative history of the record creating institution or organization."[4] Everything after the word "provenance" represents the practical modification of pure theory. Yet the heart of the record group remains the old European *fond*, defined by Canadian archivists as "the whole of the documents of any nature that every adminstrative body, every physical or corporate entity, automatically and organically accumulates by reason of its function or of its activity."[5] Record groups should be the *fonds* of administrative bodies with their own responsibilities, autonomy, and stability.

Most record groups meet this definition, which in our examples could easily apply to the Department of Natural Resources and the museum's Education Division. In addition to such "natural" groups, the National Archives created "general" record groups for executive-level departmental records and "collective" groups for the records of small but related agencies. A general group could include the records of the successive secretaries of a cabinet department, but not the records of the functional units of the department, while a collective group could include the records of many different but closely related study commissions all devoted to the same general subject.

These adaptations are responses to the need to organize and control huge bodies of government archives. They emphasize the lack of rigor in the American record group concept. The American concept represents an explicit compromise between the logical implications of provenance and the practical realities of the varying size and complexity of records produced by different agencies over different time spans. The definition of a Record Group also takes into account the extent to which an organizational unit or agency has a separate history, autonomy and identity. In our example, if the Bureau of Parks and Recreation had generated a vast amount of records and had enjoyed substantial autonomy, it might have been established as a separate record group. If all of the other bureaus were separate record groups, the DNR secretary's executive and administrative files might have become the equivalent of a general group.

The record group concept has not been without influential critics including Peter Scott in the 1960s and Max Evans in the 1980s.[6] The justification of the record group on the basis of convenient size flies in the face of reality— National Archives record groups average several thousand cubic feet. More crucially, continual reorganizations of administrative structures cause great difficulties for archives trying to maintain their records using definite record groups. Returning again to our relatively simple example, we may ask if the Park Planning files predating 1972 belong to the Conservation Department record group—since they were generated in that department—or to the new DNR record group? A plausible argument can be made for either. General archival practice assigns the records to the DNR record group, since that is the most recent department, and the one from which the records were transferred to the archives. Confronted with such situations, some archivists have urged the abandonment of the record group system in favor of concentrating on arrangement by series, with any larger administrative units described only as groupings of related series.

---

[4] Evans et al., "Basic Glossary," 428.

[5] Bureau of Canadian Archivists, *Towards Descriptive Standards: Report and Recommendations of the Canadian Working Group on Descriptive Standards* (Ottawa: Bureau of Canadian Archivists, 1985), 7.

[6] The key articles are Peter Scott, "The Record Group Concept: A Case for Abandonment," *American Archivist* 29 (October 1966), 493–504; and Max Evans, "Authority Control: An Alternative to the Record Group Concept, *American Archivist* 49 (Summer 1986), 249–261. See also Mario Fenyo, "The Record Group Concept: A Critique," *American Archivist* 29 (April 1966), 229–239; and Carl Vincent, "The Record Group: A Concept in Evolution" *Archivaria* 3 (1976–77): 3–16.

Adaptation and modification of the record group concept is generally preferable to complete abandonment. For archival administrative purposes, records should be identified, even if arbitrarily, with some creating or maintaining agency. Changes, mergers, and all kinds of administrative relationships can be represented through a variety of descriptive elements such as historical agency name lists and organizational charts, as well as traditional indexes and references within narrative descriptions.

In such a context, the strength of the record group system is apparent. For most records, it does accurately represent on the large scale the organization which created them, whether our Museum Education Division or, at the National Archives, an agency like the Federal Aviation Administration. The record group also remains a more useful unit for overall archival management, organization and description than thousands of separate series. Many of the latter will have a general and relatively uninformative title like "Case Files" in the absence of the traditional record group information that would commonly identify their provenance.

The organization of the holdings of manuscript repositories predominantly in terms of "organic" collections differs from the classic archival system in ways not always fully appreciated. Collections of organizational records and personal papers established on the basis of provenance are commonly conceived as the analogues of record groups. But in fact such collections are often the entirety of the records of their creators. Thus, *all* the records of Southside Community Services (one manuscript collection) are, in fact, equivalent to *all* the records of the Museum, not just the Education Division record group. Such manuscript collections thus represent a direct and uncompromised application of the principle of provenance. In addition, since many manuscript collections come intact as a whole from homes or offices, provenance can in those cases be maintained physically as well as intellectually.

Both manuscript collections and archival record groups can be divided into subgroups. Subgroups represent administratively discrete units or activities that produce records. The basic difference between a record group/collection and a subgroup is that all subgroups have a common origin in record groups or collections, while record groups and collections should represent reasonably autonomous agencies or organizations. However, as noted above, an organizational subgroup that is large and independent enough can be established as a separate record group, according to repository policy.

Subgroups are sometimes confused with series, because they are often small enough to be documented in one set of files. It is not at all uncommon for a small office—an archival subgroup—to have generated only one series, such as minutes, which have enough value to be retained in an institutional archives. Subgroups denote the context of records creation; series are the records themselves. Even if the subgroup and the series are physically identical, as in the case of the minutes, the distinction is important conceptually. In fact, a single minute book representing all the surviving records of a department can be simultaneously a subgroup, a series, and a file unit.

In large organizations, there can be many levels of subgroups, sub-subgroups, and so on reflecting the administrative structure. Subgroups can also be established for the records of predecessor, merged or related organizations absorbed during the organization's history. Activities and functions should be grouped where a number of related series would have no other structural link. If an individual's papers lack any formal structure, archivists sometimes create subgroups of related series of business, civic, or personal activities or functions.

Subgroups, like record groups, present the same problems of constant flux in active organizations. Such change is even more common at the office and program level of subgrouping than at the higher organizational levels. As a practical matter, subgroups should therefore be limited as much as possible to fairly stable units and functions. A business archives, for example, may create subgroups on the basis of continuing functions such as production, marketing, personnel, and finances.

Our sample collections illustrate some of these considerations. The simplest case is the museum's Education Division. The records of organizational units within the division such as the International Program and Children's Programs form obvious subgroups. In the case of the Public Relations Department, located within the Education Division until 1965, cross-references in different descriptive tools will link this records subgroup with the post-1965 Public Relations Division record group. But the pre-1965 records should remain part of the Education Division's historical materials. The Education Division itself reports to the associate director for administration, whose records form a separate record group.

The 1967–1980 park planning files are more complex. For administrative purposes the files would be part of the DNR record group, with cross-referencing to the pre-1972 Conservation Department record group. The files would also be identified with the Bureau of Parks and Recreation subgroup. The question would be whether to establish the Office of Park Planning as a separate sub-subgroup. If the office's only records were one relatively small series of planning files, they might be treated as a series within the bureau, though they could be treated as a subgroup which happened to consist of just one series. Since in this case the Office of Park Planning has been in existence since 1958 and has several other series in addition to the basic park plans, the office records become a subgroup of the bureau records subgroup. This sub-subgroup will not, however, include the records of the park planner on staff from 1935 to 1958 before the office was created, since these are already organized as a series within the records of the old Conservation Department. (See Figure 6-3.)

The manuscript collections present different challenges. One set of records—those of the Whomsoever Mission—found at Southside Community Services was identified as a separate collection during accessioning, because it always functioned as a separate organization. To the extent they can be identified separately, records of the various predecessors of the current agency will be established as subgroups, including the records of the two settlements absorbed by Southside Settlement, the Day Nurseries agency with which it merged, and the direct precursors of the agency such as the Union Mission, Southside Settlement, and Southside Community Center. In addition there will be subgroups based on the agency's recent structure, such as the Youth Services Division and the Adult Literacy Program. These subgroups will serve as a conceptual framework, though associating specific series of records with the various subgroups will be a complex task.

With the Bailey papers, the major issue will be whether any subgroups are needed. Assuming the records are in a sensible filing order, a further level of structure may not be required. Subgrouping might be convenient if there are many small sets of folders each documenting a different civic activity or financial matter. A more interesting issue would be the disposition of Mary Bailey's correspondence and her files relating to her work with the museum. If easily separable they could constitute a separate collection on the basis of a separate creator. However, if they are integrated into a much larger corpus of George Bailey's files, such a separation would violate provenance in the sense of the records' origins and maintenance, as well as violating original order. Depending on the contents of the entire collection, and the opinions of the donors, the collection could be identified as George Bailey's Collection of Bailey Family Papers. This type of decision becomes the province of policy and judgment.

3. Arrangement by Filing Structure. Archivists organize and manage physical groups of records primarily in terms of series and subseries which they identify or create. Arrangement by provenance has no direct relation to the internal order of individual series or the arrangement of series with respect to each other. Arrangement by filing structure, in contrast to arrangement by provenance, is concerned with the reality of sorting, grouping, and shelving the records themselves. It is also concerned far more with the storage, handling, and retrieval requirements of records in different physical formats. Since some series arrive as accretions over time to be stored in various locations, arrangement by filing structure is not always a physical arrangement. However, the physical aspect is usually much more important than in arrangement by provenance. The language of provenance is a language of creators— Office of Park Planning, George Bailey, Southside Settlement—while the language of series is the actual language of records—diaries, minutes, ledgers, correspondence, or grant proposals.

The standard definition of a series noted previously describes two kinds of series. The first is based on a coherent filing system in which a set of records is arranged alphabetically, chronologically, geographically, or according to some other consistent classification system. Such series include the common and easily recognizable record types like minutes, reports, correspondence, case files, and accounts. (See Figure 6-4.) The second kind of series is a set of records which may be a mixture of file types and arrangements, but which derives some unity from either a common format, such as the park planner's maps, or from a common function or activity. These may be records relating to a subject, a program, or a branch office, and may thus resemble subgroups in that they will consist of different types of files. A series entitled "Planning Review, 1980" might bring together several kinds of records, but their creation and use in a specific activity will make them part of one series. In disordered collections, archivists can establish all of these different series as needed.

The series is the key unit for processing because it combines both the file structure of records and the

Figure 6-3   Records Creating: Park Planning Institutional Contexts, 1967 and 1980

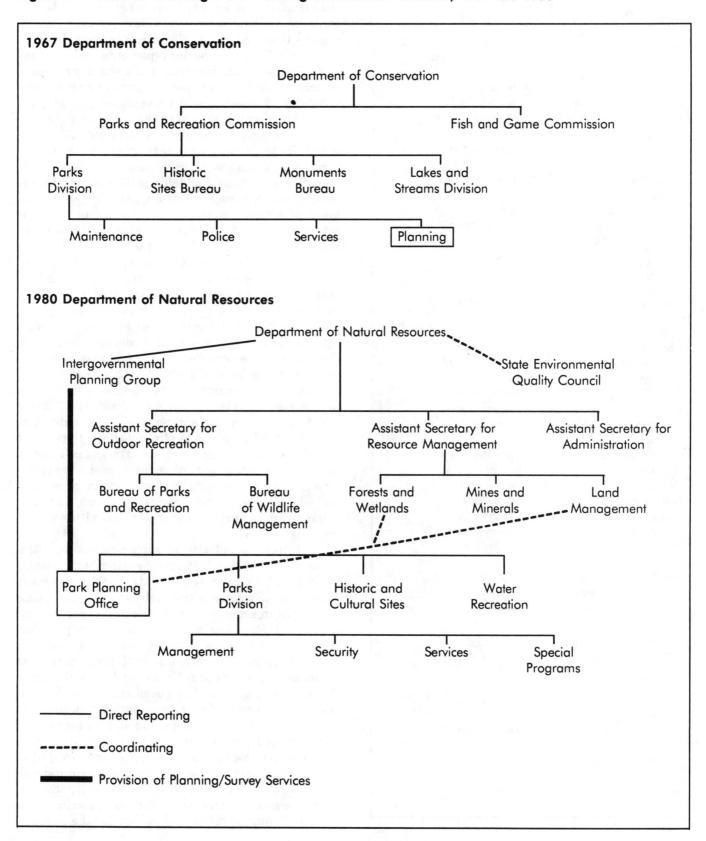

Figure 6-4   Common Types of Functional Records Series

Accounts	Manuscripts (literary)
Affidavits	Maps
Agendas	Memoirs
Agreements	Memoranda
Albums	Minutes
Annual Reports	Mortgages
Applications	Motion Pictures
Atlases	Newsletters
Audio Tapes	Notebooks
Audits	Notices
Authorizations	Orders
Awards	Organizational Charts
Bank Statements	Pamphlets
Bills	Payrolls
Bonds	Permits
Broadsides	Petitions
Budgets	Photographs
Bulletins	Plans
By-laws	Plats
Case Files	Posters
Cash Books	Press Releases
Catalogs	Printouts
Charts	Proceedings
Clippings	Proclamations
Constitutions	Programs
Contracts	Proposals
Correspondence	Publications
Daybooks	Receipts
Deeds	Recommendations
Depositions	Regulations
Diaries	Reports
Directives	Research Notes/Files
Drawings	Resolutions
Engravings	Rules
Field Notes	Schedules
Financial Statements	Scrapbooks
Graphs	Scripts
Histories	Speeches
Indentures	Statements
Indexes	Statutes
Invoices	Studies
Journals	Surveys
Laws	Testimonials
Lectures	Testimony
Ledgers	Transcripts
Legal Opinions	Videotapes
Letters (sent/received)	Vouchers
Letterbooks	Warrants
Logs	Wills
Manuals	

documentation of a record-creating activity. Experience tells us that activity is often better described in terms of tangible series—minutes, tax lists, memoranda—than in terms of constantly changing bureaucratic facades. A series represents the combination of physical file integrity and a specific function or activity. In this way, the integrity of a series preserves the values of both provenance and original order. Each type of record at the series level has its own characteristics, which archivists should understand. By their nature, minutes contain a different kind of information from annual reports or staff memoranda; annual budgets are different from ledgers. This recognition of the importance of different types of records as conveyors of different kinds of information further enhances the central role of series in archival processing and use.

Archivists denote subseries where there are significant and logical divisions within a series. Subseries must be an integral physical part of a series maintained as a unit. There are two major types of subseries. The first occurs when a series is divided into two or more parts, as in a correspondence file divided into "Letters Received" and "Letters Sent," or a unified research file divided according to different topics. The second occurs when subsets of files are "nested" in a larger set. An individual's "Financial Records" may be arranged alphabetically, but at the letter "T" a whole chronologically arranged set of tax returns may appear. These tax returns constitute a subseries. Subseries almost always derive their existence from the way they are physically embedded in the larger series structure. Original order in such situations means physical file order. (See Figure 6-5.)

Unlike the relation of subseries to series, the ordering of series in relation to each other is purely arbitrary. This issue relates both to the placement of records physically on the shelves, and to the listing of records in archival inventories and other finding aids. Traditional registry systems usually provided a fixed structure for all the different series produced by an office, and the retention of that structure was an integral part of the retention of "original order." Such registry systems have been rare in the United States, however, and archives commonly acquire series that have no predetermined relationship to other series from the same organization.

On the basis of the principle of original order, when records arrive from an organization or individual in a set order that is not purely capricious, that sequence should be retained. But there is no inherent "organic" link or ranking that dictates the physical

Figure 6-5   Series and Subseries, Park Planning Files as Transferred from Agency

Account 89–767—Park Planning Files (series)			
Box #	Subseries	Sub-subseries	Sub-sub-subseries
1–4	Departmental/Divisional Files	Annual Planning Summaries, 1976–80 (Box 1, Folders 1–5) . . . . . (Other Files)	
5–9	State Park Plans	Apple Valley S. P. Renovation (Other Parks)	Budgets, 1976–79 (Box 5, Folder 1) . . . . . (Other Aspects)
10–13	County Park Plans	Adams County (Other Counties)	Harrisville Nature Preserve, 1975–77 (Box 10, Folder 1) . . . . (Other Parks)
14–15	Park Maps	State Parks (Box 14) County Parks (Box 15)	

order in which the series constituting a collection should be arranged. There is nothing to mandate whether or not staff memoranda belong before or after financial records. Attempts by archivists to devise principles for such relationships were an outgrowth of the system which joined arrangement by provenance and arrangement by filing structure in one unified hierarchy. The ordering of series was the link between the two different types of arrangement, since it created the impression of a hierarchy of filing structures immediately subordinate to the hierarchy of record-creating bodies. But as we shall see in the next chapter, the arrangement of series is a matter of convenience and judgment, not fundamental archival principles. It is essentially an estimate by the archivist of the relative scope and importance of the various series.

In our model records, the park planning files of the Office of Park Planning represent a fairly typical series. The 1967–1980 files are actually an addition to the already existing series of 1935–1971 park planning files stored elsewhere in the archives. The four-year overlap between the two sets of files is typical of situations in which individual files remain active for varying lengths of time before being transferred to storage. The 1967–1980 files will form an addition to the existing series, rather than a new series, because in our scenario they are part of an ongoing file structure, with regular chronological breaks. Within the new addition there are records which will be stored separately from the standard paper files, such as maps, photographs, and audio and computer tapes. As has been stressed, this does not reflect on the intellectual integrity of the series. Their common

provenance will keep the textual and nontextual records linked administratively and intellectually, regardless of separate storage or even separate indexing and retrieval systems. The series also contains files which represent activities carried on and documented by other agencies before the government reorganization of 1972, but these files remain with this series. In the Office of Park Planning, the series of planning files was formally maintained in four subdivisions—DNR/Division directives, state parks, county parks, and maps; these are maintained as subseries.

The museum's Education Division records illustrate a record group which was transferred as a unit, so that the subgroups, series, and subseries are in the physical relationship to each other that was established by the division. Even if there are unpredictable sequences of file groups (perhaps International Programs has been placed before Children's Programs, or grant proposals ahead of minutes), it is best to retain this subgroup and series-level order. Here the physical and intellectual arrangement can be one.

The most difficult challenge will be the identification of series within the Southside Community Services records. Changes in organization and mission, in record formats and types, and in directors and administrative secretaries over a century could easily produce more than fifty identifiable series in fifty boxes. The Day Nursery, for example, might have retained only three cubic feet of records, but these could include four series—minutes, program files, scrapbooks, and files of the Middletown Day Nursery Association. Some of the other series could extend over the course of several organizational changes, complicating the relationship of series to subgroups. A consistent series of reports to the United Way since 1940 will carry successively the names of Southside Settlement, Southside Center and then Southside Community Services. With small sets of folders the archivist will have to decide whether to view them as subseries of larger series or group them into programmatic subgroups, such as "Health Projects." For the totally disordered records dating 1968–74, the staff will have to create series based on a study of both the pre-1968 files and the well-ordered post-1975 records.

George Bailey's files more closely resemble those of the Museum Education Division. His personal papers as transferred from file cabinets were already in file groups which can fairly easily be combined by the repository into subgroups ("Civic Affairs"), series ("Personal Correspondence"), and even subseries (Mortgages by year within "Finances-Personal"). While there will typically be some folders or documents difficult to categorize, the collection as a whole will retain its full order intact.

4. Arrangement by Physical File Units. Original order is applied most directly in handling physical file units such as folders or bound volumes. In contrast to series, whose constituent parts can be in different parts of a repository, file units really can be in only one place at a time. The order of the units imposed by the creator is the very structure which defines the files as a series. Generally that order is chronological when the series documents a regular activity, such as minutes of meetings. The order may be alphabetical when it documents programs, topics, organizations, or people, such as case files arranged by the name of the client. The arrangement can also be by some internal classification system, like a decimal subject classification, usable if the archives can find a codebook or classification scheme in the records. Series created by an archivist from loose papers will usually be arranged chronologically or alphabetically, according to the type of function or activity they document.

Within file units such as folders, individual documents will also be in some chronological or alphabetical order which should be retained. In practice, the holdings of archives and most manuscipt repositories are so large that archivists rarely review item-level arrangement. In addition, in the absence of close supervision, use itself often causes documents to become disordered within folders. Only where there are individually valuable documents should the specific location of such items be a major concern. Detailed arrangement usually ends with the ordering of file units, not their contents. The major exception is the case of records which are to be microfilmed. Such records must be in a precise and logical item-level order, since images cannot be reshuffled or viewed more than one at a time.

Our sample archival records raise few problems of file-unit arrangement. Typically the only park planning textual records needing detailed arrangement are the reports on specific parks from the park planner's office. These will be used heavily and users will ask for individual items. In contrast, the Southside records arrive with boxes of unsorted loose papers from 1968 to 1974. They also include many bound volumes which need to be brought together by provenance and type (Settlement House minutes, camp ledgers, etc.); they then must be arranged chronologically. Several series in the Bailey papers might be arranged in some detail. The autograph series will certainly have to be arranged alphabetically and listed by item. This is the procedure the historical society would use with individual "artificial collections" donated by collectors. In addition, the general correspondence series might be arranged alphabetically by incoming correspondent since that would be the way documents would normally be requested. As with the other records, the detailed arrangement of some series does not imply the detailed arrangement of all series.

The different types of arrangement described in this chapter provide the framework for the organization of records from divisions at the repository level through the placement of individual documents. That framework allows archivists to arrange records in the distinct ways appropriate to the preservation of provenance, filing systems, and physical integrity. As discussed in the next chapter, it also provides as well for the organization of completely disordered records. The arrangement of any specific body of records is a function of its own physical and intellectual characteristics. But the practices and procedures of arrangement take place within the larger system reviewed here.

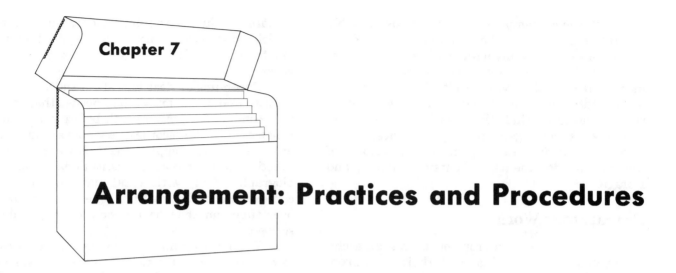

Arrangement: Practices and Procedures

Because both records and repositories are so varied, arrangement in practice can be a whole range of activities from simply approving a received filing system to establishing order in a mass of disordered documents. Whatever the initial state of a set of accessioned records, the process of arrangement should accomplish several goals. Records should be physically grouped into coherent series and subseries. Within those file structures individual file units will be either in the order received or in an order established by the archivist. Records should be identified with their administrative and/or functional origins, as part of larger record groups, manuscript collections and subgroups. Whether those identifications are purely on paper or also manifested in a physical arrangement will be determined largely by the nature of the records. Manuscript collections are more likely than complete archival record groups to be maintained as physical as well as intellectual units.

Arrangement in public and institutional archives is often a process of preservation of original order. In organizations with well-established records management programs, most records arrive in a comprehensible order from established functional entities. Archivists should verify that order and ensure that they have correct information about the creator or creators of the records. The creator will in many cases differ from the immediate source. In the majority of cases where these issues raise no problems, the basic goals of arrangement have been met. Further work (reboxing and refoldering, and listing file headings) is optional and often clerical.

The arrangement of manuscript collections very often involves much more detailed work at the folder level and occasionally even at the document level. Here archivists may have to create, replace or reconstitute a filing structure. Even well-ordered manuscript collections commonly contain some disordered or misidentified records. Because such collections often represent the entirety of an organization's or individual's records, rather than particular series, the staff must deal with both arrangement by provenance and by filing structure. Manuscript curators as well as institutional archivists can also be confronted simultaneously with changes in record-creating activity, organizational structure, and the nature and content of records, further complicating their work.

Manuscript curators may be less likely to retain arbitrary or idiosyncratic original filing order, since manuscript repositories concentrate on satisfying external research needs rather than the needs of internal administrators. The most common challenge in manuscript arrangement is to create from disordered collections a complete and detailed arrangement based upon provenance—an arrangement which reveals the reasons the files were created. In addition, individual documents of special value are more likely to be found in manuscript repositories than in aggregations of institutional and government records.

Despite these differences, there are important similarities between archival and manuscript arrangement. Archival records frequently contain some disordered files, while manuscript collections received from contemporary organizations resemble institutional archives. The overall goals and sequence of work of archival and manuscript arrangement are similar. The ultimate goal is an arrangement of records that will permit their effective use by facilitating description. The course of work at all repositories can include the following stages: preparatory work, arrangement by provenance, series-level arrangement, rearrangement, arrangement of file units and documents, and physical handling and storage.

Preparatory Work

Before arranging a group of records, an archivist should become familiar with their origin, contents, arrangement and condition. Much of this information should be available from the various forms and summary descriptions created during the acquisition and accessioning stages. However, the archivist should generally do some further research into the history and context of the creators of the records, and the activities documented. Such research should not be exhaustive at this stage, but could involve reviewing internal histories, organization charts, biographical dictionaries, local encyclopedias, and other standard reference works. The archivist should also become familiar with related records held by the repository.

Research sets the stage for the initial examination of the records and any accompanying descriptions. A review of the boxes themselves and whatever lists have been created provides a good summary of the contents, arrangement, and physical condition of the records as a whole. The archivist should take notes on existing file structures, obvious gaps in the records, loose or disordered documents, and the types of records which usually require processing at the item level. Based on previous research, the archivist should be able to recognize major subjects and events, important individuals, and the overall strengths and weaknesses of the records in terms of content. Major organizational changes not mentioned in accessioning records should also be noted. As preparation for further work, aids to processing such as annual reports, internal histories, autobiographical sketches, and organizational charts can be identified and even copied for use by the archivist.

Following the review of the records, the archivist can determine their specific processing needs. This can take the form of an explicit work plan (see Chapter 5). The plan will require the archivist to explain and justify the proposed arrangement, the associated staff assignments and required resources, and the impact of the work on reference and conservation.

Depending on decisions about the nature of the records and their processing needs, the archivist may conduct further research before beginning arrangement. If the records as a whole are in disorder or are unusually complex, the archivist may have to function for a time as an institutional historian or biographer. Only with a full understanding of the context and activities that generated the records over time can they be properly arranged and described.

The nature and order of the records also dictates the sequence in which the work of arrangement proceeds. When records arrive in order with a coherent structure, arrangement work proceeds from the largest unit to progressively more detailed subdivisions. In such situations, arrangement consists mainly of placing record containers on the shelves as received—reboxing them into archival-quality containers where necessary—and recording information about each record-creating administrative level and subdivision. This helps the archivist to prepare for the descriptive work to follow.

In our museum example, information about the Education Division record group as a whole would be derived by the archivist from an overview of the divisional records as summarized in accession forms. The archivist would then review the information about the records of each of the departments which form the subgroups. Finally, the individual series documenting functions and activities within the department subgroups would be identified. It would be possible for the whole process to proceed without any physical rearrangement of files. Arrangement of such ordered record groups can easily proceed to a given level of detail and then stop if necessary. The archivist may further refine the records later. (See Figure 7-1.)

Most collections of personal papers and disordered or complex organizational records are not so amenable to arrangement from the top down. The archivist in these cases must identify the coherent file sets which form series and then associate those series with record-creating bodies. Once established, the series will also provide the structure within which folders and documents can be placed. The Southside Community Services records typify disordered and complex collections. With no overall order to the records, the archivist cannot work from the top down. Instead, the various series, volumes, and

Figure 7-1   Museum Education Division Records, Unified Intellectual/Physical Breakdown

Subgroups	Boxes	Series	Boxes/Folders
Division Director	1-4	Administration	1
		Programs	2-3/1-15
		Personnel	3/16-27
		Correspondence	3/27-39 to 4
Children's Programs	5-6	Reports	5/1-12
		Programs	5/13-31
		Budgets	5/32-42
		Memoranda	6/1-8
		Staff	6/9-14
		Publicity	6/15-30
Adult Programs Department	7-14	Reports	7/1-9
		....	....
School District Programs	15-28	Annual Programs	15/1-16/7
		....	....
Volunteers Council	29-35	Council Minutes	29/1-18
		....	....
International Programs	36-39	Reports	36/1-9
		....	....
Administrative Secretary	40-42	Div. Accounts	40/1-16
		....	
Public Relations Department	43	General Files	43/1-27
		Publicity Lists	43/28-41
Education Division	44-45	Minutes	44/1-25
		Annual Reports	44/26-38
		Publicity	45/1-22

other documents must be assembled, and the overall order produced as a result of arrangement. Here, the work of arrangement produces an order rather than an existing order producing an archival arrangement.

The different approaches are based on the dual roles that series play—they represent file structures or types as well as document activity. Both of these functions should be respected in those situations when arrangement must begin by establishing series rather than by identifying series within subgroups. Thus in George Bailey's papers it would not be appropriate to create an all-encompassing correspondence series simply on the basis of record type. If Bailey maintained his correspondence in separate groups by activity, there should instead be a separate correspondence series for each of Bailey's activities. There might be one correspondence series for his civic affairs and another for his business affairs. Conversely, if he grouped different types of records from different creators together in documenting some civic activity, that activity should be the basis of the series regardless of the mixture of sources and record types. Thus his files on the 1956 Republican National Convention might include correspondence, local committee minutes, travel and expense documents, a convention program, and a signed thank-you note from President Eisenhower.

Some manuscript collections are so disordered that they must be painstakingly reconstructed from the documents up, reversing the whole process typical of archival groups and series. With collections of more than a few dozen documents this is naturally very time consuming. However, it really is unavoidable if the materials are to be available for use. As discussed below, the whole collection must first be examined in order to identify the different types of records and possible series. Once a framework of series is established, individual documents can be sorted accordingly.

Arrangement by Provenance

Records should have been identified by record group or collection during accessioning. However, this identification should be confirmed, and such basic information as dates and volume verified. The records may also receive a record group or collection number at this stage. The record group or collection number will be different from the accession number. It will be especially important if more than one accession is to be processed together as a group or collection. The record group/collection number will be used in all future processing and reference work.

Most of the work of arrangement by provenance concerns the identification or establishment of subgroups. It is important to recognize, however, that not all record groups or collections are necessarily divided into subgroups, nor do all series have to be clustered into subgroups. Subgroups are used by archivists only when their existence is justified by organizational structure or some type of general function or activity. Subgroups derived from existing organizational divisions should be maintained separately from each other when the records are boxed and listed. The records relating to each subgroup will be listed along with the reason for the subgroup's creation. With very large organizations, common sense and repository policies should dictate when to stop creating subgroups for every administrative unit or type of organized activity. At some point, records of activity can be established as series rather than as subgroups, even if the activity has some organizational manifestation. The Office of Park Planning will have a separate staff member for county parks, but since the permanent records generated by that individual are relatively few and form part of a larger file structure on planning, there would not be a separate County Park Planning subgroup.

Subgroups created by archivists, especially in work with manuscript collections, may lack the physical unity of subgroups maintained by original records creators. Certainly the series created by archivists will be in no preestablished order in relation to each other. Instead, the archivist will create subgroups on paper by listing together series which have some common relationship of origin, form or activity. But this work depends upon, and follows, the arrangement of the records themselves into coherent series. (See Figure 7-2.)

Series-Level Arrangement

The organization of files into series is the crux of all archival arrangement. It involves grouping records into coherent units, placing them into a provenance-based context, and ordering the series in relation to each other. There are essentially four methods by which series are generated—identification, creation, reconstitution, and rearrangement. All but the first include some physical manipulation of records. The identification and maintenance of series in a usable order is the easiest alternative. It occurs in many public and institutional archives where arrangement proceeds through a process of successive subdivision. The creation or reconstitution of series is more common in manuscript work. The tedious work of rearrangement is needed when either archival records or manuscripts arrive in an arrangement that is impossible to interpret or is positively counterproductive to research.

The identification of series in well-ordered collections is generally a matter of discerning the obvious coherent filing groups, sometimes with the assistance of an internally produced file system outline. Breaks in files caused solely by clerical action are not justifications for the establishment of separate series. If necessary, such problems can be handled as subseries. Subseries should also be used when there are two interdependent sets of records, such as old settlement house registers divided into separate books for men and women. Archivists should follow the practice of the office of origin in such determinations. The park planning files were always maintained within the office as one series with four subdivisions, so the state archives will not try to make separate series out of the county parks files and the state parks files, even though these record sets have the characteristics of series.

The creation or reconstitution of series in disordered collections is a much more complex task. The archivist faced with such a collection has to survey it completely, recording the type, dates, order, and condition of all groupings of files and all unclassifiable files. In addition to such details, this survey will provide a context in which to view the creation of possible subdivisions. It will often be necessary to compare file headings with file contents thoroughly. Relying on any lists prepared during accessioning and without physically moving any records, the archivist can prepare a tentative arrangement of series and subseries. The proposed arrangement will be reviewed with colleagues and further refined during processing.

Series will be created on the basis of type and activity as previously discussed. A chronological order will be recreated or established for series such as minutes or periodic reports, while program files and correspondence may be sorted alphabetically. Other internal systems, such as a numbering system for case files or a geographic coding for counties, will be reestablished where comprehensible. The trained

Figure 7-2 Series and Subgroups—The Bailey Papers

Series as described in file cabinets headings	Created subgroups to which series assigned
Middletown Republican Party	Political Activities
Saratoga Republican Party	Political Activities
Republican National Conventions	Political Activities
Middletown Chamber of Commerce	Civic Activities
Middletown Chamber, Executive Committee	Civic Activities
Bedford Falls Savings and Loan	Business Activities
First National Bank	Business Activities
Middletown Rotary	Civic Activities
Middletown Elks	Civic Activities
(14 Middletown Groups—1 file each)	Civic Activities
(8 Saratoga Groups—11 files)	Civic Activities
Businessman's Club	Civic Activities
Bankers' Roundtable	Business Activities
Southside Community Center	Civic Activities
Southside Community Center Board	Civic Activities
Southside Community Center, Chairman	Civic Activities
Middletown Museum of Art	Mary Bailey
Diaries—Peter Bailey	Peter Bailey collection
Diaries—Mary Bailey	Mary Bailey
Correspondence—Family	Personal
Correspondence	Personal
Scrapbooks	Personal
Saratoga State University	Personal
Elm Street House	Personal
Lake Winamonowoc Property	Personal
United Fund	Civic Activities
Financial Statements	Personal
Banking Reading Files	Business Activities
Speeches and Lectures	(To be divided)
Miscellaneous	(To be divided)

archivist's knowledge of the general characteristics of different types of series in different types of collections can be of vital assistance in identifying potential series in disordered collections. Archivists should be familiar with the general principles of records management as well as with the historical evolution of modern file creation and maintenance practices.[1] The identification of potential series in a disordered collection will be assisted by a knowledge and examination of similar types of records and record-creating bodies.

As in the creation of archival record groups, some practical considerations enter into the creation of series. In the Southside records, if there were two

---

[1] Some standard records management texts are Mina M. Johnson and Norman F. Kallaus, *Records Management*, 4th ed. (Cincinnati: Southwestern Publishing Co., 1986); Violet Thomas et al., *Records Management: Systems and Administration* (New York: John Wiley & Sons, 1983); and Patricia F. Wallace et al., *Records Management—Integrated Information Systems*, 2nd ed. (New York: John Wiley & Sons, 1987). Among the few articles on the history of file systems are JoAnne Yates, "Internal Communication Systems in American Business Structures: A Framework to Aid Appriaisal," *American Archivist* 48 (Spring 1985): 141–158; JoAnne Yates, *Control through Communications* (Baltimore: Johns Hopkins Press, 1989); and JoAnne Yates, "From Press Book and Pigeon Hole to Vertical Filing: Revolution in Storage and Access for Correspondence," *Journal of Business Communication* 19 (Summer 1982): 5–26. Chapter 9 of Schellenberg's *Modern Archives* also discusses filing.

surviving folders each dealing with the Settlement's nursing, dental, health education and medical clinic activities, they might become part of a series called "Health Activities"; but if there were a cubic foot of records on any one of those activities, it would be constituted a separate series. Such adaptations are especially important with small collections in which each folder or record type could theoretically constitute a series. It is not always necessary to divide all the files of a small collection or subgroup into series. Collections of just a few boxes would often do better with a simple alphabetical and/or chronological arrangement. Personal papers consisting of one box including a few diaries, several dozen letters, a scrapbook, some memorabilia and various financial records such as a deed and a will would not have to be formally divided into a half-dozen series. All that would be needed would be to organize and list the files by type and then chronologically by file unit.

The usual goal of arrangement is a collection physically divided into discrete series or subseries to illustrate function or activity, and assembled, at least on paper, into different subgroups to document creating organizational units. In the Southside collection, there may be a half-dozen groups of records which document the camp program over the course of fifty years, including its several changes of organization and location. Some record sets are obvious series, such as counselor's reports and lists of campers, while others might be a few folders each on various programs or activities scattered over the years. All such groupings have to be sorted and identified as series, subseries or, for all the camp records together, a subgroup.

The final stage of series arrangement is to record some basic identifying information about the series. In well-organized processing programs, this activity will draw upon work done during accessioning, and help lay the foundation for the more elaborate descriptive work to follow. Basic information to be recorded about each series includes creator, title, time span, volume, and arrangement, as well as a summary description of its contents. Series titles supplied by either the creator or the archivist generally combine a function or activity with a type, as in Director's Correspondence or County Plan Proposals. Archivists often assign or supplement titles where the identification supplied by the creator would be either misleading or inadequate for users.

In identifying creators and titles of records and papers and indicating their volume and date span, archivists should follow the descriptive rules conveyed in *Archives, Personal Papers, and Manuscripts: A Cataloging Manual* by Steven Hensen (2nd edition, 1989). As far as possible, all of the basic descriptive information recorded about each series should be compatible with internal repository policies and the national descriptive standards which will be outlined in the following chapters. However, practical considerations will usually dictate that the series-level work done during arrangement will have to be considerably refined and placed into a larger context during the final description of a group of records.

Once the records are arranged into series they may be arranged on the shelves in any sensible progression. Where records arrive in a complete and logical order, that order will naturally be maintained. In the absence of such an order, archivists have developed conventions for the progression of series, beginning with the Dutch rule that general minutes should come first. As David Gracy II wrote, series should be arranged in relation to each other "in order of the extent and value of the information within them."[2] This commonly means a progression from the general to the specific, and from policy making to implementation—such as from executive records to program records to housekeeping records. Similar procedures place the records of a central office before branches and a director ahead of an assistant director. Within clusters of series at the same level of importance, a chronological arrangement may be employed. The thrust of these conventions is to maximize the evidential value of the whole corpus of records in documenting the actual workings of an organization.

The ordering of series within record groups has long posed a challenge to American archivists, who generally could not rely on an established framework of European registry systems. Yet Holmes referred to it as "the heart of archival work" because the archival inventories were essentially reflections of a fixed ordering of the series on the shelves.[3] Archivists believed that just as subgroups had a logical relationship within record groups and file units had an order within series, so series should be arranged within subgroups or record groups and collections. While such ordering is useful, its intrinsic importance was overemphasized; the use of computers has rendered it even less vital than it had been. Instead of relying solely on one fixed series order as the link between arrangement by provenance and arrangement by series, appropriate computer data base pro-

[2] Gracy, *Arrangement and Description*, 10.
[3] Holmes, "Archival Arrangement," 29.

grams can provide a whole range of intellectual links and paper arrangements. Series can be listed in different orders, and may appear in descriptions and lists as part of more than one subgroup or record group. At the same time, the complexity and continual change of modern organizations makes it increasingly difficult to fix one appropriate order for records. Even in older collections, the notion that some types of records are more important than others has been questioned by users ranging from genealogists to social historians who bypass the minutes and concentrate instead on such "lower" ranked series as case files, personnel records, and program records.

The Southside and Bailey collections illustrate many of the problems. The parent Southside Settlement (founded in 1900) is older than the Tenth Street Settlement (founded in 1903) which it absorbed in 1946. However, placing the records of the latter chronologically in the middle of the former is awkward at best. Placing the Tenth Street files before the records of the larger Settlement has no inherent logic at all, yet it is the usual procedure. It is convenient and it preserves the separateness of the Tenth Street records. How should the dozens of program series documenting the 1920s to 1968 be ranked? Any ranking that, for example, placed files documenting the camp after those documenting the Youth Division would be purely arbitrary, though not in any sense wrong. No rule can tell the archivist dealing with Bailey's papers whether to place the business files before the civic files, or the important Republican Party papers before the more routine Chamber of Commerce files. The archivist should concentrate on ensuring that the individual series are coherent and are arranged in some sensible manner. At the conclusion of the whole process, the staff may have been through a set of records as many as four times—to determine an overall plan of work, to identify groups of files, to sort them by series and subseries, and to arrange the series and subseries in relation to each other. (See Figure 7-3.)

Rearrangement

Archivists rearrange records either by breaking up existing divisions between series or rearranging files within a series. As a violation of original order, rearrangement is a controversial practice, though we have seen that Schellenberg endorsed it in the interest of facilitating use. Some archivists have gone beyond the usual consensus that original order should be replaced only where it is incomprehensible or purely random. They argue that while original order documenting the activity of the organization should be retained, an order documenting merely the activity of file clerks has no value, even if the order is understandable and rational.[4]

The museum's Education Division can serve as an example. The division might have had an administrative secretary who at the end of every year merged reports, programs and other files from all departments within the division into one annual alphabetical file. Thus, under "1959" one might find first the *Budget* Summary for Adult Programs, followed by the Budgets for the other departments, then *Correspondence* for Adult Programs, and then the other departments' Correspondence, and so on. The whole file sequence would start over again for the 1960 records. In this case the original order hides both provenance and activity. To restore the evidence of both, the files should be rearranged by department and then alphabetically and chronologically by file type. Thus, all the Adult Programs Department files would be together, and within that subgroup all of the Budgets would be together and arranged chronologically. This type of arrangement preserves the work of the creators of the records, not their keepers.

Rearrangement of imperfect but usable file systems should be very selective. The work is extremely labor intensive. In addition, variant file orders can be created on paper without physical manipulation of the files. In most cases of an imperfect order, files should only be rearranged when the alternative is obvious and the work can be done quickly. Archivists must ensure that the new order of the files is based not on serving hypothetical research needs, but on reconstructing the activity that produced the records. Research interests are notoriously subjective and changeable. Rearranging materials to suit either one group of individuals (such as academic historians or genealogists) or one type of possible use (such as quantification or legal research) is almost guaranteed to ensure that the records will be usable only by a small group of people or for a short span of time, or both.

Arranging File Units and Documents

In most cases, the ordering of file units and documents is a routine clerical activity once the series and subseries have been established. The ordering of folders and bound volumes according to the

---

[4] See especially Frank Boles, "Disrespecting Original Order," *American Archivist* 45 (Winter 1982): 26–32.

Figure 7-3   Southside Community Services Series Organization

Record Creator	Series
Union Mission (1878–1900)	Annual Reports, Board Minutes, Relief Rolls, Dispensary Records, Matron's Reports, Donations, Cash books
Tenth Street House (1903–1948)	Director's Reports, Executive Committee Minutes, Program Files, General Correspondence, Financial Records
St. John's House (1915–1948)	Annual Reports, Monthly Board Reports, Board Minutes, Veteran's Programs, Juvenile Programs, Merger Files
Southside Day Nursery (1886–1916)	Annual Reports, Minutes of Supervisors, Donor Books, Roll Books
Southside Day Nursery and Children's Center (1916–63)	Annual Reports, Board of Managers' Minutes, Day Nursery Registers, Children's Center Programs, Day Nursery Association, United Fund, Scrapbooks
Southside Settlement (1900–1928)	Annual Reports, Board Minutes, Matron's Reports, Relief Rolls, Community Programs, Neighborhood Surveys, Accounts, Cash Books
Southside Settlement/Southside Community Center (1913–75)	34 series, including: Annual Reports, Arts Program, Board of Directors, Board of Directors Meetings, Building Fund, Building Maintenance, Camp Sunnyvale, Community Clubs, Community Relations, Contributor Lists, Dance Program, Day Nursery, Dental Clinic, Tenth Street Branch, Treasurer's Reports, Tutoring Program, United Fund, Young Adults Program
Southside Community Services (1975–)	Administration, Adult Programs, Board of Directors, Children's Programs, Community Programs, Executive Director, Finances, Membership, Middletown Human Services Department, United Fund, Young Adults Programs

inherent structure of the series or subseries precedes any work with individual documents. In most well-ordered series the main concern of the archivist will be to ensure that the file headings or volume titles are accurate and comprehensible. Clarifying information, including correct dates, can be added in pencil to folders or volumes. The most troublesome work involves the inevitable pile of loose or undated papers or papers from folders with headings like "General" and "Miscellaneous." Such individual documents should be integrated as far as possible with the existing file structure. This can be accomplished either by interfiling documents in existing folders—where this would not be a clear violation of provenance and original order—or by creating new file units. Following this procedure, on occasion there may only be one document in a folder added to a series. Undated documents will have to be examined and researched in an attempt to find at least an approximate date. Similarly, unsigned letters or letters signed with only a first name will have to be identified. Archivists should realize, however, that for all their diligence they may reach an irreducible

pile of uncategorizable documents which require too much work to justify further effort—and then they may resort to their own "Miscellaneous" folder. The specific details regarding the assignment and notation of file headings and the identification of documents should be discussed in each repository's internal procedures manual. As with many similar operations, the specific procedures are less important than the consistency with which they are followed.

Other document-level work involves records which should be arranged in item order because of their importance or likely pattern of use. These will include such records as minutes and annual reports, letters from important correspondents, valuable autograph documents and other items with monetary value, and classified or otherwise restricted records. Classified and restricted records should be in item order so that staff can retrieve one document without also either seeing or retrieving any others. Though not necessarily filed one document to a folder, all documents arranged by item should be individually marked and listed.

Figure 7-4 Physical Separation/Intellectual Unity, Southside Community Services Collection, Southside Settlement/Southside Community Center Record Group

Series/Subseries Division			
Series/Subseries	Box	Folders	Location
Arts Program, 1938–1967			
Reports (Annual/Quarterly), 1938–67	22	1–6	A3-6-1*
Program Files, 1951–66	22	7–18	A3-6-1
Middletown Arts League, 1939–62	22	19–36	A3-6-1
Participants/Prizewinners, 1939–66	23	1–5	A3-6-2
Annual Budgets, 1945–67	23	6–11	A3-6-2
Photographs, 1942–65	Ph2[1]	21–22	R5-3-8
Posters, 1951–67	MC14[2]	Drawer 6	Room 108
Scrapbooks, 1939–64	60(OV)[3]	n/a	A4-2-2

* indicates Range-Stack-Shelf (Range A3, stack 6, shelf 1)
[1] Ph2 means Photograph Box 2 of this collection
[2] MC14 means Map Case 14
[3] OV is oversize box in archives shelving area

Boxes on shelves with labels revealing appropriate information. *(Courtesy of Westchester County Archives, New York.)*

Physical Handling and Storage

Throughout the arrangement process, the work of weeding, separation and conservation begun during accessioning should continue. As archivists or clerical assistants go through series and folders, they should discard duplicates and note any groups of records of doubtful value. They will often find nontextual records or nonstandard-sized documents like photographs, folded maps, or blueprints. Such materials should usually be removed for more appropriate storage, with a note indicating the transfer left in the original folder. Descriptive tools, including inventories and other control documents, will continue to list all the records together, regardless of location. (See Figure 7-4.)

This is also the time to determine which individual documents will require special conservation treatment or copying. Clippings, scrapbooks, and brittle or mold-damaged paper should be removed for some type of corrective action; photocopying documents onto acid-free paper or microfilming are common solutions. Other records might require only unfolding, cleaning, and the removal of tape or metal fasteners such as rusting staples or paper clips. The latter can be replaced with nonoxidizing or plastic clips. All procedures relating to conservation, copying, and repair should be established and supervised by an archivist specifically qualified in this area.

Once arranged, records should be stored in acid-free boxes and folders. Many archives holding modern records find the work of comprehensive refoldering inefficient and unnecessary. Where records are refoldered, no more than about one-quarter to one-half inch of documents should be placed in any folder. Each folder should be identified at the minimum by collection name and/or number, file heading and a unique folder number. The box number and series name are commonly added as well. The records are then usually placed in standard legal- or letter-sized archives boxes, one cubic-foot record cartons or flat boxes for bound volumes and oversized records. Where possible, a box should not contain both the end of one series and the start of another. Acid-free filler materials or supports must be used to make up unused space where needed. Conversely, for conservation purposes and ease of retrieval, boxes should not be stuffed to their absolute capacity. Box labels should include the name of the repository and the record group/collection, the names of the relevant subdivisions and series, and the range of folders in the box. The exact style and format of the box label is a matter that can be left to the preference of the individual repository, but should be detailed in the procedures manual.

The last step in arrangement is the placement of the records on the shelves. After allowing for separation by physical format, repositories will find it convenient to shelve in one place records processed together. Where a collection or subgroup must be divided because of space considerations, every effort should be made to maintain together the boxes constituting a series. The goal of shelving is to use space efficiently, but also to preserve the unified filing structures that exist as series. The precise location of every box must be noted, usually in terms of its room, row, stack, and shelf number. As noted earlier, automated systems are especially valuable in this warehousing function. With the completion of this final phase of arrangement and the collection of information about the physical location of records, the foundation has been created for the descriptive work which follows.

Chapter 8

Description: The Nature of Archival Information

Archival description is fundamentally a process of communicating information about sets of records to their potential users. As an umbrella term for a group of related activities, archival description commonly includes generating or gathering information about records and their creators; organizing and controlling that information both intellectually and administratively; and providing access to it inside and outside the repository. Descriptive practice requires the employment of both historical research skills and techniques from library and information science. Description is an ongoing activity, involving the continual refinement and revision of information as sets of records grow and organizations change, as archivists process records, and as users find new meanings in them. In its full sense, archival description documents not only the records, but also the way they are used and administered.

The foundation of the whole system is the collective description in various descriptive tools, or finding aids, of the different sets of records identified and ordered during arrangement. The most common of these collective descriptive tools are series-based inventories of manuscript collections and archival record groups, and repository-wide guides. Such tools are supplemented by various types of internal indexes, catalogs, and lists of individual documents. Recently archivists have also been preparing standardized summary descriptions of records for automated library networks.

The effectiveness of a system based on collective description is directly dependent on the effectiveness of archival arrangement. Records are nor-

mally described only to the level of detail to which they are arranged. The larger aggregations (record groups and series) help provide information about origins and context which is applicable to all of their components, such as subseries and folders, without repetition. Description is also facilitated by distinct and logical groupings. A series of "Account Books, arranged chronologically" needs less explanation than "Financial Records, arranged alphabetically." It is the essence of collective description that the description depends on the collectivity. The set of records is described, not its individual components.

This dependence on arrangement raises problems in facilitating use. Archival descriptive systems are best at describing records and their origins. However, in planning such systems, archivists should remember that users really want to get at information within the records, and only seek the records as the conveyors of that information.

The distinction is made clear in the difference between what Richard Lytle termed the Provenance and Content methods of archival information retrieval.[1] In the Provenance method, records are described and retrieved primarily on the basis of originating activities and organizational structure, through the use of lists replicating the records' arrangement by creator and file structure. The Content method is based instead upon directly indexing the information contained in the records, with relatively little emphasis on the origin or context of a

---

[1] See Richard Lytle, "Intellectual Access to Archives: I. Provenance and Content Indexing Methods of Subject Retrieval," *American Archivist* 43 (Winter 1980): 64–75.

given file or document. As Lytle noted, subject access through the Provenance method "depends primarily on making the connection between a subject request and provenance related information."[2]

To find information about park planning in Middletown according to the Provenance method alone, researchers have to know first which agency in the Saratoga state government is responsible for park planning. Then they must study both the DNR's structure as expressed in the record group and the Office of Park Planning's file system to locate the appropriate records. The Content method could in theory lead a user directly to the appropriate files through an entry under "Parks—planning" in a catalog. However, it would not provide that user with the information about the institutional context or file structure provided by the Provenance method. Nevertheless, as the Dutch themselves put it at the turn of the century, writing of provenance, "we are well aware that an inventory drawn up according to our system presents certain difficulties for the user."[3]

The solution to the dilemma is a two-stage approach. Users generally go from a repository-wide index or catalog listing records under a number of appropriate terms, including subjects, first to various tools describing sets of records and second to the records themselves. In contrast to library systems, this approach forces users to examine the context in which records are created. A library user can go directly from the card catalog to a book classified under, for example, HN 387.9 without knowing the meaning of the H, HN or HN 300 classifications. In archives, rather than directing the user to a specific document or file, the catalog/index or the archival staff takes the user to an inventory or a series description listing a relevant coherent set of records. These tools in turn describe where specific records can be found. Although automation provides archives with the potential for bypassing these finding aids and linking catalog/index entries directly with individual files and documents, the temptation should be resisted. The whole point of archival description is to describe records in context as represented by provenance and original order.

Given this two-stage approach, few descriptive systems choose to rely exclusively on provenance and file structure to help users find relevant records. Public and institutional archives supplement descriptive tools such as inventories, based upon prove-

nance and filing structures, with various indexes. However, these do rely mainly on information derived from file structures and titles. Manuscript repositories have always stressed content description of files and documents through catalogs and indexes more than descriptions of file structures. However, this content-oriented method requires much more effort on the part of the repository's staff than the provenance method, because it requires information not previously gathered through arrangement. In practice, description combines both methods, with content indexing used to supplement basic provenance-centered descriptive tools. Both methods also continue to rely upon the knowledge and skills of the reference archivist. The particular nature of the combination varies according to the mission, holdings and clientele of the repository.

In this way, description is a way of both adapting and supplementing arrangement in the interests of use. Certain sets of records can be adequately described simply through their title and the context in which they appear within a collection. Other records, such as minutes and correspondence, may need much more elaborate description than that provided by their organization and placement within that same collection. But description has functions beyond providing access to researchers. It also serves important administrative purposes. Through proper description a repository knows what materials it has, where they are located, and how they are arranged. Description permits an overview of the strengths and weaknesses of the repository's holdings. These administrative functions of description are increasingly being integrated with the other components of archival information.

The Archival Information System

Archivists often identify description with its concrete manifestations in the form of various descriptive tools. But those tools are only one part of a full archival descriptive system. In the broader sense, archivists should think of description as the provision of information; hence they should think of descriptive tools as part of an archival information system.[4] Like any information system the archival

---

[2] Ibid., 71.
[3] Muller, Feith and Fruin, *Manual*, 147.

[4] See Lisa Weber, "Archival Descriptive Standards: Concepts, Principles and Methodologies," and David Bearman, "Archival Descriptive Standards: A Framework for Action," *American Archivist* 52 (Fall 1989); and H. Thomas Hickerson, "Standards for Archival Information Management Systems," *American Archivist* 53 (Winter 1990). These issues include the papers prepared for the 1988–89 Working Group on Standards for Archival Description, as well as the Working Group's final report and recommendations.

system has a number of key components, which must work together to provide effective communication with users. In very basic terms, the three essential parts of archival information systems are:

- information about records and their creators,
- the tools used to present that information, and
- the standards and rules followed in creating those tools.

These components—information, tools and standards—provide the framework for the last three chapters of this manual. Each component has its own complex history and structure, and it is easy to lose sight of the overall system while concentrating on the preparation of inventories or the application of standardized cataloging rules. A brief summary of the system will therefore be useful before proceeding to a more detailed analysis.

1. Information. Description should provide specific elements of information about records, their origins and relationships, and archival actions. The descriptive elements provided about any specific body of records fall into four broad categories. First, the descriptive elements provide information about the intellectual content of the records. Second, they provide information about how to use the records, including their accessibility and their relations to other records. Third, they inform the researcher of the physical characteristics of the records. Fourth, descriptive elements tell how to gain physical access to the records (as opposed to information about how to use them once accessed). Of equal importance in archival work is information about the records' creators, origins, and context. Archivists should also describe the nature and products of their work on the records. These categories of information form the basic components of any repository's descriptive system and are described in detail later in this chapter.

For many years, archivists thought that archival description could not be standardized and information could not be shared across repository lines because each repository's holdings are unique. This attitude changed under the influence of both library techniques and automation. Archivists have come to recognize the similarities underlying the evident diversity of descriptive practices among institutions. The same kind of information about records is collected in virtually all repositories, despite differences of procedure, format, style, and terminology. Repositories almost universally note, at a minimum, such basic pieces of information as the creator and

type of records, date spans, volume, arrangement, donor, and physical location. In addition, they typically index or catalog their holdings according to lists of subjects, names, and places, whether those lists are developed internally or follow national standards.

Identifying those various elements of information encourages both a logical, consistent control of information within a repository and the exchange of information with other repositories. Archivists should think of the possible range of information about records in terms of a list of clearly defined descriptive elements, sometimes called data elements. Taking into consideration all possible cases in all types of repositories and all types of records, the number of different archival descriptive elements is very high. The description of public records may require information about the full administrative hierarchy of the record-creating body, the process of appraisal, and the statutes and legal authorities under which records are generated, transferred to an archives, and then opened for research. The very different description of seventeenth- or eighteenth-century manuscripts in a historical society may require information about the language in which the documents are written and the availability of copies or published versions. Naturally, most records can be described using a limited selection of such elements (far less than the total number possible) and each set of records requires a different selection of elements. But any repository containing even a modest range of different types of records should establish policies and procedures for the use of all the possible descriptive elements.

2. Tools. The description of any set of records must be part of a repository-wide descriptive program implemented in a variety of related descriptive tools. These tools will be the formats in which the elements of descriptive information are presented. The descriptive program should be integrated; different tools should play different roles while avoiding duplication or contradictions by drawing on a common basis of archival information. This integrated descriptive program should control the full range of information about all of the repository's holdings and processing activities represented in the various descriptive tools.

Descriptive tools form the visible structure of the descriptive system, somewhat in the way that different levels of arrangement provide a structure for archival arrangement. As series are at the core of archival arrangement, so series descriptions, usually grouped in inventories, are at the core of collective description. Researchers are led to descriptions of series and their creators before they use the records themselves. Other descriptive tools support this two-stage approach. Control documents generated or collected during acquisitions, appraisal, and accessioning may be used for access until the records are processed. General and thematic guides, special lists, and entries into inter-institutional systems can be derived from the core descriptions of records and records creators. In all, a comprehensive set of descriptive tools begins with accessioning and ends with the reporting of standardized information through national data bases. The range of descriptive tools forms the subject of Chapter 9.

3. Standards. Descriptive elements and tools must be presented and prepared according to some documented standards in order to form a consistent, predictable, and efficient descriptive system. Standards in the archival world range from generally accepted guidelines, such as the principle of collective description, to precise technical requirements, such as the use of certain terms in automated cataloging systems. Descriptive information should always be conveyed in structures and utilize terminology and rules that are consistent within the repository. Preferably, these institutional standards should follow existing and evolving national standards for archival information exchange. In this way, information will be presented to users in a format, sequence, and vocabulary that they will always be able to recognize and understand. No longer should it be necessary for each repository to devise its own descriptive standards and rules, or for users to learn a new system at each repository.

The three crucial areas in which there are national descriptive standards usable by archivists are formats, descriptive (or cataloging) rules, and terminology. The first, descriptive formats, sometimes called data structures, are the tools or containers in which archival information is presented. The only formally standardized data structure for archival information is the USMARC AMC (Archives and Manuscripts Control) format. This is analogous to the cataloging record for a book, but it also has special features applicable to archival materials.

Second, descriptive rules govern the way information, such as names and dates, is formed within descriptive formats. Such standardization also extends to the use of common punctuation and spacing. The main source of rules for the description of archival materials is *Archives, Personal Papers, and Manuscripts (APPM)* by Steven Hensen. Archivists also use the library standard *Anglo-American Cata-*

loguing Rules 2nd edition, revised (*AACR 2*) in areas not covered by *APPM*.[5]

Third, terminology in this context refers to the lists of terms that are used in archival description. There are many standard lists, the most familiar of which is the *Library of Congress Subject Headings (LCSH)*.[6] Archivists also use standard lists of terms for occupations, physical formats, and organizational activities, as well as more detailed subject lists for various specializations. Lists of subject terms often take the form of a thesaurus, which is defined as a "compilation of words and phrases showing synonyms, hierarchical and other relationships and dependencies."[7] Archivists commonly employ all three types of standards when they use *LCSH* terms in USMARC AMC records cataloged according to *APPM* in the national library data bases like RLIN and OCLC. The various descriptive standards and rules form the subject of Chapter 10.

Rules and standards should apply not only to the description of specific collections, but also to the entire repository descriptive system. Thus standards should be applied in the same way to all of the repository's holdings. For example, the same descriptive element, such as a description of functions, should not appear as as an index term in one finding aid and only in a free form narrative in another. If all agencies that do strategic planning are indexed under that specific term, the planning records should also be so indexed even if the phrase appears as well in the narrative of the planner's responsibilities. Similarly, the same type of finding aid should serve the same purposes for all similar collections. One collection should not have an inventory that includes a folder list while another has only series descriptions in the inventory but a card catalog describing the folders.

Standardization of terms is commonly applied to subjects, places, names, events and other topics. But standard terminolgy applies as well to identifying descriptive elements themselves. For example, the state archives should be consistent about using the term provenance for the creator of the records; the term should not also be used for the immediate source or custodian. The somewhat different stan-

[5] Michael Gorman and Paul W. Winkler, eds, *Anglo-American Cataloguing Rules*, 2nd edition, revised (Chicago: American Library Association, 1988).

[6] Library of Congress, Subject Cataloging Division, *Library of Congress Subject Headings*, 10th ed. (Washington: Library of Congress, 1986).

[7] American National Standards Institute, *Guidelines for Thesaurus Structure, Construction and Use, ANSI Z39.19-1980* (New York: ANSI, 1980).

dardization of terminology describing information means that, for example, volume should be described as cubic feet or linear feet, but not both, or that metric measurements be used consistently if they are used at all. The archival profession is gradually moving towards formal agreement on these various aspects of terminology.

Archival standardization has generally been driven by automation. Even sophisticated computer programs demand some standardization of format and terminology to work most effectively. At the same time automation allows the archivist to generate, control, and manipulate whatever number of indexing terms is appropriate to each group of records. In the past, concern over the hundreds or even thousands of names mentioned in inventories limited the use of catalogs in archival description; it was feared that the number of names would make the catalogs unmanageably large. By freeing archival description from such restrictions, as well as by forcing increased standardization, automation has led archivists to focus on the elements of information about records that are at the core of any descriptive system.

Descriptive Elements

Many archivists, from the earliest theorists through Schellenberg and beyond, analyzed the different characteristics of records and the information collected about them.[8] The virtue of the descriptive or data element approach is that it clearly separates the essential issue of information gathering from both descriptive tools and descriptive standards. A given descriptive element can appear in several descriptive tools, while standardization is clearly independent of the specific information collected. The focus on descriptive elements emphasizes the primacy of the information itself. As noted earlier, the descriptive elements in an archival information system will provide information about the records, their origin and context, and archival actions and descriptive control.[9]

1. Information about Records.

A. Intellectual content. Information about content includes creator, record type, time span, origin/function of the records and a summary narrative,

or "scope and contents" note. Other common data elements include creator's occupation/function, immediate source of the records, and place of creation. All such information about content can be employed as is or used to derive specific terms for indexing and cataloging the records.

B. Intellectual access. Access here refers to information needed by researchers to use a specific set of records, as distinct from repository rules governing the conditions of use of all records. This type of information about access describes the arrangement of the records, relevant finding aids, and any technical and language requirements for using the records. Other records related in some integral way to the records being accessed, such as their source, summary, index, or supplement, should also be noted.

C. Physical description. Elements of physical description include total volume, number, and type of storage units, physical format and recording medium, physical condition, and any technical data about scale or information-recording techniques.

D. Physical access. Information about physical access includes location, restrictions, required authorizations for use, and the nature and location of copies of original records.

2. Information about Origins and Context.

Information about the organizational unit or individual which created the records should be conceived of as distinct from information about particular records. The information about the creator may be applicable to more than one set of records. Once again, this emphasizes the critical difference between records and their creators. Information about an organizational unit should include its current and previous names; superior, predecessor, and successor units, with dates; and a summary of its legal basis, administrative history, and major functions or activities. Information on individuals will consist of a short summary biography with dates. As with information about record content, the names and titles of record creators will also be used as index terms in repository-wide catalogs and indexes. Much of this information about both individuals and organizations can also be conceived of as "authority file" entries, described below in more detail.

3. Information about Archival Actions and Descriptive Control.

A. Archival actions. Because processing is an ongoing activity, information about archival actions forms an important part of archival descriptive systems. Such information can be of use not only to archivists and administrators, but also to researchers. A number of separate descriptive elements can

---

[8] A good example is the chart in Schellenberg, *Management of Archives*, 121.

[9] The basic categories were first outlined systematically in NISTF, "Standard Data Elements for Archives and Manuscript Information Systems: A Report to the Archival Profession," February 1982. The associated Data Elements Dictionary can be found in Sahli, *MARC for Archives and Manuscripts*.

Figure 8-1   Matrix of Some Common Descriptive Elements

	Records Set		
Descriptive Element	*Museum Education Division Children's Programs Department*	*Union Mission Board Minutes*	*Bailey Family Papers*
I. Information about Records			
Intellectual Content			
Creator	Children's Program Department, Education Division	Union Mission	George Bailey
Title/Type	Records	Board Minutes	Family papers
Dates	1935–1982	1878–1900	1789–1986
Bulk Dates	1938–1979	1878–1900	1928–1986
Origin/Function	Program files	Minutes	Personal papers
Level	Subgroup	Series	Collection
Content	(narrative text)	(narrative text)	(narrative text)
Descriptive Terms	Education, School District, Children, Community Programs...	Charities, Social Settlements, South Middletown...	Banking, Politics, Philanthropy, Bedford Falls...
Intellectual Access			
Arrangement	Alphabetical/chronological	Chronological	Subgroups/series
Finding Aids	RG Inventory, Box list	Box list, minutes indexed	Inventory/folder list
Language	English	English	English
Related records	Education Division (RG 6)	Union Mission Southside Settlement	Peter Bailey, Chamber of Commerce, Businessman's Club, . . .
Physical Description			
Volume	2 cubic feet	1 cubic foot	38 cubic feet
Number of containers	2 cartons	4 flat boxes	117 archives boxes
Format	paper files/foldered	bound volumes	paper files
Condition	satisfactory	bindings deteriorating	some brittle paper
Physical Access			
Location	15/3/3	A3/5-8	Rm 32/6/5
Restrictions	unrestricted	unrestricted	Autograph collection, restricted
Use Authorization	n/a	n/a	Autograph collection, Estate permission
Copies	n/a	microfilmed	Autograph collection photocopied
II. Records Creator			
Name	Children's Program Department, Education Division	Union Mission	George Bailey
Dates	1935–	1878–1900	1911–1987

Figure 8-1   Matrix of Some Common Descriptive Elements—_Continued_

Records Set			
Organization level			
Predecessor	Education Division	none	n/a
Successor	n/a	Southside Settlement	n/a
Occupation	n/a	n/a	Banker
History/biography	(narrative text)	See Union Mission entry	(narrative text)
III. Archival Actions and Descriptive Control			
Provenance	Education Division	Southside Community Services	George Bailey
Immediate Source	Administrative Secretary, Education Division	Director, Southside Community Services	Mary Bailey
Acquisition Date	2/18/89	3/14/89	4/6/89
Accessioned	2/18/89	5/27/89	11/15/89
Processing Status	accessioned	series/box descriptions	completed
Preservation review	2/22/89	7/19/89	5/6/90
Control #	A89077	M 725/1	MS 90-105

be employed to provide information about all the acquisition, appraisal, processing, and preservation activities a repository performs with respect to each group of records. In addition to the type of action, this information should include the date of the action, the individual responsible, authorizations, and contingencies for taking any future action. In automated systems, information on archival actions is often in part of the descriptive information created about a set of records from the moment it is authorized for transfer to a repository. Thus the description of the park planning series should list the dates when different groups of records were transferred to the state archives, provide continually updated information on the state of processing for each group, and indicate when future additions to the series will occur.

B. Control of descriptive information. Archival information systems include information about the control documents themselves in which the various descriptive elements are contained. These control documents range from internal catalog entries to full inventories and standardized USMARC AMC descriptions. They are the archival equivalents of the bibliographic records in a library's catalog. Information about such descriptive control documents is especially crucial in automated systems, though it can be useful in the administration of all descriptive programs. Descriptive control documents often include a summary and layout of the kind of information

they contain about the archival materials described, and how that information was gathered and maintained. In the case of the Bailey papers, the accession record should indicate that it is in fact an accession record, that it is number 89062, that it follows a certain sequence or structure in the presentation of information, and that it was last updated on 18 November 1989. Eventually this accession record may be linked to more elaborate descriptive tools as processing proceeds. On the national level, when a summary of a collection is entered into _NUCMC_, that entry receives a _NUCMC_ number. The number refers not to the collection's number within the repository, but simply to the _NUCMC_ entry.

Authority Control

All of these descriptive elements produce a very large number of terms which can be used to lead users to records, relate records to each other and link them to their creators. Archivists, like librarians, should employ authority files to control this blizzard of information. _Authority files_ are standardized vocabularies which indicate the one agreed form for terms, names and phrases. They indicate as well the variant forms which should not be used.[10] In effect,

---

[10] See Jackie M. Dooley, "Introduction to Authority Control for Archivists," in Avra Michelson, ed., _Archives and Authority Control: Proceedings of a Seminar Sponsored by the Smithsonian Institution, October 27, 1987._ Published as Part 2 of _Archival Informatics Newsletter and Technical Report_ 2:2 (Summer 1988): 5–18.

authority files form a distinct part of any repository's descriptive system, separate from the descriptions of the records themselves. The great value of authority files is that they help insure that similar inquiries will produce similar results. As in library systems, the purpose of authority control is to create entities that are distinguishable from each other but will subsume all possible forms of that entity.

In the case of the Bailey papers, George Bailey may in the course of his life have used a full middle name, initials, a combination thereof and a nickname. The function of an authority file is to decide unequivocally that George Rogers, G. Rogers, G. R. and Rog Bailey are all in fact to be described as George Bailey. In the absence of authority files, processors, reference archivists and/or researchers would have to know or guess all the relevant variations on a term; otherwise records not indexed under the precise term being used would not be retrieved even by the best descriptive systems.

Because archival holdings are unique, each repository will need authority files specific to its records. These are in addition to the standard lists of names and subjects used in libraries and discussed in Chapter 10. These archival authority files will include the correct form for local names, places, events, and organizations. Records will be listed under as many relevant authority file headings as are applicable. It is especially important to recognize that information about individuals and organizational units is similar to the "origins and context" descriptive elements noted above, but is viewed here in its technically correct role as authority information. Information about records creators is in fact best regarded as authority file information. Thus the history, structure, and functions of the DNR are authority-file data which can be used in the description of all records mentioning the department in any way, including records from other departments.

Such authority information can also be shared among repositories. In addition to the established national networks, authority files can be shared within a geographical area or among repositories documenting the same subject or type of activities. George Bailey's name will appear in the Southside records at the university library and the Southside Settlement will be documented in his papers at the historical society. Regional authority files should ensure that both names are formed the same way in both repositories. Authority files will also play an important role in linking the Mary Hatch who was active in the museum before she married and the

Mary Bailey who continued those activities after her marriage.

Authority records can be used more broadly by archivists to describe types of records and activities found in virtually all repositories. Agreement on standard terms for records like "diaries" or activities like "taxing" allows archivists to "capture in cultural shorthand a description of the intellectual content of records."[11] A standard list of *Form Terms for Archives and Manuscripts Control* was published in 1985 to standardize the description of record types.[12] When a researcher asks for "case files," it is very helpful to be able to find such records across collection and even repository lines. Archivists are also working to standardize the description of organizational activities.[13]

Descriptive Practice

The effectiveness of all the different parts of the archival information system discussed above depends ultimately upon the quality of the information gathered and presented by archivists. Description requires a detailed understanding by the archivist of the nature and probable uses of the records to be described and the appropriate roles of different descriptive tools. Archivists must know what information is required for effective description and how to find such information both in the records and from other sources. Tools discussing record creators will require capsule histories or biographies. Those describing sets of records must include precise analyses of activities and functions. Integrative indexes are based on terms appearing in all finding aids, and terms added by the archivist. The level of further detail provided in the finding aids should be decided on the basis of probable use and repository policy. The state archives might concentrate on the need for indexing records by relevant statutes, while the historical society may emphasize the full forms of name and dates for individuals and families.

In finding and preparing the information for various finding aids, archivists use both historical research skills and methods drawn from information science. Historical skills will be used in researching

---

[11] Bearman and Lytle, "The Power of the Principle of Provenance," 22.

[12] Research Libraries Group, *Form Terms for Archival and Manuscript Control*, (Stanford, CA: RLG, 1985).

[13] A list of terms describing activities, processes and functions was developed as part of an RLG project involving state archives. The list has been included in Toni Peterson, director, *Art and Architecture Thesaurus*. 3 vols. (New York: Oxford University Press, 1990). The *AAT* also incorporates the *Form Terms* list cited in note 12.

histories and biographies, and in identifying major activities, functions, events, participants, and processes. Here the archivist may be the first researcher in the records being described. Even in the age of automation, archivists should be able to organize and write a narrative description of the content and context of records. Information and library science techniques are especially relevant in the selection and formatting of precise indexing terms from finding aids and standard library lists. Such techniques are also central to the entire process of employing standardized descriptive formats, rules, and terminology, and to the creation of integrated archival information systems. Information science also emphasizes the systematic study of user needs and, in combination with historical skills, can help archivists adapt description to changing patterns of use.

Description is an entire system of communication. To extend the analogy, the information about specific records and the terms used for people, places, organizations, and subjects together provide the vocabulary. Formats and rules are the structure or grammar of the language. Descriptive tools are the voice. They all must be brought together to communicate effectively. In archives, that goal is accomplished by creating an integrated network of finding aids, summary descriptions, and indexes—a coordinated system of descriptive tools.

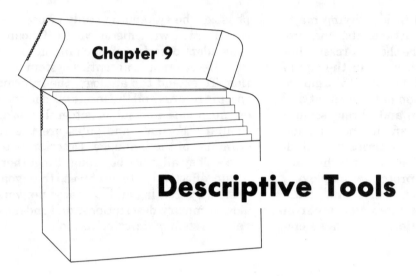

Chapter 9

Descriptive Tools

Archival description is often identified with the various descriptive tools used by researchers to gather information about the holdings of a repository. Descriptive tools, or finding aids as some are also called, are in that respect the public side of the archival information system. Users of archives often find themselves consulting the whole range of descriptive tools within a repository. They also become accustomed to the variations among similar tools produced by different repositories. Beyond their essential function of intellectual control, descriptive tools of various types provide as well physical and administrative control over records. Some tools, such as inventories and series descriptions, describe specific sets of records in depth while others, like guides, provide capsule summaries of whole collections and record groups. Still other tools, like repository indexes and catalogs, cut across provenance to bring together records sharing a common theme. These various descriptive tools are discussed in detail in this chapter, but it is important to first see them together within a larger context.

An Integrated Descriptive Program

The different specific types of descriptive tools should not be analyzed or created in isolation. Repositories should have a coordinated and integrated network of descriptive tools. In an effective integrated system, the different descriptive tools should be complementary and reinforcing, not duplicative and parallel. Each part of the system should have a particular role and provide a particular type or level of information. Thus a catalog or index should not un-

necessarily repeat information available in an inventory, but instead should lead users to the inventory. Where the same descriptive element, such as the record type, does recur in several tools, the information should be derived from the records only once and then exchanged, thus avoiding both needless work and possible inconsistencies. (See Figure 9-1)

An integrated system is not necessarily an automated system—nor is an automated system necessarily integrated. An integrated system is simply one which provides a logical, efficient, comprehensive, and substantially self-explanatory presentation of information. In the last sense, an integrated descriptive system should reduce the traditional dependence on the archivist as the personal intermediary between users and records.

A program that is comprehensive as well as integrated will describe all of the repository's holdings at some minimal level for administrative control even if not for full intellectual access. It will therefore include unprocessed records as they are described at the time of accessioning, and records in all physical formats. It will describe records at all subsequent stages of processing, and will provide for the regular revision of descriptions as processing proceeds. A major function of description is to restore the intellectual coherence that may have been lost through the separation of records by format. The descriptive program must be able to reunite on paper all of the records, regardless of form, which have been produced by a given records creator or are related to a common topic. This is one of the functions performed by a repository-wide catalog or index, as well as by various types of published guides and lists.

Figure 9-1   Matrix of Descriptive Elements Recorded in Descriptive Tools, Saratoga State University Library, Regional History Center

Descriptive Element	Accession Form	Inventory	Repository Data base	Bibliographic Network Entry
Rec. Creator	X	X	X	X
Creator's Dates		X	X	X
Hist./Biog.		X	X	X
Rec. Title	X	X	X	X
Rec. Dates	X	X	X	X
Bulk dates		X	X	X
Rec. types		X	X	X
Physical format	X	X	X	X
Volume	X	X	X	X
# Containers	X	X	X	X
Physical Condition	X		X	
Scope/Contents		X	X	X
Index terms		X	X	X
Provenance	X	X	X	X
Immed. Source	X	X	X	
Acquis. date	X	X	X	
Acquis. authority	X		X	
Arrangement		X	X	X
Processing Status			X	X
Series Titles		X	X	X
Dates		X	X	X
Volume		X	X	X
Arrangement		X	X	
Contents		X	X	
Box Summaries	X			
Folder Lists		X		
Access Restrictions	X	X	X	X
Location	X		X	
Related Records		X	X	X
Bibliog. Citations		X		

Note: *This is an example of how one university library might structure its descriptive system. Other repositories might decide to include different elements in different tools, or even to have other tools, such as a comprehensive guide.*

The descriptive program should also be flexible. One important reason that the network of descriptive tools should encompass records in various stages of processing is that description usually proceeds in accordance with the practice called progressive refinement. Progressive refinement means that in the case of records which are already arranged, descriptions are created in a sequence from the broadest down to the most detailed—from record groups or collections to series and individual files. Such a procedure assumes the prior existence of some systematic arrangement and of preliminary container listings.

Progressive refinement does not mean that all records are described to the same level of detail, but only that work on all records should proceed in the same direction, even if the stopping place varies with different materials. Items should not be described before the folders of which they are a part, nor series before the larger collection. However tempting, Bailey's autograph letters should not be cataloged as items before the autograph series and the Bailey collection as a whole are described. Similarly, the state archivists should not analyze the individual park proposals before describing the entire planning series. Sometimes records will be described to one level of detail and then be left for later refinement. Records such as those of the planning office could be described to the subseries level, whose titles would convey considerable information, without proceeding immediately to the preparation of a detailed folder listing. This building block approach to description provides flexibility for administrative needs and priorities as well as for the needs of different types of records and users.[1]

The descriptive program should also allow for the growth and evolution of collections. Public and institutional archives and manuscript repositories working with ongoing organizations all need systems which can accommodate regular additions of material. The state archives will have organized the various DNR records into subgroups and series, but the individual series descriptions will have to change regularly as new material arrives according to the records management schedules. Yet descriptive systems should not be so specific to archives that they become isolated from other information resources such as libraries and records management programs within the same institution. Some compromises in

the areas of common formats, such as the USMARC AMC format, and the use of terminology, such as the *Library of Congress Subject Headings*, are usually necessary and even desirable.

Archival Descriptive Programs

Archives and manuscript repositories naturally have somewhat different types of descriptive programs. Archives have relied mainly on inventories of records groups. Such inventories are broken down by subgroup and list records by series and subseries. If users know the governmental or organizational structure, they can find relevant records by going directly to the inventories for the appropriate agency or department. But in the absence of other indexing they would have to know that park planning, for example, is now a function of the DNR in order to go that record group inventory. This type of descriptive system assumes that the archival arrangement outlined in the inventory provides a structure replicating the organization's history and activities. The title and nature of a series together with its provenance would thus provide in theory a self-explanatory analysis of the contents of the records.

In a typical archival descriptive program, each level of arrangement by provenance or file structure has a corresponding finding aid. The center of the system is the series-based inventory describing together all of the series produced by a records creator. An increasingly common variation which gathers the same type of information is the preparation of separate descriptions of series, records creators, and the links among them. Guides are summaries of record groups and collections as described in inventories. Thematic and special lists of records should also be drawn from inventories, through the identification and selection of relevant series, folders, or even documents.

Index entries can be generated from file lists as well as from information about the larger record sets. In most systems, entries in card catalogs and data bases are based mainly on terms and information derived from inventories. The indexes to individual inventories and box/folder listings can all be combined into a repository-wide index, especially if consistent terminology is employed in all the inventories. Because archival descriptive tools naturally describe organizational and file structures better than processes and subjects, such indexes will have to be supplemented by terms drawn from outside the tools themselves.

[1] Lydia Lucas, "Efficient Finding Aids: Developing a System for Control of Archives and Manuscripts," *American Archivist* 44 (Winter 1981): 24.

Manuscript Descriptive Programs

Compared to archival description, the descriptive programs of most manuscript repositories represent a blend of the provenance/inventory approach and the content orientation of library cataloging by names and subjects. Collections are arranged according to archival principles and inventories prepared to describe them. But in a manuscript repository the catalog—automated or manual—serves most researchers as the main integrative tool, rather than the set of inventories themselves as in a pure archival system. The catalog contains index entries derived from all the inventories. In manuscript repositories, inventories normally describe records to the folder level. The catalog will also contain subject, geographic, personal, and topical terms supplied by the staff after examining the collections. Most users will use the catalog as an index to find the inventories describing records relevant to their needs.

Like archival systems, a modern manuscript descriptive system forces users to see records in context by leading them from the catalog to the inventory, not to the records themselves. In contrast to past practice, the catalog is understood primarily as an index to the inventories. Manuscript catalogs therefore do not need to duplicate most of the descriptive information found in inventories. The catalog can simply provide index terms and a notation of the names and numbers of the relevant records sets. This catalog or index should have only enough information to direct the user to the appropriate inventory or series description.

Catalogs have the added virtues of being easily expandable and, unlike inventories, compatible with other information systems. However, they still demand an additional level of work after the arrangement and basic description of the records. For example, after arranging and creating an inventory for the Southside Community Services records, the staff of the Regional History Center will have to provide subject and other indexing terms for the catalog. Not all of the terms can simply be drawn from the inventory, since some general themes and topics may not be mentioned in the specific record descriptions. Without the catalog and the indexing terms, however, the repository would have to rely on the abilities of the staff to connect the Southside collection with researchers' inquiries. Even the memories of the best and most senior archivists are not equal to the challenges posed by the bulk and complexity of contemporary records. Only a comprehensive set of descriptive tools can provide both archivists and users with the required control of and access to records.

Descriptive Tools

Although descriptive tools vary among repositories in format and structure, they generally fall into several clearly identifiable categories. One useful overall distinction is between descriptive tools designed primarily for use within the repository and those designed primarily to inform outside researchers about holdings. The major categories of descriptive tools are as follows:

1. Internal tools

    A. Accession documents
    B. Creator-supplied finding aids
    C. Inventories
    D. Series-record creator linking systems
    E. Indexes and catalogs

2. External descriptions

    A. Guides
    B. Specialized descriptions
    C. Summary collective descriptions

1. Internal Tools.

A. Accession documents. As explained in Chapter 4, by the end of accessioning, a repository should have collected basic information about the nature and contents of a group of records, and produced a summary box listing. The further elaboration of this information depends upon two factors; the length of time before the records are likely to be processed, and the repository's policies on access to unprocessed materials. In automated systems, the accessioning information can be used as the first stage of a continually refined bibliographic record. Where appropriate, the box listings can be expanded into folder listings. Without any further arrangement, such listings can be sorted alphabetically and chronologically and indexed by computer. Their value for researchers will be greatly enhanced by these relatively simple steps. Similarly, box and folder listings can be photocopied and added to internal repository-wide control files arranged by provenance, donor, format, topic, and similar categories. These actions will aid in the physical and administrative control of the records, as well as in their intellectual control.

In public and institutional archives, box and folder lists can also serve a vital role as permanent location registers for records that arrive already in satisfactory order. Most inventories provided to researchers in archives describe records only down to the series or subseries level. To retrieve the actual boxes and folders, which may well be in a variety of locations, a separate system of documentation on the box and folder level is needed. Accession documents, especially those based on creator-supplied lists, are well adapted to the purpose. The locations of individual boxes should be noted on the container lists, and the archivist should ensure that the repository's internal files link inventories to such container/location lists.

 B. Creator-supplied finding aids. Finding aids generated by the creators of records for their control during active use are a special boon to archivists. Not only do they offer a savings in work, but they also have the uniquely archival virtues of preserving a full original order reflecting ongoing activity. Before relying on such tools, archivists should check them for accuracy and comprehensibility. Where not capricious or unusable, they should be integrated into the final descriptive system.

 The most useful creator-supplied finding aids are complete outlines of internal filing structures, such as classification systems or lists of file headings. The best outlines include explanations of all codes and abbreviations. (See Figure 9-2.) A second type of internal finding aid is the separate catalogs, indexes and registers used to control files. They can be in the form of cards, lists, or computer data bases. Internal indexes commonly provide access to individual file units under a variety of headings devised or adapted by records creators. Bailey might have kept such a personal catalog for his autograph collection, and it should be retained for use with that collection. Registers in this traditional sense of the term are chronologically-arranged summaries of each document generated or received, including information on the document's location. The park planner's secretary might have retained such a list of the incoming correspondence that required a specific official response.

 Registers and indexes supplied by creators should be seen as both finding aids to organizational records and as part of those records. Thus volumes which consist of indexes to minutes or lists of letters dispatched will themselves be series or subseries within a set of records as well as function as a finding aid to the subset of records they describe. In addition to filing system descriptions, registers, and indexes, an archives should also acquire internal filing and indexing rules, thesauri, and lists of authorized indexing terms used in internal catalogs.

 Creator-supplied finding aids can comprise systems almost as elaborate as that of an entire repository, if the agency or organization documented is

Figure 9-2   Department of Natural Resources, Bureau of Parks and Recreation, Office of Park Planning

Filing System for Bureau/Departmental Records
Effective 9/1/70
(Discontinued 3/1/76)

1. Reports to Bureau Chief
    1a. Annual Reports
    1b. Monthly Reports
2. Planning Summaries
    2a. Annual Summaries
    2b. Monthly Summaries
3. Budgets—Office
4. Budgets—Parks
5. Bureau of P&R
    5a. Meetings
    5b. Reports
    5c. Memoranda
    5d. General
6. Contracts
    6a. Acquisition
    6b. Maintenance
    6c. Repair
    6d. Planning Services
7. Correspondence
    7a. Public
    7b. Legislative
    7c. Executive Agencies
    7d. Planning Groups and Agencies
    7e. General
8. Department of Natural Resources
    8a. Meetings
    8b. Reports
    8c. Memoranda
    8d. General
9. Education
10. Forests and Wetlands (Bureau)
    10a. Surveying Services
    10b. Planning Services
    10c. General
    .
    .
    .
41. Wilderness Areas
    41a. Surveys
    41b. Planning
    41c. General
42. Youth Employment Program
    42a. Positions
    42b. Applicants
    42c. Trainees

large enough. While very rare in manuscript work, it is not uncommon for archives to receive large bodies of records which are not only in order, but which come with a full descriptive system. Often this will be the result of the existence of a formal files management system within an agency, which can produce its own classification system, lists, and indexes. But such specific descriptive systems and the records themselves still have to be integrated into the repository-wide descriptive program. Archivists still must provide access terms, standardized according to repository usage, and prepare finding aids such as standard inventories compatible with those for other groups of records.

C. Inventories. Archival inventories are essentially descriptions of all the series identified with a record group or collection, preceded by a description of the organization or individuals which created the records.[2] Inventories are sometimes called registers, especially in manuscript repositories, though they have nothing to do with traditional public archives registry systems. In inventories, the individual series descriptions are often grouped under descriptions of subgroups. Inventories are thus representations of provenance; in Jenkinson's words "a summary but complete exposition on paper of the Arrangement we have given our Archives."[3] Over the decades archivists have achieved a large measure of agreement about the form of inventories and the information they should contain. Even when computer generated, the form is usually like a pamphlet—a document meant to be read. The information is essentially those descriptive elements described in the last chapter.

Inventories have persisted because, for a large proportion of records, they are an effective way of conveying information in a manner consistent with basic archival principles. By grouping records into appropriate series and subgroups, inventories display the full context in which records were created and functioned. Inventories allow archivists to avoid repetition of general contextual information for each set of records. They encourage the integrated description of related records regardless of physical format or location. While difficult to use for growing and changing record sets, inventories are well adapted to the description of personal papers, small bodies of organizational records, and the records of defunct agencies or organizations.

Ironically, because of the complexity, continual change and bulk characteristic of modern public records, the inventory is now least useful in the public archives environment in which it originally developed. Manuscript repositories still find inventories a very effective way to provide the overview of a collection that traditional item-based catalogs cannot provide. However, the role of the inventory in manuscript repositories should not be overstated. Although there should be such collective descriptions for all collections, the numerous small collections can often be summarized through some basic information such as title, provenance and a list of file units. The most important access to such collections will still be through the repository catalog/index.

Standard inventories for larger manuscript collections, and for archives, include the following components:

(1) Introductory Information. The nature of introductory material depends on the complexity of the inventory and the likelihood of its possible distribution outside the repository. Such material can include a title page, table of contents, introduction to the repository, acknowledgments, a foreword by the preparer, and an abstract describing the records. Finding aids intended for publication should meet both repository and general publishing guidelines for format and content. Even unpublished inventories will benefit from a simple title page including the collection name and number and the name and address of the repository. A clear table of contents will always be useful. It should indicate subdivisions of the records, as well as subdivisions of the inventory, and include a list of appendices.

Introductory text will vary according to repository policies and the level of processing of each collection. Acknowledgments should be made of donors or depositors, personnel involved, and any financial support used to purchase or process the records. In a foreword, the preparer can discuss any special aspects of the finding aid and how it should be used, but should not discuss the records themselves. An abstract is especially useful in introducing users to large and complex collections. The abstract should be a brief summary of the provenance, contents, volume, dates and form of the records. It should caution users about any restrictions or difficult physical formats which may affect access. (See Figures 9-3, 9-4, and 9-5.)

(2) Agency History/Biography. Histories of organizational units or biographies of individuals are summaries of functions, activities, events, and changes essential to understanding the records.

---

[2] See Edward Hill, *The Preparation of Inventories.*
[3] Jenkinson, *A Manual,* 115.

Figure 9-3

(Cover Page)

Middletown Museum of Art
Museum Archives
Education Division
Record Group 6
Inventory

123 High Street	Prepared by:
Middletown, SA	Rose Pallette
(122) 555-1212	9 September 1990

Figure 9-4

(Page 1)

TABLE OF CONTENTS

They are neither definitive narratives nor interpretive works. They are mainly chronological expositions of either formal organizational structures and responsibilities or the major events in an individual's life. Most are brief, consisting of not more than a few pages, and often only a paragraph or two. Where the records or papers concentrate on a certain period or subject, the history or biography should follow that emphasis. After the main text, it is common to mention relevant published histories, biographies, or reference sources.

The use of narrative here is the subject of some debate among archivists.[4] The goal of the history or biography seems to lend itself better to listing than prose, and much prose in inventories strongly resembles lists formed into paragraphs. One solution is to abandon any attempt at narrative and rely on organizational charts and chronological outlines. Instead of the traditional narrative history of the Southside Community Services, there would simply be a list of all the major organizational changes starting in 1878. Such a form is also more easily indexed than a narrative, since it consists of essential names and phrases without the surrounding verbiage. Whichever form is used, the description should concentrate on major factors crucial to using the records, not on every change of structure or function. (See Figure 9-6.)

(3) Scope and Contents Note. The distinction between describing records and describing their creators is reflected within traditional inventories in the difference between the history/biography and the scope and contents note. This note is a summary description of the records making up the record group or collection. It may include information about the way the records were generated, used, and maintained; the time span and contents of major subdivisions; the availability of copies; and the overall arrangement. The note should document the appraisal and processing decisions made by archivists. The archivist can here assess the strengths and weaknesses of the records, including gaps in their coverage, and their relation to other record groups or collections. Like the history/biography, the scope and contents note rarely exceeds a few pages.

The scope and contents note has often been regarded as the place where the archivist may write an interpretive narrative about the records, in contrast to the typically dry, factual summary of the agency history/biography. Such a narrative is appropriate as long as it emphasizes areas where the records are unusually rich, notes unexpected gaps in documentation, and discusses relations to other records and subjects that would not be noted explicitly anywhere else in the inventory. An observation concerning ethnic change and distribution in the Southside neighborhood would be a good example of the latter, as would documentation of the environmental movement in the park planning files, or a notation

---

[4] For example, see the contrasting views of narrative in Mary Jo Pugh, "The Illusion of Omniscience" *American Archivist* 45 (Winter 1982), 42; and Richard Berner and Uli Haller, "Principles of Archival Inventory Construction," *American Archivist* 47 (Spring 1984): 152.

Figure 9-5 Education Division Inventory—Continued

(Page 3)

Introduction

The records of the Education Division described in this inventory cover the years 1927 to 1982 and total 45 cubic feet. They form Record Group 6 in the Museum Archives. Post-1982 files are still in the possession of the Division and can be viewed with the permission of the Director. Other records related to the Museum's educational efforts can be found in various Record Groups in the Archives, especially the Director's Records (RG 1), the Board Minutes (RG 3) and the Women's Committee files (RG 4). Users should consult the Archives' Comprehensive Index, available in both hard copy and through the in-house computer system.

The Education Division records were surveyed and appraised during the initial creation of the Archives in 1987. They were transferred to the Archives in 1988. R. Pallette completed processing them in 1989. The processing was supported by a grant from the Middletown Foundation.

The records are open for research without restrictions under the conditions of the Archives' access policy. Records may be copied for use in individual scholarly or personal research. Researchers are responsible for obtaining copyright permission to use material not produced by Museum personnel.

The suggested citation to these records is "Middletown Museum of Art Archives. Education Division. (Record Group 6)."

Figure 9-6

(Page 5)

History of the Division

The Middletown Museum of Art first established a Division of Education and Instruction in 1927. The first regularly scheduled Museum lectures were offered in 1897 and the first formal classes were taught to school children in 1909. Organized tours began in 1911. As such activities gradually increased, the need for a separate education department became evident. In 1925 an education department was proposed by Mrs. Latimer Hetherington, Museum Board member, and Dr. Harley Hansworth, Superintendent of Schools. The Division was formally created by a motion of the Board on February 10, 1927. Miss Julianne Helms was appointed first Director.

In its first years the Division worked mainly with public and private school groups. It was also responsible from the beginning for tours and lectures. During the 1930s, several programs were conducted in coordination with such New Deal agencies as the WPA and the NYA. A formal curriculum within the public school system was offered beginning in 1935. At that point the Division created the two separate departments: Children's Programs and Public Education Programs. From the late 1930s, lectures and tours came increasingly under the purview of the Women's Committee rather than the Division.

Miss Helms left the directorship in 1942. After several short term directors, the post was assumed by Mrs. Violet Hughes. Mrs. Hughes served from 1947 to 1965. In 1948 the Public Relations Department was transferred to her supervision, and it remained within the Division until her departure. As a result of programs begun in World War II and continued after the war, an Adult Department was created in 1955. Increased use of the Museum also led to the creation of a Volunteer's Council within the Division in 1958. However, during the 1950s the School District reduced the number of formal classes which it allowed Museum personnel to offer and these classes finally ended in 1961. The Division then dropped the term "Instruction" from its name, becoming simply the Education Division. In general, formal instructional programs became relatively less important than they had been in the first thirty years of the Division's history. However, the Division did begin to reassume primary responsibility for tours and lectures.

In 1965, Lillian Krasnow became the Director of the Division. She emphasized the Museum's international collections and in 1966 established an International Department. She was also responsible for moving the offices of the Division from the original Museum building to the new Extension wing opened in 1970. When Ms. Krasnow retired in 1978, the Division began to report to the Associate Director for Administration, rather than to the Director as it had previously done.

For further information see also:

Armitage, C. Schuyler, *To Truth and Beauty: The Cultural Life of Middletown, 1880–1945* (Middletown: Homer Press, 1971).

Fourier, Charlene, "Social Control through Cultural Hegemony: A Critical Look at One Midwestern Museum," *Journal of Metacritical Aesthetics* 27 (March 1985): 12–34.

---

of coverage of a longstanding controversy with the school district in the museum files. More questionable are attempts to identify specific research questions that the records address. Archivists can certainly write such essays, but not as parts of inventories. (See Figure 9-7.)

(4) Series Descriptions. The heart of an archival inventory is the description of the series estab-

Figure 9-7 Education Division Inventory—Continued

(Page 7)

Scope and Contents of the Records

The records of the Division cover the years 1927–1982. Material on early education programs and the discussions leading to the formation of the Division in 1925–27 can be found in the Director's Records (Record Group 1) and the Minutes of the Board (Record Group 3). Except for some gaps in 1930–31 and 1941–42, the policy making files are essentially complete. The correspondence of the various directors has been preserved since 1941. In addition to the Division, all of the Departments and subdivisions are well-documented at the policy and general programmatic levels. The largest group of files documents the work of the Division with the Middletown School District. Most of these records are formal reports required by the District for all classes and programs involving schoolchildren. The best overall view of the Division's work can be found in the minutes, annual reports, and directors' correspondence. Among the most interesting and best documented topics are relations with local New Deal agencies in the 1930s, programs for servicemen and veterans in the 1940s, disputes with the School District over the role of the Museum in the late 1950s, and the creation of international programs in coordination with the federal government in the mid-1960s. A number of prominent artists and critics have delivered the annual Hetherington lecture, beginning in 1940. They are listed in Appendix IV. Information on tours and lectures can also be found in the Women's Committee Records (Record Group 4).

The records are arranged in subgroups. Each of the constituent departments of the Division is a subgroup, as are the records of the Director, the administrative assistant, and the general divisional records. Within the subgroups, records are arranged in series by type of file (minutes, memoranda) or subject, usually in some order of priority. The file organization established by the office staff has been maintained. Within the series the records are arranged in either alphabetical or chronological order.

All of the records in this Record Group are textual files. There are many published guides and brochures, but the vast majority of the material is typewritten paper records. All of the slides which have been used in education programs are in the possession of the Slide Library. The Public Relations Division has a collection of posters used to advertise education programs.

As a result of the appraisal of the Education Division records, a large volume of housekeeping and routine records from the years 1927–1982 was destroyed. These records included duplicates, multiple announcements of events, office maintenance files, staff time sheets, weekly or monthly reports if they were summarized on a quarterly basis, most personnel files and virtually all lists of attendees at various events and tour participants. Approximately 5% of the lists for each year were retained as a sample of the population using the Museum.

lished as part of the process of arrangement. Series descriptions usually start with a "title line," including the series number, title (usually the records' function plus the type of records), dates (in terms of both the full span and the bulk of the material where they differ), volume, and physical format. Such basic information should be presented in accordance with internal and national standards.

Following this title line, the description contains what is, in effect, a small scope and contents note. It should summarize the activity or function which the records document or the format of a typical record in the case of a series consisting of a uniform record type such as survey forms. Any particular strengths or weaknesses of the series should be noted. This short narrative should also mention subseries, relevant information about the physical condition of the records, the existence of copies, restrictions on use, and any closely related records. Finally, the series description should briefly explain how the records are arranged, noting any creator-generated finding aids. Using the simplest automated systems, series descriptions can easily be modified and updated as new records arrive. The 1967–1980 park planning files are an addition to an already existing series whose description will be changed to reflect the new material.

Where series are clustered into subgroups, the description of the subgroup should precede the descriptions of those series in the inventory. The subgroup description should deal with the history of the organizational unit or the common activity that brings the series together, not with the records forming the constituent series. Whether or not they are part of subgroups, series are listed in archival inventories according to the same principles of series arrangement outlined in Chapter 7; that is, in some order from the general to the specific, and from policy making to implementation. Because of changes and additions this order within the inventories will not necessarily reflect the physical arrangement or placement of the records. (See Figure 9-8.)

(5) Container Lists. Container lists are simply lists of the folders, volumes, or other file units in each box of a set of records. In archives, inventories often provide no information about the boxes and folders making up the series and subseries they describe, nor do they indicate the physical location of the records. The size and continual growth of archival record groups together with the existence of cre-

Figure 9-8   Saratoga Historical Society—Department of Manuscripts, Bailey Inventory

George Bailey, Family Papers

Subgroups and series

The Bailey Papers were arranged into subgroups by the staff of the Department of Manuscripts during the processing of the collection. The series represent the groupings of files created by Mr. and Mrs. Bailey, unless noted otherwise. The subgroups are:

    I. Business Activities, 1928–1986, 10.5 cubic feet
    II. Civic Activities, 1936–1986, 15 cubic feet
    III. Political Activities, 1940–1982, 6 cubic feet
    IV. Personal Files, 1911–1986, 4 cubic feet
    V. Mary Hatch Bailey Papers, 1915–1986, 2 cubic feet
    VI. Autograph collection, c.1789–1978, .3 cubic feet (150 items)

I. Business Activities, 1928–1986, 10.5 cubic feet
    1. Bedford Falls Savings and Loan
       1931–1970, 6 cubic feet
       Arranged alphabetically by type of record.
       Annual reports, minutes, and agendas of annual meetings of Board of Directors and stockholders, audits, financial statements, journals, ledgers, legal papers, and some correspondence relating to investments, property assessments, and taxes.
    2. First National Bank of Middletown
       1966–1982, 2.5 cubic feet
       Arranged alphabetically by type of record.
       Annual reports, minutes, and agendas of annual meetings of the Board of Directors and stockholders, financial statements, and files relating to absorption of Bedford Falls Savings and Loan.
    3. Bankers' Roundtable
       1947–1985, 1 cubic feet
       Arranged alphabetically by subject.
       Minutes, speeches, subject files on various banking and economic development issues, correspondence with legislators and others during term as chairman (1962–67).
    4. Banking "Reading File"
       1928–1986 (bulk, 1940–1974), 1 cubic foot
       Arranged alphabetically by subject.
       Material retained covers banking, financial, and economic development issues in Saratoga and Middletown, and reports and studies annotated by Bailey.

II. Civic Activities, 1936–1986, 15 cubic feet
    1. Businessmen's Club of Middletown
       1936–1980, 1 cubic foot
       Arranged alphabetically by type of record.
       Annual reports, meetings of board (1942–53), programs,...

Figure 9-9

(Container List)

George Bailey, Family Papers

II. Civic Activities

Box	Folder	File title	Dates
		Series 1. Businessmen's Club	
32	1	Constitution and Bylaws Revision	1943–55
	2–13	Annual Reports	1936–78
	14–23	Annual Meetings	1936–65
33	1–5	Annual Meetings	1965–80
	6–13	Board Meetings	1942–53
	14–16	Membership Committee	1939–42
			1957–60
	17–22	Community programs	1947–71
	22–25	Legislative File	1941–63
	26–27	Bailey Correspondence	1938–77
	28	General	1935–85
		Series 2. Chamber of Commerce	
34	1–15	Annual Reports	1940–86

Figure 9-10

Index

Note: Numbers indicate Box/Folder. They do not refer to pages of the inventory.

Accounts (Financial)	8/11–12, 98/1–5
Adams, John	112/2
Adams, John Quincy	112/3
American Association of Bankers	25/20, 28/6–7
Art Museum *see* Middletown Museum of Art	
Arts Council of Middletown	108/9–14
Associated Services of Middletown	60/3–6
Audits—Bedford Falls Savings and Loan	2/1–8
Averington, Clifford	23/8–15, 26/1, 84/11, 86/16–18, 101/24–17
see also First National Bank of Middletown	
Averington, Celeste (Mrs. Clifford)	109/3
Awake and Sing Club	108/16

ator-generated finding aids mean that box and folder lists are maintained as location aids separate from inventories in most public archives and many large institutional archives. Sometimes these aids take the form of very simple lists of boxes noting the range of folders in them and their physical locations. The most important point is to ensure that, whatever the level of detail of the container list, archivists' internal files link the list with the series described in the inventories.

Most manuscript inventories, in contrast to archival inventories, do include box and folder lists, even for their large collections. These container lists usually follow all the other information in the inventory. Listings of box and folder contents allow manuscript inventories to serve as location aids as well as descriptive tools. For purposes of security and to allow for internal reorganizations, it is best not to record locations on the inventories available to researchers. Location information should be noted only on staff copies or in the protected sections of automated descriptive systems.

The container list includes each file unit in its series context, even if it is stored separately for physical reasons. For each file unit, the list should indicate a unique number, a title, dates, and a container number. Repetitious file headings, such as "Monthly minutes", are often summarized using a range of dates and folders, though this may not be advisable in some automated systems. For very important series, container lists can include item or document listings. A set of folders in the museum Education Division records containing transcripts of lectures by eminent artists could be described in some detail by giving the name of the lecturer and the title and date of the lecture, even if there were several lectures in a folder. Separation sheets can be placed at the end of the container list to describe accessioned materials not listed elsewhere in the inventory, such as the Southside Settlement lantern slides. (See Figure 9-9.)

(6) Indexes. Inventories of more than a few pages should contain their own index. Index terms should be derived from all parts of the inventory, from the history/biography through the container lists. Information provided by these components of the inventory is necessary but not entirely sufficient for effective access. The archivist will therefore have to add terms describing the content and form of the whole collection and its subdivisions. Since the inventory indexes can be used to create a repository-wide index, these terms should be standardized and consistent. Such a repository-wide index would allow

a researcher at the historical society interested in, for example, the 1956 Republican convention to find an entry in that index for the George Bailey inventory under "Republican Party—1956 National Convention." The researcher could then locate in the Bailey inventory's index the pages in the inventory containing the appropriate references. Finally, the researcher could request the specific files described in the inventory. (See Figure 9-10.)

(7) Appendices. Inventories often have appendices providing supplementary information about records creators and/or records. Public and institutional archivists commonly provide organizational charts from different periods and lists of key officials. Creator-generated classification systems can be outlined in appendices. They may also include specialized glossaries and legal citations and statutes. In manuscript inventories, appendices can be used to list major correspondents or documents of special value, such as the Bailey autographs.

The inventory format outlined above has proven to be a widely applicable and straightforward method for describing archives according to the basic principles of arrangement. Automation has allowed archivists to both update and index inventories quickly and efficiently through the application of word-processing or data base software. The inventory format is flexible enough to describe small collections requiring just a few lines for each of the sections discussed above, or large collections of personal papers and records from old organizations and closed agencies. However, the truly massive and complex records of modern organizational life are not so amenable to description through standard inventories. An alternative system of manipulating the basic descriptive elements, discussed below, can better meet the demands of such records.

D. Series-records creator linking systems. Despite acquiring increased flexibility through automation, inventories as traditionally prepared present a number of problems. They are essentially fixed lists of series in which each series is identified with one immediate record creator, whether that is a subgroup, or a record group or collection. The more this structure diverges from real organizational life, in which change is the norm, the less useful is the inventory. By their nature, inventories are not well adapted to representing growing and evolving collections. Their usability is also reduced by the size of modern record groups. Researchers are usually interested in only a few specific series, but are confronted with long inventories containing literally hundreds of series entries. Such extensive documents with large sections of narrative are difficult to integrate into modern information systems based on automation and indexed summary descriptions.

A sensible solution to these problems is to maintain series descriptions separately from descriptions of record creating entities and then to link the two systems as appropriate.[5] For administrative purposes each series may be identified with the most important or most recent creator. However, that will not be the crucial aspect of these richer and fuller descriptions of the interrelationships of records and their creators. The series-records creator system is especially applicable to public and institutional archives and large manuscript collections. It represents modern organizational environments and records sytems better than traditional inventories. It also emphasizes the crucial distinction between records and records creators which is blurred in inventories. (See Figure 9-11.)

In this type of system the park planning files will be described as part of the complete listing of all the records series in the State Archives. For administrative purposes the files can be identified with the DNR, but they will be linked as well with information about the old Department of Conservation. At the museum, the problem of the pre-1965 Public Relations Department files in the Education Division would be handled by linking them with data about the post-1965 Public Relations Division.

The system represents a disassembling of the traditional inventory in order to create a more flexible description. The same descriptive elements are gathered and recorded as in the inventory system. However, they are organized somewhat differently, and there is a particular emphasis on links among records and between records and record creators. The links can take the form of index terms, pointers analogous to the "see" and "see also" references familiar in library catalogs, and sections of automated descriptive systems dedicated to describing interrelationships. The broadest description of actual records is of individual series, not subgroups, record groups, or collections. The emphasis on individual series descriptions also facilitates integration of archival information with other information systems and with records management systems, because series are in many ways the most coherent units of archival information. Their relationship to records creators is somewhat like the relationship of different books created by one author to that author. Further encouraging integration with other information, the descriptions of records creators function as

standardized authority file information, somewhat like information about authors.

The four basic components of the system are series descriptions, record creator/agency descriptions, linking information and aggregate finding aids.

(1) Series Descriptions. Records in this system are organized primarily according to the name of the individual series. This should be a carefully conceived combination of function/activity and record type, such as "Day Nursery Attendance Registers" in the Southside collection. In addition to all the information about a series provided in inventories, the freestanding series descriptions in this approach must also record the name of one primary creator with which the series is identified—a relevant subgroup, record group, or manuscript collection. Series descriptions should stress the role and function of the records over time. The description should include indexing terms designed to provide access by subject, place, personal names, form, and function. A box/folder list should form part of the series description, or there should be an indication of where and how such a list can be located. It should be noted that this format can also be used to describe subseries, as long as the system links them to their parent series. As a general rule, in a series-creator linking system all types and sets of records are treated equally, and peer relationships replace hierarchies. (See Figure 9-12.)

(2) Record Creator/Agency Histories. A description should be prepared for every record creating body with which any series will be associated. As with series, the information will be essentially the same as in the agency history/biography of the inventory, though it can be somewhat more detailed. This description should also include index terms. It is important to stress that it will contain no information about any records. As Max Evans wrote, "an agency entry in the authority control file can be established and maintained independently of any knowledge of the record material produced by the agency."[6] (See Figure 9-13.)

(3) Linking Information. Series descriptions should indicate relationships between the series described and other series, and the relationship of the series to one or more records creators. This information will include not only the titles and/or control numbers for related records, but also the nature of the relationships. Similarly, each entry for a record creator/agency history will describe its history and organizational relationships—its links—with other agencies and series associated with it. Just as all

---

[5] The basic explication of this system is in Max Evans, "Authority Control," 249–261.

[6] Ibid., 256.

Figure 9-11   Series-Records Creator Schematic

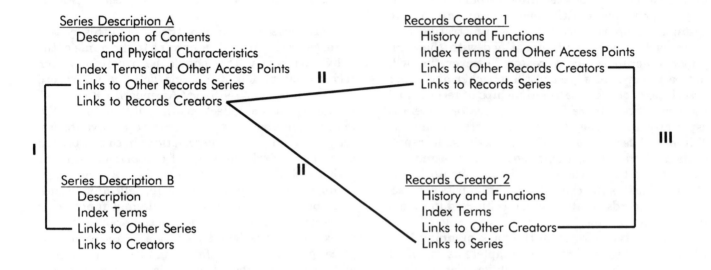

Series Description A
    Description of Contents
        and Physical Characteristics
    Index Terms and Other Access Points
    Links to Other Records Series
    Links to Records Creators

Records Creator 1
    History and Functions
    Index Terms and Other Access Points
    Links to Other Records Creators
    Links to Records Series

Series Description B
    Description
    Index Terms
    Links to Other Series
    Links to Creators

Records Creator 2
    History and Functions
    Index Terms
    Links to Other Creators
    Links to Series

I = Links among series
II = Links among series and records creators
III = Links among records creators

Park Planning as an example of the system

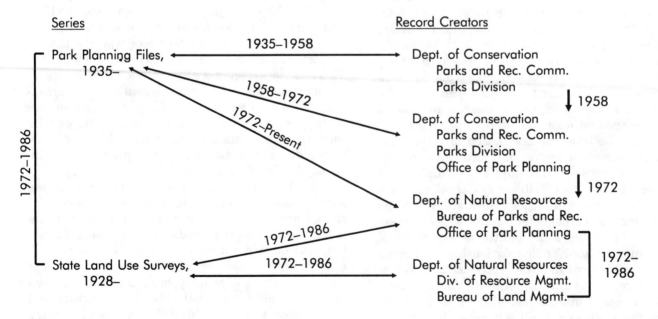

Series

Park Planning Files,
    1935–

State Land Use Surveys,
    1928–

Record Creators

1935–1958

1958–1972

1972–Present

1972–1986

1972–1986

Dept. of Conservation
    Parks and Rec. Comm.
    Parks Division

Dept. of Conservation
    Parks and Rec. Comm.
    Parks Division
    Office of Park Planning

Dept. of Natural Resources
    Bureau of Parks and Rec.
    Office of Park Planning

Dept. of Natural Resources
    Div. of Resource Mgmt.
    Bureau of Land Mgmt.

1958

1972

1972–1986

1972–1986

Figure 9-12   Saratoga State Archives, Series Description

Series # 137
Title Park planning files
Creating Department/Division Natural Resources/Outdoor Recreation, Parks & Recreation. Office of Park Planning
   Subunits
Dates 1935–1983
Bulk dates 1938–1980
Volume   *Textual files* 68 cubic feet
                             Graphic records 2 cubic feet of photographic prints and 10 trays of slides
                             Machine-readable 4 computer tapes
                             Other c. 625 maps
                                      38 reel-to-reel and 104 cassette audio tapes

Contents Records document state and county park planning, from initial proposals and surveys through final approval and creation of parks. Records also document some land use planning and general survey functions and work with other executive agencies, the state legislature, and the general public.

Subseries Departmental/divisional files; state parks; county parks; natural resource planning; maps.

Arrangement By subseries, and alphabetically or chronologically within subseries

Finding Aids Inventory to Department of Conservation (RG 33) records
              Box/folder list in Archives

Related Series Office of Park Planning. Administrative Records (#135), Legislative Files (#136), Research Files (#138), and Land Acquisition Files (#139); Parks Commission. Commissioner's Records (#87) and General Files (#89) Department of Conservation. Director's Files (#102); Department of Natural Resources. Bureau of Parks and Recreation. Director's files (#118), Parks Division Blueprints and Sketches (#127), Construction Files (#128), Park Maintenance Files (#129); Bureau of Land Management. Planning Records (#130); Bureau of Forests and Wetlands. Planning and Survey Records (#146); Department of Transportation. Office of Transportation Planning. Highway Planning Records (#218); Governor. Office of Capital Budget. Capital Budget Meetings (#31) and Plans (#32).

Related Agencies Department of Conservation. Parks Commission; Department of Transportation; DNR Bureau of Parks and Recreation. Parks Division; DNR Office of Forests and Wetlands; DNR Office of Land Management

Authorization for Transfer Records Schedule 12-345

Source of Records Administrative Secretary, Parks & Rec. Div.

Access Unrestricted

Date of last addition 081789

Locations
           Acc# 80-323   Archives 5/8/15/2–7
                                     5/8/16/1–8
                 84–009   6/11/22
                                     6/11/23/1–3
                 89–767   6/33/14/2–8
                                     6/33/15/1–5
                 89–768   6/35/7/1–8
           For photographs, audio, and computer tapes see listings under Office of Park Planning in relevant catalogs.

Figure 9-12 Saratoga State Archives—Continued

Index terms:

        Subject: County parks—planning
                 Land use—planning
                 Land use surveys
                 Parks—planning
                 State Parks—planning

        Place: Assiniboin National Park
                (Individual names of the 14 state parks)
                Middletown—Parks—Riverside Park
                Saratoga City—Parks—Buckram County Park

        Form/Genre: Planning files
                    Maps
                    Land surveys
                    See also Audio tapes
                             Computer tapes
                             Photographs
                             Slides

        Function: Planning
                  Land surveying

        Personal names: (Names of 13 of the 15 planners since 1935)
                        (Names of 5 state legislators and 2 governor's aides especially involved in park planning)

Prepared by: J. Muir   Date: 021990

types and levels of records are allowed in the system, so all types of links and relationships can be represented equally.

Access to one series or record creator thus opens up pathways that can be followed into a whole network of relationships of records and record creators. A researcher looking for information on Saratoga county roads in the late 1960s might find his or her way from a series in the Transportation Department files to that agency's history entry. The researcher might see there a reference to the DNR's activities and through the DNR history entry find the park planning files. Facilitating the description of such relationships is at the core of the linking system. In fact, the links and information about the nature of various relationships form a body of data with its own structure and characteristics that is distinct from the information about specific records and record creators.

(4) Aggregate Finding Aids. Series descriptions, agency histories and biographies, and linking information can be brought together to generate a variety of descriptive tools. Assembling all the series linked with a specific agency under the descriptions of immediate records creators (subgroups) and the agency as a whole will produce a basic inventory-type series list. Adding some introductory information, an ordering of series descriptions, appendices and an index would essentially provide a standard inventory. Of course in this system both series and subgroups can easily appear in one or more inventories.

The special strength of the system, however, is that such inventories are only one potential product. With separate series descriptions, archivists can generate series lists under any indexing term or combination of terms, rather than handing researchers a number of different inventories in response to queries. They can better answer subject requests. For example, they could locate all series at the state archives relating to parks in the 1970s regardless of record creator. Archival administrators can obtain series-level information on such variables as size, location, and format, as well as subject and agency

Figure 9-13 Saratoga State Archives, Record Creator Entry

Department   Natural Resources
Division   Outdoor Recreation
Subdivision   Bureau of Parks and Recreation
Subdivision   Office of Park Planning
Subdivision   n/a
Date unit established   1958
Date of current structure   1980
Authority   Code of Saratoga 1982 (Chapter 56), Natural Resources Act of 1972 (See Saratoga Government Manual, 1990)

Administrative History

The Department of Conservation (est. 1927) first retained a permanent park planner in 1935 within the Division of Parks and Recreation. In 1958 a separate Office of Park Planning was created. The position of Park Planner became a civil service position in 1964. The Office is responsible for planning and coordinating the development of state parks and for coordinating the state's role in the development of county and local parks. Specific responsibilities include overall statewide planning, physical planning of state parks, budgeting, public presentations, the acquisition of land, and coordination with other state agencies and the legislature. From 1972 to 1986 the office was also responsible for state land use surveys, and planning for wetland, wildlife preservation, and soil conservation districts.

Organization Since 1980 the Office of Park Planning has been a separate unit of the Bureau of Parks and Recreation. The park planner is a member of the Interdepartmental Planning Group within the Department of Natural Resources. The office also has formal responsibilities for coordination with the Bureaus of Forests and Wetlands and Land Management within the department's Division of Resource Management.

Predecessor Units Parks Commission (1911–1927); Department of Conservation. Parks Commission (1927–1938) and Division of Parks and Recreation (1938–1958)

Successor Units n/a

Related Units
        Department of Natural Resources. Bureau of Parks & Recreation
           "   "   "   "   Parks Division
           "   "   "   Bureau of Forests & Wetlands
           "   "   "   Bureau of Land Management
        Department of Transportation. Office of Transportation Planning
        Governor. Capital Budget Office

Series Created Directly (Numbers)
        135–139

Related Series (Numbers)
        31, 33, 127–134, 140–142, 145–149, 216–218, 308

Location   DNR Building, Room 506
               527 Averington Street
               Middletown, SA

Index terms
                Subject: County parks—planning
                         Land use—planning
                         Parks—planning
                         State parks—planning

                Place: Assiniboin National Park
                       (Individual names of the 14 State Parks)

        Personal Names:
                       (Names of all 15 Park planners since 1935)
                       (Names of 5 other key staff people)

coverage. On the repository level, the system creates a complete data base which can either substitute for or be used to produce a continually current guide. Instead of guides being derived from inventories, both inventories and guides are differing products of the combined data base of series descriptions and record creator authority files. At the same time, the data base can serve a variety of administrative needs, providing overviews of series according to such factors as location, size, date of arrival in the repository, processing and preservation status, and restrictions on access.

A series-records creator linking system is not necessarily an automated system or a system appropriate only for use with large collections. Separate descriptions of records and creators can be maintained in a manual system and can be linked through the simple means of photocopying. In the case of small and simple collections, the descriptions of both the materials and their source can be similarly brief. However, the value of series-creator linking is undoubtedly maximized by automation. The value of this type of descriptive system increases with the capacity of a computer system to allow researchers to explore the many possible pathways and relationships. As sophisticated computer data base software increasingly emphasizes such links and networks rather than simple sequences of data, the description of archives through linking systems represents an effective response to changes in both automation and archives.

E. Integrative tools: indexes and catalogs. Whether a repository relies primarily on inventories or a series-creator linking system to describe its various sets of records, it will still need some integrated tool to describe all of its holdings. This is the function of the comprehensive index, whose most common forms are the card catalog and the automated data base. More important than the specific format is the provision of access to all sets of records sharing the common characteristic identified by a name, place, subject, or other index term. The records can be identified in the index by any number, records creator name or record title that will lead users to the finding aid describing them. Only through such an index will most users be able to find that there are Chamber of Commerce records in the Bailey papers. Without it, they might never discover data about juvenile delinquency in the 1960s in the Youth Division sub-subgroup of the Southside Community Center subgroup of the Southside Community Services records.

Terms for the repository-wide index are drawn in the first instance from the finding aids. These relatively objective terms are supplemented by the more interpretive subject terms. All the terms then lead the users back to indexed inventories or descriptions of series and records creators. Primarily because of limits on staff time and the size of catalogs, nonautomated systems will generally index only the most important names, topics and record characteristics as determined by the archivists. Automated indexing can allow the comprehensive representation of all terms mentioned in the finding aids. Because archival inventories generally do not include box/folder lists, specific terms for archival repository indexes will have to be derived from other sources that do contain such information, such as accession lists. All of these terms will be supplemented by terms that do not appear in any finding aid but are vital to understanding the records, such as "social services" for the Southside records. Whether using inventories or separate series and records creator descriptions, the repository index should include terms derived from descriptions of creators as well as records, rather than being confined to records indexing alone.

There are instances where detailed indexing of specific file units may be appropriate. The most useful intellectual access to such essential records as minutes, annual reports, executive correspondence, and internal publications is through some analysis of their contents. Indexing by the words in the folder title "Minutes, January–March 1970" provides little information. Where there is any indexing of the contents of documents not listed individually in the existing finding aids, such as indexing of the most important matters mentioned in such minutes, the archivist should ensure that either the repository index or the finding aid allows the researcher to locate the specific document. The preferable approach would be to utilize the index to individual inventories to point to the location within folders of specific documents.

In addition to selecting index terms, archivists also have to adopt indexing rules and an appropriate format. In the past, manuscript repositories prepared a master card for each collection or document filed under the name of its creator. These cards closely resembled catalog cards for books and were based on rules developed for book cataloging, including the identification of the records creator as the "main entry." The master card usually identified the equivalent of the descriptive information normally provided for books—creator, title (including dates), and volume. They often also added short summaries of the material. The collection cards could be duplicated and filed under the index terms which were typed in as "added entries."

The manuscript card catalog system with its carefully formatted information about provenance, title, dates, content and location, was often criticized for ignoring archival principles. It led researchers directly to specific records, ignoring contextual information, and tried to condense unduly information about collections. But its compatibility with library systems made it in some ways the basis for the various systems of archival information exchange, from *NUCMC* in the 1950s to USMARC AMC in the 1980s.

For purposes of internal repository-wide indexing, however, the preparation of elaborate descriptive catalog cards or their equivalent is unnecessary. The key requirements are simply the use of standard terms and a way to get from those terms to the finding aids where the elaborate description is properly located. As we shall see in Chapter 10, such terms can be derived from different types of standard references and also be established locally. The use of standardized terms should be supplemented by the use of the type of "see" and "see also" references familiar in library catalogs—these hold the index together and guide users from variant to standard terms. The format and rules for constructing and ordering the index should be consistent and as simple as possible. Archivists should consult specialized works on the creation and maintenance of indexes before establishing one.[7] Whatever rules are adopted, they should be available to, and comprehensible by, researchers.

2. External Description.

A. Guides. The descriptive tools reviewed above are all designed primarily for use inside the repository. Archivists have always supplemented these internal tools with other descriptive media designed for external audiences. Published guides consisting of short descriptions of collections and record groups are external counterparts to the internal integrative indexes. Like those indexes, comprehensive guides are designed to bring together all the holdings of a repository. Such guides were traditionally regarded as the culmination of a repository's descriptive program; as the way it presented itself to the world. Before cooperative automated systems, published guides were indeed the only way to disseminate comprehensive information about holdings. They were especially important for manuscript collections. While the basic holdings of a public or insti-

tutional archives would be evident from the institution's name, the holdings of a historical society or library could not be so easily determined. Guides still provide an important method of access to the holdings of many repositories, although of course the information is only current to the date the guide was completed.

Guides are essentially abstracts of inventories with an index keyed to those abstracts. For each record group or collection, a guide entry should at minimum include information about history/biography, time span, volume, contents, physical formats, and arrangement by major subgroups and series. (See Figure 9-14.) A guide should include all holdings in all formats. Manuscript repositories sometimes cluster many small collections under some general rubric like "Eighteenth Century Diaries" for summary listing. At the same time, the preparation of short abstracts of extensive inventories requires skill in concise summarization of vital information. Within the guide, entries can be arranged by any arbitrary numbering system used in the repository, since access will usually be through the index. Some guides are arranged by subject or type of record, but this is simply a matter of convenience. The guide should include introductory information about the repository and about the guide's own preparation and use.

In addition to comprehensive guides, repositories sometimes publish guides to records on specific themes, like the Civil War, or in certain formats, like photographs. Specialized guides are often responses to emerging research interests not easily satisfied by traditional provenance-oriented tools. Nevertheless, such guides should be prepared only if resources can be spared, and only by an archivist familiar with both the records and their uses. The selection of material for inclusion in a guide relating to a given subject is really a historical research project of great complexity. The records included in such guides are not limited to the record group/collection level but often extend to series, folders, and even items. Again, unlike general guides, they are often arranged topically, and contain an interpretive introductory essay.

Guides of all kinds present serious conceptual and practical difficulties. Most repositories never publish comprehensive guides. The conceptual problems are those of traditional inventories writ large, since guides are firmly based on the identification of each records set with one records creator, and represent modern organizational records only with difficulty. Usually taking years or even decades to

Figure 9-14   Saratoga State University, Regional History Center, Guide to the Collections

.
.
.
.

32. Southside Community Services, Inc.
    Records, 1874–1983 (bulk, 1878–1980)
    61 cubic feet

The origins of the present agency date to the founding in 1878 of the Union Mission at 234 South Kendall Street. The mission provided fuel, food, clothing and shelter to the immigrant and black communities of South Middletown. It was affiliated with the Episcopal Church. In 1900, after a steady expansion of its neighborhood services, the mission became the Southside Settlement House and its formal church affiliation ended. As a result of a reorganization of local social services in 1948, the settlement took over the nearby Tenth Street House (established 1903) and St. John's House (established 1915). Both were run as branches until closed in the 1970s. In 1963 the settlement merged with the Southside Day Nursery and Children's Center. The Day Nursery had been founded in 1886 and had taken a new name when it expanded its services in 1916. The consolidated agency, located in a new building at 814 S. Main Street, was called the Southside Community Center. From the mid–1960s, the center became increasingly responsible for encouraging and administering local community development and urban renewal programs. To reflect these changes, the center was renamed Southside Community Services, Inc., in 1975.

Records include the board minutes, matron's reports and general correspondence of the Union Mission (1878–1900) and minutes and other records of the Tenth Street and St. John's Houses. Policy, administrative and program records of the Southside Settlement, Community Center and Community Services (1900–1980) total 41 cubic feet and provide comprehensive documentation of the agency's history. Reports, minutes, and some program files document the work of the Day Nursery and Children's Center. The collection includes photographs, scrapbooks, clippings and pamphlets.

   Post–1920 case files and employee records can be researched only with the permission of the agency.
   Arranged by organizational unit and then by file series.
   Inventory with container list in the Library (Collection M725)
   Microfilmed materials: Union Mission records; Board minutes and matron's reports of the Southside Settlement, Tenth Street House and St. John's House.
   Records deposited by the agency in 1989.
   See also records of the Whomsoever Mission (Guide entry 55).

produce, they are out of date even before they are published because of both organizational change and repository growth. Guides also have to be publicized so that potential users are aware of their existence. While users find guides helpful, they do not seem to lead to an increased volume of use. The scholars to whom they are typically directed are generally more interested in collections on a given topic from a variety of repositories. This is the type of information provided by cooperative bibliographic networks rather than single-institution guides.

Under these cirumstances, few archival situations will demand the publication of a traditional comprehensive guide. Instead, repositories can use relatively simple automated systems to produce both comprehensive and specialized overviews of holdings on a regular basis. Such overviews can describe ap-

propriate selected descriptive elements from each set of records. For example, to produce something analogous to a traditional guide, those descriptive elements can include all of the agency histories or biographies and the associated scope and contents notes. Rather than general guides, repositories might produce guides for particular subjects, time periods, or locations. The comprehensive guide may survive for reasons of tradition and public relations. However, in the age of automated archival data bases, such a guide will more often be a by-product of the descriptive system than its culmination.

B. Specialized descriptive tools. Repositories sometimes find it useful to prepare specialized tools to highlight or control certain records. Lists of commonly requested records focused on a topic, a type of record, or a type of research, such as genealogy,

Figure 9-15   Saratoga Historical Society, The Bailey Autograph Collection, Item Listing

1. Adams, John (1735–1826). D.S., 1 p., Braintree, MA, April 8, 1811. To William Hawthorne, carpenter. Note concerning bill for repairs, drafted in unknown hand.

2. Adams, John Quincy (1768–1848). A.L.S., 2 pp., Washington, DC, December 10, 1837. To Isaac Lovett, a constituent from Massachusetts. Letter concerning tariff legislation and post offices.

3. Allen, Julia (Mrs. Henry), (ca. 1780–1818). A.L.S., 3 pp., "Near New Worcester," SA, July 11, 1816. To Rebecca Willings, her sister. Describes arrival in area and condition of the new town.

4. Arthur, Chester Alan (1829–1886). D.S., 1 p., New York, NY, Nov 22, 1878. To Julius Davis, dry goods merchant. Receipt for goods provided to office of Port of New York.

5. Babbitt, George (1886–1967). T.D.S., 6 pp., Middletown, SA, July 4, 1927. Speech delivered at July 4 Chamber of Commerce observances.

6. Bransom, William Henry (1767–1834). A.L.S., 4 pp., New Worcester, SA, February 2, 1821. To Congressman Richard Smith. Discusses Bransom's plans for his inauguration as governor and some personnel decisions.

7. Bransom, William Henry (1767–1834). A.L.S., 3 pp., Middletown, SA, May 9, 1830. To David Harriman, lawyer. Discusses transfer of capital to Middletown.

8. Buchanan, James (1791–1868). A.L.S., 2 pp., Wheatland, PA, November 5, 1866. To Samuel Jones, neighbor and longtime friend. Reports on health and discusses local farm conditions.

9. Carter, James Earl (1924–   ). T.L.S., 1 p., Atlanta, GA, November 19, 1975. To George Bailey. Thank you for expressing interest in campaign.

10.   Cartwright, Captain James "Buckskin" (ca. 1765–1811). L.S., [n.p.], [April 1789?]. To William Livingston, Pittsburgh merchant. Request for supplies for exploration, drafted in unknown hand.

.
.
.

Note: A.D.S. = Autograph document signed
         A.L.S. = Authograph letter signed
         D.S.   = Document signed
         T.D.S. = Typed document signed
         T.L.S. = Typed letter signed

are useful in expediting reference work. Such lists differ from thematic guides in that they are not published and are often focused more on individual documents. A related type of aid to research is a file of records retrieved to answer different requests. Having once identified all the records on child care in Middletown's immigrant communities around 1900, the university library staff should not have to repeat the exercise, at least for the records in the repository at the time of the initial search.

The most common type of special list is a list of individual documents with research and/or monetary value. These lists are often prepared as part of an exhibit of the items. Documents to be listed must be assigned a unique number, which can simply be an addition to an existing sequence such as Collection/Box/Folder and then the document number. A summary listing will include the date and place of the document's creation, the donor or other provenance, and the creator, recipient and type of document. (See Figure 9-15.) The most elaborate form of item listing is calendaring, which includes a narrative summary of each item and a description of its physical condition. As illustrated in Chapter 3, calendars usually describe a unified set of documents arranged chronologically. For security purposes and most uses, a summary listing will suffice for all but the rarest and most valuable records. Such summary lists can be incorporated into the repository-wide index as indexed appendices of the relevant inventories. Except in the case of an individual document not part of any larger record set, repositories should avoid cataloging items directly into the repository-wide catalog.

C. Summary collective descriptions. Since guides are so expensive and time consuming to produce, archivists have developed other means of publicizing their holdings after final processing. Short summaries of records should be sent routinely to internal publications, scholarly publications, and even local news media. Descriptions sent to journals should follow their standards and should include basic information about the time span, volume, contents, and restrictions on use of the records.

On the national level, manuscript repositories should report their holdings to the *National Union Catalog of Manuscript Collections (NUCMC)* based at the Library of Congress. *NUCMC* has been published since 1959 and its volumes list over fifty thousand manuscript collections held by well over a thousand repositories. The regularly-issued volumes of *NUCMC* are indexed according to standardized name and subject terms. *NUCMC* has its own forms that repositories should use in reporting collections, and *NUCMC* staff use the forms to prepare summary collection entries and appropriate index terms. Information about reporting to *NUCMC* can be obtained from the *NUCMC* office at the Library of Congress.[8] As its name implies, public and institutional archives are not included in this catalog of manuscript collections.

Another method of publicizing holdings, and one that does include archives, is the *National Inventory of Documentary Sources in the United States (NIDS)*. Published by Chadwyck-Healey, *NIDS* is essentially a compilation on microfiche of inventories submitted by hundreds of repositories.[9] As in *NUCMC*, there are master subject and name indexes.

However, *NIDS* provides far more detail about the actual contents of collections, since it includes the full inventories, including folder-level descriptions, in contrast to the catalog card-like listings found in *NUCMC*. *NIDS* regularly updates information about the holdings of libraries, historical societies, state archives, and academic repositories.

Since the development in 1983 of a USMARC format for archives and manuscripts compatible with other library-based USMARC formats, the most important vehicles for external information sharing in the archival community have become the Research Libraries Information Network (RLIN) of the Research Libraries Group, headquartered in Mountain View, California, and the OCLC On-Line Computer Library Center, headquartered in Dublin, Ohio. Most academic, public, and research libraries participate in these networks in some way, as do a large number of historical societies and public archives. The RLIN archives data base also includes information from *NUCMC*. In terms of the descriptive tools discussed in this chapter, archivists whose repositories are involved in these networks prepare summaries of their holdings according to the USMARC AMC format. These summary descriptions are entered into the automated descriptive data bases. The summaries can be at any level of description from collection, record group, and subgroup to series, subseries or even document. However, as in *NUCMC*, the emphasis is on collection-level descriptions.

As the next chapter explains, these summary descriptions not only follow the USMARC standardized format, but they are also prepared according to standardized rules and indexed for the national systems under a variety of standardized terms. Such standardization for the purpose of sharing information demands a certain amount of discipline and consistency in following rules. Archivists had previously minimized these characteristics of the library and computer worlds, but they now have a vital place in descriptive practice.

---

[8] The address is *NUCMC*, Library of Congress, Washington, DC 20540.

[9] Information about *NIDS* is available from Chadwyck-Healy Ltd., 1101 King Street, Alexandria, VA 22314.

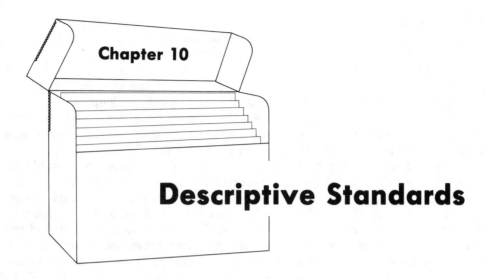

Chapter 10

Descriptive Standards

Repositories standardize information about their holdings for both internal and external reasons. Internally, standardization allows archival information to become part of integrated systems describing all types of institutional holdings. Externally, standardization allows the inclusion of archival descriptions in automated multi-institutional information networks. In both internal and external settings, the goal of standardization is to produce unique descriptions for each set of records according to rules and procedures that are explicit, consistent, and comprehensive.

Formal standardization came to the archival world mainly because in library-based bibliographic networks "participation requires conformity to certain standards, through the networks' incorporation of certain enforcement mechanisms that encourage standardization."[1] But standardization is not an isolated part of the descriptive process applicable only in supplying information to networks. The need to produce standardized descriptions at the end of processing has a reverse ripple effect, affecting all aspects of archival work. Thus the demands of standardization have clarified and rationalized descriptive practice from accessioning through the reporting of information to national networks.

Standardized practice in both cooperative network data bases and internal information systems is usually based on bibliographic systems originally designed for traditional library books and periodi-

cals. Such systems require that archival information be presented in a form compatible with the description of those materials. At the same time, archivists have to preserve the unique aspects of archival description which their materials require. It is important to remember that what is being standardized is information about record groups, series, inventories, and all the other aspects of archival processing reviewed in the preceding chapters; that in the end effective information exchange depends more on effective processing than on advanced technical capabilities.

Several different types of standards are used in archival information exchange. In general, such standards are "shared practices that are set up and established by authority, custom or general use with more or less formal endorsement."[2] As this definition indicates, standards can include guidelines outlining general principles, such as provenance and original order, rules such as those governing the selection of record titles, and more exacting technical standards such as those applying to USMARC cataloging. Rules and standards in all professions are typically created and adopted through careful deliberation by professional associations. Elaborate systems of national and international organizations and procedures exist to publicize and enforce standards. For archivists, the most immediately relevant standards are those adopted by the National Information Standards Organization (formerly Committee Z39),

[1] H. Thomas Hickerson, "Archival Information Exchange and the Role of Bibliographic Networks," *Library Trends* 36 (Winter 1988): 566.

[2] Henriette D. Avram, Sally H. McCallum, and Mary S. Price, "Organizations Contributing to the Development of Library Standards," *Library Trends* 31 (Fall 1982): 197–198.

which is in turn accredited by the American National Standards Institute (ANSI). The USMARC format is in accordance with standards formally adopted by both national and international information standards organizations.[3]

Because archival processing can precede and be independent of information exchange, archives and manuscript repositories can often make their own decisions about the extent of their participation in internal and external systems. This is a sharp contrast to contemporary libraries, in which participation is in effect mandatory because it is the cooperative system which provides for most of the processing—the cataloging and classification of books and journals. Libraries have a strong economic incentive to use standardized processing because few of their holdings are unique. They can thus utilize a common data base for both cataloging and interlibrary loan. There are few such practical incentives for archivists. While standardized information exchange systems are at the core of library processing, archivists joined and adapted to them to solve certain problems and meet certain needs specific to their profession.

Until as late as the mid-1980s, archival description was remarkably isolated from the rest of the national information system. There were useful multi-institutional published tools such as *NUCMC* and the *Directory of Archives and Manuscript Repositories* first published by the National Historical Publications and Records Commission in 1976 and updated in 1988. However, there was no systematic representation of archival information in either a library network or a national archival data base. In fact many archives and manuscript collections were not even represented in the new automated data bases of the libraries of which they were a part. Much archival "information exchange" was through informal professional contacts and the "invisible college" of scholars. There were neither firm rules or standards for any aspect of archival processing, nor a mechanism to enforce them.

In contrast, after 1968 the library community possessed a standard format for sharing computerized information about books—the MARC (Machine Readable Cataloging) format. The American version is now called USMARC. The MARC format built upon a century-long accumulation of shared cataloging centered around the Library of Congress and conducted according to standardized rules, subject classifications, and other authority files. National library networks—also called bibliographic utilities—were established to share MARC records produced by the Library of Congress. Through the 1970s, MARC formats were developed for such materials as periodicals, films, musical scores, and maps, in addition to books.

Attempts to develop comparable formats and descriptive rules that would be acceptable to the archival community foundered until the early 1980s. Finally, the work of the SAA's National Information Systems Task Force and the desire of the members of the Research Libraries Group (RLG) to integrate archival materials into its MARC-based Research Libraries Information Network (RLIN) system spurred the successful creation of a national system for archival information exchange. Several RLG libraries began using the MARC format for Archival and Manuscripts Control (now USMARC AMC) in 1984. In 1983, as the format was being adopted, the Library of Congress issued the *Archives, Personal Papers and Manuscripts* cataloging manual (*APPM*), explaining to archivists how to adapt the standard library cataloging rules so that archival description would be compatible with library systems.

The use of the new USMARC AMC format spread rapidly, especially through RLIN, which included data from many major historical societies, specialized centers, and state archives. The other national bibliographic utility, OCLC, also adopted the USMARC AMC format. *NUCMC* records began to be described in the USMARC AMC format in 1988. As archivists began adding descriptions to the national bibliographic networks, they also increasingly followed standard cataloging rules and employed accepted thesauri and authority files. The 1980s thus witnessed the rapid development of a system of standardized archival information exchange and integration barely conceivable at the start of the decade. Tens of thousands of collections, record groups and series were represented in automated bibliographic networks along with books, periodicals and other types of information resources.

Each repository must weigh the benefits and costs of standardization and network participation. The most obvious benefits accrue to researchers, who will be able to find archives and manuscripts within internal and multi-institutional library data bases. The major benefits to a repository may be the same increased integration with the larger information community as well as increased numbers of users.

---

[3] The international body is called the International Organization for Standardization (IOS). *Library Trends* 31 (Fall 1982) is devoted to standards and the standard-making process. See also Walt Crawford, *Technical Standards: An Introduction for Librarians* (White Plains NY: Knowledge Industry Publications, 1986).

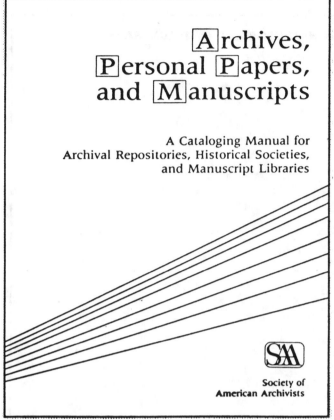

Archives, Personal Papers, and Manuscripts

A Cataloging Manual for
Archival Repositories, Historical Societies,
and Manuscript Libraries

SAA

Society of
American Archivists

Archives, Personal Papers, and Manuscripts: A Cataloging Manual for Archival Repositories, Historical Societies, and Manuscript Libraries is a useful tool for an increasing number of archivists. (Courtesy of the Society of American Archivists.)

More tangible benefits can include the sharing of authority file information about names, functions, and subjects, although the inherent uniqueness of archival materials means that such benefits will never approach the scale of library savings from automation. Archivists can also use the USMARC AMC format for better administrative control over their holdings. It was specifically designed to allow them to describe all of the actions they take with respect to a set of records over time as well as the conditions governing access to them. Such information can be held for purely internal use, so that neither users nor other repositories can see it.

The new procedures also bring challenges and difficulties. Library-dominated bibliographic networks organize information about holdings in ways not easily reconcilable with archival practice. The identification of a single author-like "main entry" and the use of nationally standardized subject headings are often inappropriate or insufficient for archival records. Bibliographic systems are not designed

for the complex and changing provenance information and elaborate file structures that often characterize modern archives and manuscript collections. Neither are they designed to accommodate the hundreds of index terms which can be derived from an institution's inventories. In order to adapt successfully archival information to such bibliographic systems, archivists should fully understand the interrelated trinity of standardization—format, descriptive rules, and vocabulary.

Standardized Descriptive Format

Although archivists have evolved some guidelines for descriptive tools such as inventories and guide entries, the only descriptive tool definable as an explicit technical standard is the USMARC record. The format for archives and manuscripts, USMARC AMC, is a structure for listing the elements of information about the content and control of a given set of records under designated machine-readable field identifications. A field is a specifically identifiable section of the USMARC record which always carries the same piece of information. Thus, field 110 is always used for "main entry" by "corporate name," such as Southside Community Services, and field 245 for "title statement," such as "Records, 1878–1980." There are more than seventy-five such fields usable for archives and manuscripts, though the vast majority of descriptions can be accomplished using no more than about fifteen of them. Each field can have several subfields, such as duration and authorizing official under the Restrictions field. In addition, each MARC record contains technical information relating to its own structure and computer processing requirements. (See Figure 10-1.)

Archivists should understand that the use of USMARC in itself does not imply or demand membership in any bibliographic network such as RLIN or OCLC; it can be used by one institution on its own or by any combination of institutions. An institution can purchase computer software which will enable it to create records according to the USMARC formats without importing or exporting any information. The formats are simply means of organizing information in a common structure which makes possible mutual comprehension and the exchange of data in computerized networks.

Two essential features of the USMARC AMC format are that it applies equally to archives and manuscripts and that it integrates both types of material with other information resources. A re-

Figure 10-1

USMARC ARCHIVAL AND MANUSCRIPTS CONTROL FORMAT: FIELD SUMMARY

TAG	FIELD
Leader/00–04	Logical record length
Leader/05	Record status
Leader/06	Type of record
Leader/07	Bibliographic level
Leader/08–09	Undefined legend character positions
Leader/10	Indicator count
Leader/11	Subfield code count
Leader/12–16	Base address of data
Leader/17	Encoding level
Leader/18	Descriptive cataloging form
Leader/19	Linked-record code
Leader/20	Length of the length-of-field portion
Leader/21	Length of the starting-character-position portion
Leader/22	Length of the implementation-defined portion
Leader/23	Undefined entry map character position
Directory/00–02	Tag
Directory/03–06	Field length
Directory/07–11	Starting-character position
001	Control number
002	Subrecord map of directory
005	Date and time of latest transaction
007/00	Category of material
007/01	Specific material designation
007/02	Original versus reproduction aspect
007/03	Polarity (microforms)
007/04	Dimensions (microforms)
007/05–08	Reduction ratio
007/09	Color (microforms)
007/10	Emulsion on film (microforms)
007/11	Generation
007/12	Base of film (microforms)
008/00–05	Date entered on file
008/06	Type of date code
008/07–10	Date 1
008/11–14	Date 2
008/15–17	Place of publication, production, or execution code
008/18–22	Undefined
008/23	Form of reproduction code
008/24–34	Undefined
008/35–37	Language code
008/38	Modified record code
008/39	Cataloging source code

Figure 10-1   continued

USMARC ARCHIVAL AND MANUSCRIPTS CONTROL FORMAT: FIELD SUMMARY—CONTINUED—2

TAG	FIELD
010	Library of Congress control number
020	International Standard Book Number (ISBN)
033	Date and place of capture/finding
035	Local system control number
039	Level of bibliographic control and coding detail
040	Cataloging source
041	Language code
043	Geographic area code
045	Time period of content
046	Type of date code, date 1, date 2 (B.C. dates)
052	Geographic classification code
066	Character sets present
072	Subject category code
09X	Local call numbers
100	Main entry—personal name
110	Main entry—corporate name
111	Main entry—conference or meeting
130	Main entry—uniform title heading
240	Uniform title
242	Translation of title by cataloging agency
243	Uniform title, collective
245	Title statement
250	Edition statement
260	Publication, distribution, etc. (imprint)
300	Physical description
340	Medium
351	Organization and arrangement
500	General note
502	Dissertation note
505	Contents note *(formatted)*
506	Restrictions on access
510	Citation note (brief form)/references
518	Date and place of capture/finding note
520	Summary, abstract, annotation, scope, etc., note
521	Users/intended audience note
524	Preferred citation of described materials
530	Additional physical form available note
533	Reproduction note
535	Location of originals/duplicates
540	Terms governing use and reproduction
541	Immediate source of acquisition
544	Location of associated materials
545	Biographical or historical note
546	Language note
555	Cumulative index/finding aids note
561	Provenance
562	Copy and version identification
565	Case file characteristics note

Figure 10-1   continued

USMARC ARCHIVAL AND MANUSCRIPTS CONTROL FORMAT: FIELD SUMMARY—CONTINUED—3

TAG	FIELD
580	Linking entry complexity note
581	Publications note
583	Actions
584	Accumulation and frequency of use
59X	Local notes
600	Subject added entry—personal name
610	Subject added entry—corporate name
611	Subject added entry—conference or meeting
630	Subject added entry—uniform title heading
650	Subject added entry—topical heading
651	Subject added entry—geographic name
655	Genre/form heading
656	Index term—occupation
657	Index term—function
69X	Local subject added entries
700	Added entry—personal
710	Added entry—corporate name
711	Added entry—conference or meeting
730	Added entry—uniform title heading
740	Added entry—title traced differently
752	Added entry—place of publication or production
755	Physical characteristics access
773	Host item entry
851	Location
870	Variant personal name
871	Variant corporate name
872	Variant conference or meeting name
873	Variant uniform title heading
880	Alternate graphic representation
886	Foreign MARC information field

---

searcher at the historical society interested in George Bailey materials could thus find his papers listed along with any books by or about Bailey at the society. If the museum archives were part of the same bibliographic network as the historical society, a search about museum education in that network would reveal both the organizational records of the Education Division and the personal papers of Mary Hatch Bailey.

In adapting the USMARC AMC format for their own use, archivists should understand that the format can be used to describe any type of records set and link those records to other records. Thus a separate USMARC record can be prepared not only for the park planning files, but for each of the subser-

ies. The subseries USMARC records would indicate the link to the larger series. The bibliographic record describing the whole series would indicate its links to the creating office hierarchy, from the Office of Park Planning to the Parks and Recreation Bureau up to the DNR record group designation. Similarly, the format could accommodate item cataloging of all the Bailey autograph documents, while indicating that they form part of Bailey's papers. In general, however, the format works most efficiently with collection- and series-level descriptions. The extent of its internal application is a matter that each repository staff must determine as part of its processing policy.

Such flexibility is vital to the effective use of bibliographic exchange formats by archivists. The

Figure 10-2 USMARC AMC Record for the Bailey Papers

This example does not include the Leader and Record Directory information which precedes the data fields. This information is usually generated automatically by a specific automated system and serves to identify the record and allow a computer to process it. The example also does not include the control fields (001-009) which are also used mainly for automated information retrieval.

The three-digit numbers identify the variable data fields. One- or two-digit numbers following them are "indicators" which convey coded information about the information which follows. Within the data fields, various pieces of information are separated into subfields, denoted by a "$" sign and a letter. In this example, where the first subfield is essentially the same as the field title itself, the initial "$a" has been omitted. The symbol "$3" indicates that only part of the collection is about to be described.

010		$bMS 90001166
035		(SaH)MS90-077
040		SaH$cSaH$eappm
100	1	Bailey, George Rogers,$d1911-1987
245	00	$kFamily Papers, $f1789-1986, $g1919-1982 (bulk)
300		3a35$fcubic feet (archives boxes)
300		3a150$findividual autographed manuscripts
351		Organized into 6 subgroups: I. Business Activities, 1928-1986; II. Civic Activities, 1936-1986; III. Political Activities, 1940-1982; IV. Personal Files, 1911-1986; V. Mary Hatch Bailey Papers, 1915- 1986; VI. Autograph Collection, 1789-1978
506		Access unrestricted.
520		Papers include business records relating to Bedford Falls Savings and Loan Association, First National Bank of Middletown and local banking activities; civic activities, especially involving the Southside Settlement and Community Center; poltical activities, especially involving the Republican Party; various personal files; a collection of autographs of famous Saratogans and U. S. Presidents; and diaries, papers and correspondence of Mary Hatch Bailey (Mrs. George Bailey).
524		George Bailey, Family papers, Saratoga Historical Society
540		$3Autograph collection$aPhotocopying prohibited$bexcept with permission of Mrs. Bailey or the estate.
541		Mary Hatch Bailey,$b123 Elm Street,$cGift,$dMarch 22,1989,$e89062$n4$ofiling cabinets
544		Associated material: $dPeter Bailey Papers (MS90-067)
545		George Bailey was born in 1911 in Bedford Falls, SA, where his father, Peter Bailey (1879-1934) was President of the Savings and Loan. Upon his father's death he took over the Savings and Loan. He served as President until the bank closed in 1970. He then served until 1981 as Vice President of the First National Bank of Middletown. Among his many local activities the most prominent were his service as Chairman of the Board, Southside Community Center, 1961-1966 and member of the Chamber of Commerce Executive Committee, 1971-1976. He was also a Delegate to the 1956 and 1960 Republican National Conventions. He married Mary Hatch (1913-) in 1932 and they had four children. Mrs. Bailey was active in the Middletown Museum of Art and served as Chair of the Women's Committee, 1965-1973
555		$3Entire collection$aInventory with folder listing.
555		$3Autograph collection$aItem listing.
561		Gift of Mary Hatch Bailey, 1989
583		Processing completed$dMay 17, 1990
600	10	Averington, Clifford,$d1885-1963
600	10	Ellis, William,$cGovernor,$d1878-1949
600	10	Sherman, Joseph,$d1912-
610	20	Middletown Museum of Art
610	20	Republican Party of Saratoga
610	20	Southside Settlement
610	20	Southside Community Center
650	0	Banks and banking$zSaratoga
650	0	Charities$zMiddletown, SA
650	0	Political parties$zSaratoga
651	0	Bedford Falls, SA
651	0	Middletown, SA
655	7	Autographs$2ftamc
656	7	Bankers$2lcsh
691	4	South Middletown (Middletown, SA)
696	14	Lindquist, George$d1909-1967
696	14	Hetherington, Winston, $cMrs.,$d1914-1988
697	24	Banker's Roundtable (Middletown, SA)
697	24	Bedford Falls Savings and Loan
697	24	Businessmen's Club of Middletown
697	24	First National Bank of Middletown
697	24	Middletown (SA) Chamber of Commerce
697	24	United Fund of Saratoga
700	1	Bailey, Mary Hatch$d1913-
851		Department of Manuscripts$bSaratoga Historical Society$c200 West High Street, Middletown SA

Figure 10-3   USMARC AMC Record as Seen by a Researcher

The following is one example of how the Bailey record could be made to appear to users of the Saratoga Historical Society's on-line public catalog.

Bailey, George Rogers, 1911-1987
    Family Papers, 1789-1986, 1919-1982 (bulk)
    35 cubic feet (archives boxes), 150 individual autographed manuscripts

    George Bailey was born in 1911 in Bedford Falls, SA, where his father, Peter Bailey (1879-1934) was President of the Savings and Loan. Upon his father's death George took over the Savings and Loan. He served as President until the bank closed in 1970. He then served until 1981 as Vice President of the First National Bank of Middletown. Among his many local activities, most prominent were his service as Chairman of the Board, Southside Community Center, 1961-1966 and member of the Chamber of Commerce Executive Committee, 1971-1976. He was also a Delegate to the 1956 and 1960 Republican National Conventions. He married Mary Hatch (1913-) in 1932 and they had four children. Mrs. Bailey was active in the Middletown Museum of Art and served as Chair of the Women's Committee, 1965-1973.
    Organized into 6 subgroups: I. Business Activities, 1928-1986; II. Civic Activities, 1936-1986; III. Political Activities, 1940-1982; IV. Personal Files, 1911-1986; V. Mary Hatch Bailey Papers, 1915-1986; VI. Autograph Collection, c. 1789-1978
    Access unrestricted.
    Summary: Papers include business records relating to Bedford Falls Savings and Loan Association, First National Bank of Middletown and local banking activities; civic activities, especially involving the Southside Settlement and Community Center; political activities, especially involving the Republican Party; various personal files; a collection of autographs of famous Saratogans and U. S. Presidents; and diaries, papers and correspondence of Mary Hatch Bailey (Mrs. George Bailey).
    Cite as: George Bailey, Family papers, Saratoga Historical Society
    Autograph collection: Photocopying prohibited except with permission of Mrs. Bailey or the estate.
    Associated material: Peter Bailey Papers (MS90-067)
    Finding Aids: Entire collection, Inventory and folder listing; Autograph collection, Item listing.
    Gift of Mary Hatch Bailey, 1989
    Location: Department of Manuscripts, Saratoga Historical Society, 200 West High Street, Middletown SA

1. Averington, Clifford, 1885-1963. 2. Ellis, William, Governor, 1878-1949. 3. Sherman, Joseph, 1912- . 4. Lindquist, George, 1909-1967. 5. Hetherington, Winston, Mrs., 1914-1988. 6. Middletown Museum of Art. 7. Republican Party of Saratoga. 8. Southside Settlement. 9. Southside Community Center. 10. Banker's Roundtable (Middletown, SA). 11. Bedford Falls Savings and Loan. 12. Businessmen's Club of Middletown. 13. First National Bank of Middletown. 14. Middletown (Sa.) Chamber of Commerce. 15. United Fund of Saratoga. 16. Banks and banking—Saratoga. 17. Charities—Middletown, SA. 18. Political parties—Saratoga. 19. Bedford Falls, SA. 20. Middletown, SA. 21. South Middletown (Middletown, SA). 22. Autographs. 23. Bankers. I. Bailey, Mary Hatch, 1913-

archivist still has to rely on the available descriptive tools and institutional policies in deciding exactly what information is to be exchanged in the form of USMARC AMC records. The descriptive tools from which those records are derived usually contain too much information for the summary USMARC descriptions. The length of archival finding aids thus often demands rigorous selection of information to be included in a collection-level USMARC AMC record. Further, the system or network can demand information not contained in the finding aid. However, the USMARC AMC format is structured so that

there is a field or subfield for each of the descriptive data elements discussed in Chapter 8, from basic title and dates through organizational history and series arrangement to the many different types of index terms.

In most descriptive systems, a USMARC AMC record is in effect an abstract of the core finding aid, traditionally the inventory, together with a summary of archival actions taken with regard to the materials described. The latter can include information about donors, accessioning, appraisal decisions, records management, microfilming, physical location, access restrictions, and similar administrative activities. In a sound descriptive program, the archivist should be able to establish procedures for the smooth transfer of already existing information from administrative files and finding aids to a USMARC AMC record. (See Figure 10-2.)

The USMARC format is far from static. The 1980s saw the creation of formats for visual materials and computer files as well as the archives and manuscripts format. In 1988 the library community decided to move towards integrating all of the separate formats into one common format in the 1990s. The USMARC format may also be adapted to the description of material objects.[4] In such a scenario, all of the holdings of an institution like the Middletown Museum of Art could be described in one integrated cultural data base. The Society of American Archivists is involved in the continued evolution of the USMARC format, but archivists are only a small part of the information and cultural communities. Some of the changes in the format are naturally more beneficial to archival description than others. Yet once a repository has begun creating USMARC records about its holdings and adding them to a network or bibliographic utility, the repository must remain current with the development of the system. In addition to SAA publications, archivists should be aware that detailed documentation of all aspects of the format is available from the Library of Congress in the regularly updated volumes of *USMARC Format for Bibliographic Data* and *USMARC Format for Authority Data*.[5]

Standardized Descriptive Rules

The USMARC AMC format is simply a collection of fields and subfields, with no rules governing how information is recorded within them. As with the format itself, archival rules had to be reconciled with library practices represented by the *Anglo-American Cataloguing Rules*, 2nd edition, revised (*AACR 2*). This has been the function of the *Archives, Personal Papers and Manuscripts* (*APPM*) cataloging manual, first issued in 1983 and revised in 1989. The

basic goal of the manual is to interpret and adapt *AACR 2* rules so that archivists can describe such aspects of their holdings as creator, title, dates, volume, and content in a manner and style compatible with the description of other library materials. The *APPM* manual can be used for any archival descriptive tool and is not necessarily tied to USMARC fields.[6]

APPM succeeded where previous efforts had failed because it preserved key archival practices. In the absence of a traditional title page—the chief source of cataloging information about books—the manual provides that the equivalent source of information about a set of archival records is the finding aid for those records. In accordance with the two-stage nature of archival description, the cataloger, like the researcher, goes first to the basic descriptive tool, not to the records themselves. The basic point is that "finding aids are as reliable and concrete a source of information on descriptive elements such as title, dates and extent as the title page of any book."[7] Further, the manual stressed collective description of record groups, collections, series, and their components, though it does allow for item description in exceptional cases. This reversed the traditional item-level emphasis of manuscript cataloging as expressed in Chapter 4 of the standard *AACR 2*.

APPM and *AACR2* deal with issues archivists long ignored, such as the derivation, selection, style, and structure of titles, added entries and indexing terms. *APPM* legitimates the usual archival practices of using the creator of the records as the "main entry" analagous to the author of a book (George Bailey; Middletown Museum of Art. Education Division). The type of records together with dates functions as a common form of title supplied by the archivist (Papers, 1919–1986; Records, 1927–1985). *APPM* establishes the minimum archival descriptive entry as a creator, a title including type and dates, and an indication of volume. Guidelines are offered for indicating record type, dates and volume. *APPM* also provides a suggested form, punctuation and order for all the different kinds of descriptive narrative text commonly found in an inventory or a USMARC AMC record. (See Figure 10-4.)

For compatibility with library practice, archivists should follow *AACR 2* in the areas not expressly covered by *APPM*. These include the selection and

---

[4] For a discussion of this issue see David Bearman, "Archives and Manuscript Control with Bibliographic Utilities: Challenges and Opportunities," *American Archivist* 52 (Winter 1989): 37–39.

[5] *USMARC Format for Bibliographic Data: Including Guidelines for Content Designation* is available, along with regular updates, from the Library of Congress's Cataloging Distribution Service. An overview of the whole USMARC structure can be obtained in *USMARC Concise Formats for Bibliographic, Authority and Holdings Data* (1988), also available from the Library of Congress.

[6] See Steven L. Hensen, "Squaring the Circle: The Reformation of Archival Description in AACR2," *Library Trends* 36 (Winter 1988): 540–542 for the origins of *APPM*.

[7] Ibid., 545.

Figure 10-4   Museum Records Described According to *APPM* and *AACR 2* Rules

Middletown Museum of Art. Education Division.
    Records, 1927-1982.
    45 cubic feet.
    Forms Record Group (RG) 6 of the Middletown Museum of Art Archives.

    Established as the Division of Education and Instruction on February 10, 1927. Departments of Children's Programs (1935), Public Education (subsequently School District) (1935), Adult Programs (1955), Volunteer's Council (1957) and International Programs (1966) function within the Division. The Division also included the Public Relations Department, 1948-1965. Name changed to Education Division in 1960. Division Director reported to Museum Director until 1978; reports to Associate Director for Adminstration since 1978.

    Records include the administrative, policy and general programmatic files of the Division and all of its constituent Departments.

    Organized into the following subgroups: I. Division Director, 1927-1982; II. Children's Programs, 1935-1981; III. Adult Programs, 1955-1982; IV. School District Programs, 1933-1979; V. Volunteer's Council, 1949-1982; VI. International Programs, 1961-1980; VII. Administrative Secretary, 1945-1982; and VIII. Education Division—General, 1927-1982.

    Deposited by the Administrative Secretary of the Education Division, 1988.

    Records are open to scholarly researchers and museum personnel.

    Inventory available in the Archives.

    Described in: *Guide to the Middletown Museum of Art Archives* (Middletown: Museum of Art, 1990).

structure of nonsubject access points and indexing terms. They also include such distinctive library practices as the preference for the form of a personal name used in authoring a publication rather than an exact but more obscure form, or the "common" name rather than the full legal term for a government agency. Thus George Bailey may really be George Rogers Bailey, but his "official" name according to *AACR 2* will be the former if it appeared that way on a publication's title page. Such names, once established in national authority files, discussed below, must be used by all libraries and participating archives. To some extent, the uniqueness and local emphases of so many archives will allow archivists to establish the form of names most important to

themselves. Archivists are thus in a position to greatly enrich national name authority files. They can also include full variants of already established names as long as all the variants and the standard form are included in authority files. Once again, standardization requires a combination of compromise and skillful adaptation of established rules.

In addition to *APPM*, archivists should be aware that there are similar manuals for cataloging maps, films, photographs and computerized records. *APPM* should be used for multi-format historical collections, although the media-based cataloging manuals should be consulted for specific points of physical description and access terms.[8]

Standardized Vocabulary

Automated information exchange has very little tolerance for vocabulary that is not standardized and structured. Archivists have to accept some common standards and structure not only within the archival community, which is no small undertaking in itself, but also between archives and the larger cultural and intellectual communities. Standard vocabularies should be used in all relevant aspects of archival description. It is especially important that a common vocabulary be used for records creators, indexing terms and archival actions, since in all these areas terms can be applied to many sets of records.

The basis for a common descriptive vocabulary is the use in archival description of word and phrase authority lists developed for the most part by the library community. When an archivist wants to describe the contents of a collection within that larger community in terms of subjects, places and occupations, he or she should use as many of the terms listed in the most recent edition of the *Library of Congress Subject Headings* (*LCSH*) as are appropriate. (See Figure 10-5.) Thus for the park planning records, *LCSH* indicates that "Recreational use" is an approved term, so that should be used rather than something like "recreational activities." In addition to approved terms, *LCSH* also indicates nonauthorized terms and the appropriate substitutes, and provides a whole network of broader, narrower, subordinate, and related terms. Finally, a separate volume

---

[8] The manuals issued by the Library of Congress include Elizabeth Betz, *Graphic Materials: Rules for Describing Original Items and Historical Collections* (1982); Sue Dodd, *Cataloging Machine-readable Data Files* (1982); and Wendy White-Hensen, *Archival Moving Image Materials: A Cataloging Manual* (1984). See also Hugo Stibbe, *Cartographic Materials: A Manual of Interpretation for AACR2* (Chicago: American Library Association, 1982).

Figure 10-5   Library of Congress Subject Heading Page for Parks

Parji language *(PL4741)*
  xx Dravidian languages
Park administration
  See Parks—Management
Park and ride systems
  See Fringe parking
Park Cemetery (Columbus, Kan.)
  xx Cemeteries—Kansas
Park districts *(Indirect)*
  sa Parkways
  xx Express highways
      Parks
      Special districts
Park family
  sa Parker family
  x Parke family
      Parkes family
      Parks family
  xx Parker family
Park interpretation
  See National parks and reserves—
          Interpretive programs
        Parks—Interpretive programs
Park management
  See Parks—Management
Park planning, National
  See National parks and reserves—Planning
Park policy
  See Parks policy
Park Range (Colo. and Wyo.)
  xx Mountains—Colorado
      Mountains—Wyoming
      Rocky Mountains
Park rangers *(Indirect)*
  sa Forest rangers
  x Rangers, Park
  xx Forest rangers
      National parks and reserves
      Parks
  — Scotland
      sa Speyside Project
Park Top (Race horse) *(SF355.R)*
Parkard family
  See Packard family
Parkateyê Indians
  See Gaviões Indians
Parke family
  See Park family
Parker family
  sa Park family
  x Parcher family
      Parkers family
  xx Park family
Parker Lake (Sask.)
  xx Lakes—Saskatchewan
Parker shotgun *(TS536.8)*
Parkeriaceae
  xx Filicales
      Water ferns
Parkers family
  See Parker family
Parkes family
  See Park family
Parkes process *(TN785)*
Parket (Game) *(GV1295.P2)*
Parkhill Site (Sask.)
  xx Excavations (Archaeology)—
          Saskatchewan
      Indians of North America—
          Saskatchewan—Antiquities
      Paleo-Indians—Saskatchewan
      Saskatchewan—Antiquities
Parkin Indian Mount (Ark.)
  See Parkin Site (Ark.)
Parkin Site (Ark.)
  x Parkin Indian Mount (Ark.)
      Stanley Mounds (Ark.)
  xx Arkansas—Antiquities
      Excavations (Archaeology)—Arkansas
      Indians of North America—Arkansas—
          Antiquities

Mississippian culture
  Mounds—Arkansas
Parking, Automobile
  See Automobile parking
Parking, Bicycle
  See Bicycle parking
Parking, Campus
  See Campus parking
Parking, Motorcycle
  See Motorcycle parking
Parking, Trailer
  See Trailer parking
Parking, Truck
  See Truck parking
Parking garages *(Indirect)*
  xx Automobile parking
      Garages
      Transportation buildings
  — Law and legislation *(Indirect)*
Parking lots *(Indirect)* *(TL175)*
  sa Truck parking
  xx Automobile parking
  — Landscape architecture
      xx Landscape architecture
Parking meter collectors *(Indirect)*
  xx Parking meters
Parking meters
  sa Parking meter collectors
  x Automobile-parking meters
      Meters, Parking
  xx Traffic regulations
Parkinson disease
  See Parkinsonism
Parkinsonian syndrome
  See Parkinsonism, Symptomatic
Parkinsonism *(Indirect)* *(RC382)*
  sa Antiparkinsonian agents
      Cycrimine
      Parkinsonism, Postencephalitic
      Parkinsonism, Symptomatic
  x Palsy, Shaking
      Paralysis agitans
      Parkinson disease
      Parkinson's disease
      Shaking palsy
  xx Brain—Diseases
      Movement disorders
  — Chemotherapy
Parkinsonism, Postencephalitic *(Indirect)*
  x Postencephalitic parkinsonism
  xx Parkinsonism
Parkinsonism, Symptomatic *(Indirect)*
      (RC382)
  x Parkinsonian syndrome
      Symptomatic parkinsonism
  xx Parkinsonism
Parkinson's disease
  See Parkinsonism
Parks *(Indirect)* *(SB481-5)*
  sa Amusement parks
      Botanical gardens
      Landscape gardening
      Military parks
      National parks and reserves
      Park districts
      Park rangers
      Parkways
      Picnic grounds
      Playgrounds
      Skateboarding parks
      Zoos
      subdivision Parks *under names of cities*
  x State parks
  xx Cities and towns
      City planning
      Commons
      Landscape architecture
      Municipal engineering
      Outdoor recreation
      Playgrounds
      Recreation areas

  — Interpretive programs *(Indirect)*
      (SB481–485)
      x Interpretation, Park
          Interpretive programs of parks
          Park interpretation
      xx Public relations—Parks
  — Law and legislation *(Indirect)*
  — Maintenance
      Example under Grounds maintenance
  — Management *(SB481)*
      x Park administration
          Park management
  — Officials and employees
  — Tort liability
      See Tort liability of parks
  — Visitors
  — Vocational guidance

GEOGRAPHIC SUBDIVISIONS

— Alabama
    sa Mound State Monument (Ala.)
— Alaska
    sa Bering Land Bridge National
        Preserve (Alaska)
      Denali National Park and Preserve
        (Alaska)
      Gates of the Arctic National Park
        and Preserve (Alaska)
      Glacier Bay National Park and
        Preserve (Alaska)
      Misty Fjords National Monument
        (Alaska)
— Alberta
    sa Dinosaur Provincial Park (Alta.)
      Waterton Lakes National Park
        (Alta.)
— Argentina
    sa Parque Nacional Los Glaciares
        (Argentina)
      Parque Nacional Nahuel Huapf
        (Argentina)
— Arizona
    sa Canyon de Chelly National
        Monument (Ariz.)
      Grand Canyon National Park (Ariz.)
      Petrified Forest National Park
        (Ariz.)
— Arkansas
    sa Arkansas Post National Memorial
        (Ark.)
      Buffalo National River (Ark.)
      Hot Springs National Park (Ark.)
— Australia
    sa Carnarvon National Park (Qld.)
      Centennial Park (Sydney, N.S.W.)
      Kakadu National Park (N.T.)
      Kosciusko National Park (N.S.W.)
— Bonaire
    sa National Park Washington-Slagbaai
        (Bonaire)
— Brazil
    sa Itatiaia National Park (Brazil)
      Parque Nacional da Serra da
        Canastra (Brazil)
      Parque Nacional da Tijuca (Brazil)
      Parque Nacional das Emas (Brazil)
      Parque Nacional de Aparados da
        Serra (Brazil)
      Parque Nacional de Brasília (Brazil)
      Parque Nacional de Monte Pascoal
        (Brazil)
      Parque Nacional de Sete Cidades
        (Brazil)
      Parque Nacional de Ubajara (Brazil)
      Parque Nacional do Amazonas
        (Brazil)
      Parque Nacional do Caparaó (Brazil)
— British Columbia
    sa Manning Provincial Park (B.C.)
      Pacific Rim National Park
        (Vancouver Island, B.C.)

issued by the Library of Congress called the *Subject Heading Manual* governs the use of acceptable subdivisions under main place and subject terms.[9]

Archivists often find that the book-oriented terms in *LCSH* are too broad for their very detailed and unique holdings, or do not reflect concepts employed in current research. Even with the appropriate subdivision, the term "Parks—planning" is of limited assistance in describing the state archives' park planning files, and the term "State Parks" is disapproved in *LCSH*. In such cases, archivists must draw on one of the many subject specialized vocabularies as well as use whatever *LCSH* terms are appropriate. In general, they must ensure that they maintain as much consistency with national standards as is possible while accurately describing their holdings. Fortunately, cataloging rules and the USMARC format allow several methods of providing terms from other standardized vocabularies for specialized and local subjects, events, and topics. Many such terms may be derived from the crucial agency history/biography and scope and contents narratives. Archivists should not feel constrained to abandon the use of local terms or specialized index terms where they are appropriate, since in most systems users will be able to search under such terms when they are applied.

The second major general authority list is the *Library of Congress Name Authorities* (*LCNA*). Archivists will find here the standardized form of many corporate, personal, and place names established by the Library of Congress and the hundreds of libraries which participate in the Name Authority Cooperative Organization (NACO). As in the case of subject terms, the use of standard names will allow researchers and repositories to discover related materials across institutional lines. *LCNA* also includes names used in *NUCMC* entries, thus including thousands of local as well as national entries. Local names not already in the *LCNA* should be established by archivists in accordance with the rules in *AACR 2*, as supplemented by *APPM*. They should be aware that if they do choose to establish such names according to these standards, these forms will become the national standard. If archivists establish terms in a manner at variance with the established rules, they may not be acceptable to the larger bibliographic networks.

The national subject and name authority files have been supplemented in three ways. First, a number of thesauri are available for specialized topics and types of material. Among the most important are the *Art and Architecture Thesaurus* (*AAT*), part of the Getty Art History Information Program, and the *Medical Subject Headings* (*MeSH*) thesaurus of the National Library of Medicine. There are also thesauri for different literary and graphic genres, physical material characteristics, and occupations.[10] Second, the archival profession is standardizing many of the terms used mainly in archival work, including types of records, types of official actions, and different aspects of archival activity. The *Form Terms for Archives and Manuscript Control*, published by the Research Libraries Group in 1985, is a particularly valuable listing of hundreds of different types of documents. Archivists can obtain the publications covering these standardized terms from the relevant library and archival organizations.

Third, groups of repositories sharing common themes have developed or adapted their own local and subject based authority networks and thesauri. Our four sample repositories in Middletown will share hundreds of individual names, places, and events not recorded in any national systems. The Baileys appear in both the Southside Community Services and Museum of Art records and collections, while those two organizations are the subject of various state government records. All of the repositories should use the same form of these personal and corporate names. Similarly, the Saratoga State Archives should use the same subject terms for park planning as other state archives, and the Art Museum should describe its activities and structure in a manner consistent with those of other art museums. Here standardization can result in savings comparable to those of library cataloging, if the archives can derive many of the authority terms used in a description from an outside source. Archivists in the future may draw upon the whole range of available information sources for their authority information about records and records creators.

The standardization of vocabulary is in some ways more difficult for archivists than the standardization of format, which is based on longstanding practice. The inherent uniqueness and level of de-

---

[9] Library of Congress, *Subject Cataloging Manual: Subject Headings* is a looseleaf publication prepared by the Subject Cataloging Division, Processing Services.

[10] See especially American Library Association, Association of College and Research Libraries, *Genre Terms: A Thesaurus for Use in Rare Book and Special Collections Cataloging* (1983), *Provenance Evidence: Thesaurus for Use in Rare Book and Special Collections Cataloging* (1988), and *Relator Terms for Rare Book, Manuscript and Special Collections Cataloging* (1981); and Helena Zinkham and Elizabeth Betz Parker, *Descriptive Terms for Graphic Materials: Genre and Physical Characteristics Headings* (Washington, D.C.: Library of Congress, 1987).

tailed description in archival holdings make standard terms harder to apply than a standard format and rules. But there can be no integration of archival information into larger information resources without a common vocabulary. Without giving up their grounding in local detail, archivists can select terms from standard sources that will link their holdings to each other and to larger systems. At the same time, they enrich the vocabularies of the standard bibliographic networks through their very concentration on specific subjects and localities.

Applying Standardization

Applying standardization to archival description is a relatively straightforward procedure. Archivists should prepare a summary description based on core finding aids and utilizing the USMARC AMC format, *AACR 2* rules as interpreted in *APPM*, and at least some standard indexing terms. This description should become part of an internal repository system and one of the national information exchange systems, such as RLIN, OCLC, or *NUCMC*. In an efficient integrated descriptive system, this entry can be used in various types of guides and in internal automated information retrieval systems. The primary goals of information integration and exchange will thus be achieved.

In reality, the application of standardization to description can and often should have a profound impact on internal operations. The creation and gradual refinement of a USMARC AMC record should be part of the entire internal processing of every group of records from the initial acceptance of the material by the repository. Information should flow as easily as possible from accessioning forms and basic finding aids into the USMARC AMC record. Thus the requirements of standardization for USMARC AMC records become requirements for the standardization of considerable sections of the whole descriptive process as well. Index terms in the finding aids should be understood as index terms for USMARC AMC records as well as for the internal repository index. In addition, as we have seen, in the place of traditional static guides standardized automated descriptions can be used to generate regular summaries of the whole of a repository's holdings or of holdings selected by topic.

Some features of USMARC AMC records can encourage more radical changes in descriptive practice. Inherent in bibliographic exchange and the USMARC AMC format is an absence of hierarchical structures within and among individual sets of rec-

ords. The emphasis instead is on linking related materials, on cross-format compatibility, and on controlled vocabulary through authority files. All these features encourage the development of systems based on series descriptions linked to provenance-based authority files, rather than the traditional comprehensive archival inventory. The USMARC format and rapidly evolving internal automated systems also encourage the integration of archival description with information about the whole range of collection management operations and the entire "life-cycle" of a set of records. Some repositories prefer to maintain such information separately, based on considerations such as the complexity of their operations or a concern for confidentiality.[11]

The most important commitment of repository resources may be required not for the creation and initial implementation of a system for information exchange, but rather for its application to existing holdings already described in traditional tools. If an archives does not add the holdings described in nonstandardized formats and terms to a new and standardized system, those holdings will not appear anywhere in that system. Yet for many years nonstandardized descriptions will represent the vast majority of that repository's holdings. In general, if a library does not do such a "retrospective conversion" that simply means its own holdings of certain books are not recorded in a national network, but the books will usually be represented nevertheless, through information supplied by other libraries. However, without a determined effort to convert retrospectively as many archival and manuscript collections as possible, archival information exchange will be only a shadow of its true potential.

Unfortunately, the difference between libraries and archives in this respect has national implications. As long as there is more than one national bibliographic data base—such as RLIN and OCLC—the archival network will be seriously divided. If the university library is a member of network A, then the university's Southside Community Services records will usually not appear in network B, whereas the great majority of books and journals will appear in both networks. As both economics and technology encourage the formation of a unified national system, such problems will diminish. However, the evolution of national networks will bring further extensions and refinements of standardization by national

---

[11] See William Holmes, Edie Hedlin and Thomas Weir, "MARC and Life Cycle Tracking in the National Archives: Project Final Report," *American Archivist* 49 (Summer 1986): 305–309.

Figure 10-6   Descriptive Standards

STANDARD SOURCES FOR DESCRIPTIVE ELEMENTS (TERMINOLOGY)

Subject Terms:

Art and Architecture Thesaurus, directed by Toni Peterson. 3 vols. New York: Oxford University Press, 1989. The *AAT* is an ongoing program of the Getty Art History Information Program.

Library of Congress. Subject Cataloging Division. *Library of Congress Subject Headings,* 10th ed. Washington: Library of Congress, 1986.

Library of Congress. Subject Cataloging Division. Processing Services. *Subject Cataloging Manual: Subject Headings*. Washington: Library of Congress, 1984.

National Library of Medicine. *Medical Subject Headings*. Bethesda, MD: National Library of Medicine, 1960-.

Personal and Corporate Names:

Library of Congress. *Name Authorities*. Washington: Library of Congress, 1974- .

Place Names:

Library of Congress. *Subject Headings* and *Subject Cataloging Manual* cited above.

Forms and Genres of Material:

Association of College and Research Libraries. *Genre Terms: A Thesaurus for Use in Rare Book and Special Collections Cataloging.* Chicago: ACRL, 1983. Available from American Library Association.

Research Libraries Group, Inc. *Form Terms for Archival and Manuscripts Control*. Stanford, CA: Research Libraries Group, 1985. This has been incorporated into the *AAT*.

Zinkham, Helena and Elizabeth Betz Parker. *Descriptive Terms for Graphic Materials: Genre and Physical Characteristics Headings*. Washington: Library of Congress, 1987.

Functional Terms (functions, activities, processes):

A list originally developed by the Research Libraries Group for the "Seven States Project" has been incorporated into the AAT.

Occupations:

Department of Labor. Dictionary of Occupational Terms. Washington: Department of Labor.

STANDARDS FOR DESCRIPTIVE TOOLS

Formats:

Evans, Linda J. and Maureen O'Brien Will. *MARC for Archival Visual Materials: A Compendium of Practice*. Chicago: Chicago Historical Society, 1988.

Hill, Edward. *The Preparation of Inventories*. Staff Information Paper 14. Washington: National Archives and Records Service, 1982. Originally published in 1950.

Library of Congress, Network Development and MARC Standards Office. *USMARC Formats for Bibliographic Data*. Washington: Library of Congress, 1988. Updated periodically.

——————————. *USMARC Concise Formats for Bibliographic, Holdings and Authority Data*. Washington: Library of Congress, 1988.

Sahli, Nancy. *MARC for Archives and Manuscripts: The AMC Format*. Chicago: Society of American Archivists, 1985. With 1987 Update #2, by Lisa Weber.

Content:

Gorman, Michael and Paul W. Winkler, eds. *Anglo-American Cataloguing Rules,* 2nd edition revised. Chicago: American Library Association, 1988.

Hensen, Steven L. *Archives, Personal Papers and Manuscripts: A Cataloging Manual for Archival Repositories, Historical Societies and Manuscript Libraries*. Chicago: Society of American Archivists, 1989.

Betz, Elizabeth. *Graphic Materials: Rules for Describing Original Items and Historical Collections*. Washington: Library of Congress, 1982.

Dodd, Sue. *Cataloging Machine-readable Data Files*. Washington: Library of Congress, 1982.

Stibbe, Hugo. *Cartographic Materials: A Manual of Interpretation for AACR2*. Chicago: American Library Association, 1982.

White-Hensen, Wendy. *Archival Moving Image Materials: A Cataloging Manual*. Washington: Library of Congress, 1984.

organizations. The archival profession will have to monitor and participate in the ongoing process of standard establishment and enforcement.

Individual archivists should also play a direct and active role in the creation of local and thematic networks. A group of repositories in the same geographic or subject area having compatible systems can not only maintain common authority lists, but can also produce common guides and other summary descriptions. Beyond descriptions of holdings, they can exchange information about the appraisal, processing, preservation, and management of similar holdings, as well as providing access to a shared user population.

Such improved access to archives remains the ultimate justification for information exchange, as it does for the entire processing program. Effective access is not only vital for users, but also improves all archival operations, from appraisal and administration through preservation and outreach. Archival standardization and information exchange do not have the same financial and administrative rationales as traditional bibliographic exchange. The justification for joining the larger world of information resources is instead the same justification that led nineteenth-century curators to laboriously prepare their detailed calendars. Archives and manuscript repositories exist not only to collect and preserve historical records, but equally to facilitate their use. That connection remains fundamental to every principle and practice of archival arrangement and description.

Bibliographic Note

This bibliographic note includes three types of sources:

1) ongoing publications which allow archivists to keep up with developments in arrangement and description;

2) writings illustrating the historical development of current practices; and

3) recent publications discussing some of the policies and practices covered in the preceding chapters.

This is not intended as a comprehensive bibliography. For more extensive listings, see:

Berner, Richard C. *Archival Theory and Practice in the United States*. Seattle: University of Washington Press, 1983, 199–211.

Evans, Frank B. *Modern Archives and Manuscripts: A Select Bibliography*. Chicago: Society of American Archivists, 1975.

Evans, Frank B., comp. *The History of Archives Administration: A Select Bibliography*. Paris: UNESCO, 1979.

Myers, Katherine, comp. "Select Archival Descriptive Standards Bibliography," in Bureau of Canadian Archivists. *Toward Descriptive Standards: Report and recommendations of the Canadian Working Group on Descriptive Standards*. Ottawa: Bureau of Canadian Archivists, 1985, 103–192.

In addition to these individual publications, the *American Archivist* published annual bibliographies from 1943 to 1980, with the last issue covering literature of the year 1978. The next four years are covered in Andrews, Patricia A. and Bettye J. Grier. *Writings on Archives, Historical Manuscripts and Current Records, 1979–1982*. Washington: National Archives, 1985. For coverage after 1983, consult the indexes of the annual issues of the *American Archivist* since 1986 to find the issue containing the bibliography. A good deal of the current archival literature relating to arrangement and description is included in the periodical index *Library Literature*.

1. Ongoing sources.

The most efficient way to remain current with the archival literature is through the following four major North American archival journals:

American Archivist, published quarterly by the Society of American Archivists;

Archivaria, published semi-annually by the Association of Canadian Archivists;

Midwestern Archivist, published semi-annually by the Midwest Archives Conference; and

Provenance, published semi-annually by the Society of Georgia Archivists.

For technical information, including information about descriptive standards and bibliographic networks, archivists should monitor the publications issued by the following:

American Library Association (request the catalog "American Library Association Publications") and Association of College and Research Libraries, 50 East Huron Street, Chicago, IL 60611;

Library of Congress. Cataloging Distribution Service (request "Catalogs and Technical Publications" from the Distribution Service's Customer Section), Washington, DC 20541;

Society of American Archivists, Suite 504, 600 S. Federal, Chicago, IL 60605 (request the SAA publications list).

2. Historical background.

For an excellent introduction to the historical roots of modern archival practices, see Ernst Posner *Archives in the Ancient World*. Cambridge, MA: Harvard University Press, 1972; "Max Lehmann and the Genesis of the Principle of Provenance," in *Archives and the Public Interest: Selected Essays by Ernst Posner*, ed. by Ken Munden. Washington: Public Affairs Press, 1967, 36–44, and "Some Aspects of Archival Development since the French Revolution" (1940), reprinted in Maygene Daniels and Timothy Walch, eds. *Modern Archives Reader: Basic Readings on Archival Theory and Practice*. Washington: National Archives, 1984, 3–14 provide Also see the commentary by Gregg Kimball, "The Burke-Cappon Debate: Some Further Criticisms and Considerations for Archival Theory," *American Archivist* 48 (Fall 1985), 369–376.

Modern archival arrangement and description was first codified in the Dutch manual by Samuel Muller , J.A.Feith and R. Fruin, *Manual for the Ar-*

rangement and Description of Archives. Translation of the 2nd edition by Arthur Levitt. (New York: H.W. Wilson, 1968). The British counterpart, first published in 1922 before Muller et al. had been translated into English, is Hilary Jenkinson, *A Manual of Archival Administration*. (London: P. Land, Humphries, 1937). The closest equivalents published in United States are two books by Theodore R. Schellenberg, *Modern Archives: Principles and Techniques*. (Chicago: University of Chicago Press, 1956) and *The Management of Archives*. (New York: Columbia University Press, 1965). R. Stapleton "Jenkinson and Schellenberg: A Comparison," *Archivaria* 17 (Winter 1983–84), 75–85 provides an interesting comparison of the two major English-language archival theorists.

For overviews of the development of archival practice in the United States, see Berner, *Archival Theory and Practice in the United States*; O. Lawrence Burnette, *Beneath the Footnote: A Guide to the Use and Preservation of Historical Sources*. (Madison: State Historical Society of Wisconsin), 1969; Donald McCoy. *The National Archives: America's Ministry of Documents*. (Chapel Hill: University of North Carolina Press, 1978); and Ernst Posner, "The National Archives and the Public Interest," in *Archives and the Public Interest*, 131–140.

Among the publications that best document the development of American arrangement and description prior to 1980 are the following (listed chronologically):

Leland, Waldo G. "American Archival Problems," in American Historical Association, *Annual Report* (1909) vol. 1: 302–348.

Leland, Waldo G. "The National Archives: A Programme," *American Historical Review* 18 (1912): 1–28.

Fitzpatrick, John C. *Notes on the Care, Cataloguing, Calendering and Arranging of Manuscripts*. (Washington: Government Printing Office, 1913).

Peckham, Howard W. "Arranging and Cataloguing Manuscripts in the William L. Clements Library," *American Archivist* 1 (1938): 215–229.

Norton, Margaret Cross. "The Classification and Description of Archives," in Mitchell, Thornton W., ed. *Norton on Archives: The Writings of Margaret Cross Norton on Archives and Records Management*. (Carbondale: Southern Illinois University Press, 1975), 106–131. Originally published in 1940 as "Classification in the Archives of Illinois," in A. F. Kuhlman, ed. *Archives and Libraries* (Chicago: American Library Association, 1940).

Hamer, Philip M. "Finding Mediums at the National Archives: An Appraisal of Six Years Experience," *American Archivist* 5 (April 1942), 82–92.

National Archives. *The Control of Records at the Record Group Level*. (Washington: Government Printing Office, 1950).

National Archives. *The Preparation of Preliminary Inventories*. Washington: Government Printing Office, 1950. Reprinted in 1982.

National Archives. *Principles of Arrangement*. (Washington: Government Printing Office, 1951).

Brand, Katherine. "Developments in the Handling of Recent Manuscripts in the Library of Congress," *American Archivist* 16 (April 1953): 99–104.

Brand, Katherine. "The Place of the Register in the Manuscripts Division of the Library of Congress," *American Archivist* 18 (January 1955): 59–67.

Cappon, Lester. "Historical Manuscripts as Archives: Some Definitions and their Application," *American Archivist* 19 (April 1956): 101–110.

Holmes, Oliver W. "Archival Arrangement—Five Different Operations at Five Different Levels," *American Archivist* 27 (January 1964): 21–41.

Evans, Frank B. "Modern Methods of Arrangement of Archives in the United States," *American Archivist* 29 (April 1966): 251–263.

Brubaker, Robert L. "Archival Principles and the Curator of Manuscripts," *American Archivist* 29 (October 1966): 505–514.

Papenfuse, Edward C. "The Retreat from Standardization: A Comment on the Recent History of Finding Aids," *American Archivist* 36 (October 1973): 537–542.

Abraham, Terry. "NUCMC and the Local Repository," *American Archivist* 40 (January 1977): 31–42.

As a unified archives/manuscripts practice emerged, several manuals based on modern principles were published in the United States. The most significant were:

Bordin, Ruth B. and Robert M. Warner. *The Modern Manuscript Library*. (New York: Scarecrow Press, 1966).

Duckett, Kenneth W. *Modern Manuscripts: A Practical Manual for their Management, Care and Use*. (Nashville: American Association for State and Local History, 1975).

David B. Gracy, II. *Archives and Manuscripts: Arrangement and Description*. (Chicago: Society of American Archivists, 1977).

One major aspect of archival processing which can be viewed historically even though it is relatively new is automation. Early developments were summarized in *American Archivist* 30 (April 1967), which was entirely devoted to automation. See especially Frank Burke, "The Application of Automated Techniques in the Management and Control of Source Materials," 255–278. H. Thomas Hickerson, *Archives and Manuscripts: An Introduction to Automated Access.* (Chicago: Society of American Archivists, 1981) covers developments of the 1970s prior to the creation of the USMARC AMC format.

3. Current practice.

Two processing manuals published in the 1980s are Hugh A. Taylor, *The Arrangement and Description of Archival Materials.* Munich: K. G. Saur, 1980 (ICA Handbook Series, vol. 2) and Michael Cook and Kristina Grant, *A Manual of Archival Description.* London: Society of Archivists, 1985. See also the chapters on Accessioning, Arrangement and Description, and Finding Aids in Ann Pederson, ed. *Keeping Archives.* (Sydney: Australian Society of Archivists, 1987) and Sharon Thibodeau, "Archival Arrangement and Description" in James Gregory Bradsher, ed. *Managing Archives and Archival Institutions.* (Chicago: University of Chicago Press, 1988).

Significant articles on traditional processing practices are:

Berner, Richard C. and Uli Haller. "Principles of Archival Inventory Construction,"*American Archivist* 47 (Spring 1984): 143–155.

Boles, Frank. "Disrespecting Original Order," *American Archivist* 45 (Winter 1982): 26–32.

Duchein, Michel. "Theoretical Principles and Practical Problems of *Respect des Fonds* in Archival Science," *Archivaria* 16 (Summer 1983): 64–82.

Lucas, Lydia. "Efficient Finding Aids: Developing a System for Control of Archives and Manuscripts," *American Archivist* 41 (Winter 1981), 21–26.

For the development of the USMARC AMC format and related changes in the early 1980s see Richard H. Lytle, "An Analysis of the Work of the National Information Systems Task Force," *American Archivist* 47 (Fall 1984), 357–365 and David Bearman, *Towards National Information Systems for Archives and Manuscript Repositories: The National Informations Systems Task Force (NISTF) Papers, 1981–1984.* (Chicago: Society of American Archivists, 1987). Three articles in *American Archivist* 49 (Winter 1986) discuss the use of the USMARC AMC format: Nancy Sahli, "Interpretation and Application of the AMC Format," 9–20; Katherine D. Morton, "The MARC Formats: An Overview," 21–30; and Steven L. Hensen, "The Use of Standards in the Application of the AMC Format," 31–40. See also Avra Michelson, "Description and Reference in the Age of Automation," *American Archivist* 50 (Spring 1987): 192–208.

Further discussions of archival standards can be found in a number of special isssues of periodicals. *Library Trends* 36 (Winter 1988) contained several articles on archival description. See especially Steven L. Hensen, "Squaring the Circle: The Reformation of Archival Description in AACR2," 539–552 and H. Thomas Hickerson, "Archival Information Exchange and the Role of Bibliographic Networks," 553–571. Authority control in archives is the subject of *Archival Informatics Newsletter* 2:2 (Summer 1988), edited by Avra Michelson, which contains the proceedings of a 1987 Smithsonian Institution Seminar on the topic. *American Archivist* 52 (Fall 1989) and 53 (Winter 1990) contain the report, recommendations and papers of SAA's Working Groups on Standards for Archival Description. A 1990 issue of *Cataloging and Classification Quarterly* edited by Richard Smiraglia is devoted to cataloging archival materials.

Index